THE BEGINNINGS OF PHILOSOPHY IN GREECE

The Beginnings of Philosophy in Greece

Maria Michela Sassi

Translated by Michele Asuni

PRINCETON UNIVERSITY PRESS

PRINCETON & OXFORD

Originally published as *Gli inizi della filosofia in Grecia*, copyright © 2009 by Bollati
Boringhieri; this English translation is published by arrangement with the publisher and
is copyright © 2018 by Princeton University Press.

Published by Princeton University Press,
41 William Street, Princeton, New Jersey 08540

In the United Kingdom: Princeton University Press,
6 Oxford Street, Woodstock, Oxfordshire OX20 1TR

press.princeton.edu

First Paperback Printing, 2020
Paperback ISBN 9780691204567

The Library of Congress has cataloged the cloth edition of this book as follows:

Names: Sassi, Maria Michela, 1955– author.
Title: The beginnings of philosophy in Greece / Maria Michela Sassi ; translated by
    Michele Asuni.
Other titles: Inizi della filosofia in Grecia. English
Description: hardcover [edition]. | Princeton, NJ : Princeton University Press, 2018. |
    Includes bibliographical references and index.
Identifiers: LCCN 2017031659 | ISBN 9780691180502 (hardcover : alk. paper)
Subjects: LCSH: Pre-Socratic philosophers.
Classification: LCC B187.5 .S2713 2018 | DDC 180—dc23
LC record available at https://lccn.loc.gov/2017031659

Editorial: Ben Tate and Hannah Paul
Production Editorial: Debbie Tegarden
Cover Design: Pamela Schnitter
Cover Credit: Jean-Baptiste Hilaire (1753–1822), *The Ruins of Miletus
    and the Maeander Valley*. Courtesy of Sotheby's Picture Library
Production: Jacquie Poirier
Publicity: Amy Stewart
Copyeditor: Anne Cherry

British Library Cataloging-in-Publication Data is available

This book has been composed in Miller

Printed on acid-free paper. ∞

Printed in the United States of America

To Bruno and Nicola
lovers of knowledge in different ways

CONTENTS

A Note on This Edition · ix

Introduction · xi

Chronological Chart · xix

CHAPTER 1   Thales, Father of Philosophy?   1

Before the Presocratics   1

Ex Oriente Lux?   8

Back to Aristotle   19

Knowledge Has Many Faces   26

CHAPTER 2   Philosophy in the Cosmogonies   32

Hesiod: Cosmic Masses and Divine Personas   32

Anaximander in a World "without Gods"   37

The Invention of the Cosmos   44

The Horizon of the Theogonies   47

Pherecydes's "Mixed Theology"   51

A Cosmogony in the Temple of Thetis?   53

A New, Self-Conscious Knowledge   57

CHAPTER 3   Writing Experiments   64

A "Hot" Society   64

Egotisms   70

The Power of Writing   73

Anaximander: The Treatise and the Map   81

Xenophanes, Satirist and Polemicist   93

The Obscure Heraclitus   98

CHAPTER 4   Adventures of the Soul   110

The Soul, the Cosmos, and an Orange   110

From Breath to the Self   112

Restless Souls   119

Empedocles and His Daimōn   120

To Each His Own (Compound)   136

CHAPTER 5   Voices of Authority   139

The Odd Couple   139

Farewell to the Muse   142

Power Games   148

The Truth Revealed in Song   151

Between Muses and Other Gods   160

The Specialization of Reason   168

Bibliography · 179
Index · 203

A NOTE ON THIS EDITION

THIS EDITION PRESENTS a few changes compared to the Italian one. Besides the necessary corrections to oversights found during translation, it contains a revised introduction and several updates to the footnotes. Since neither the essential lines of my argument nor any specific parts of it have changed, I simply added references for works published after 2009 that are particularly relevant to the topics covered in the book, and for a few essays in which I myself have expanded on some points.

This book is also meant for readers who do not know Greek. All of the texts quoted have been translated into English (by Michele Asuni, from my Italian translations unless otherwise noted), but for important terms and passages I have also given the Greek in transliterated form (always in parentheses for direct quotations). Accents are not marked, except for one rare instance of two homographs (Heraclitus's *bìos* and *biòs*); the macron sign has been used to indicate long *o* and *e* vowels.

The fragments of the Presocratics are cited from Diels and Kranz's edition (where A indicates a testimony, B a fragment). Quotations from Plato and Aristotle use the Stephanus and Bekker pagination, respectively.

For works of secondary literature that have been translated into English, the page numbers indicated in the footnotes refer to the English translation. The date of the original publication is given in brackets.

I BEGAN TO THINK about *The Beginnings of Philosophy in Greece* during a conference organized in Lille by André Laks ten years before the book's publication in Italian in 2009. The conference dealt with a fundamental question: "What is Presocratic philosophy?" (Laks-Louguet 2002). That question expressed the difficulty of giving a unitary definition of so-called "Presocratic" thought, but more important was that it brought to the fore an intriguing basic issue: is it appropriate to call this thought "philosophy," and even to say that it is precisely with that thought that Philosophy with a capital *P* is born?

Looking in hindsight twenty years later, that conference seems to have marked the rebirth of an already noble research trend on the Presocratics. In fact, there has been an extraordinary increase in publications on early Greek philosophy, whose authors are often, not by chance, scholars who participated in the Lille conference. As just a few examples, limited to the English-speaking world, we must mention at least the *Oxford Handbook of Presocratic Philosophy*, edited by Patricia Curd and Daniel Graham (2008); Daniel Graham's two-volume edition and translation, *The Texts of Early Greek Philosophy: The Complete Fragments and Selected Testimonies of the Major Presocratics* (2010); and the completely revised edition, in 2011, of Richard McKirahan's *Philosophy Before Socrates. An Introduction with Texts and Commentary*, first published twenty years before. The last, most important result of this rich season of scholarship has been the publication of the fragments and testimonia of *Early Greek Philosophy* by André Laks and Glenn W. Most in nine volumes of the Loeb Classical Library (2016; a French version of the same work was published simultaneously by Fayard). This edition is destined to change our perception of early Greek philosophy in a significant way, thanks to a series of choices that represent a firm break away from (though not a complete unhinging of) the patterns of reception consolidated during the course of the last century in the framework set up by Herman Diels's *Vorsokratiker*; the most remarkable indication of this is the inclusion of Socrates (in the section devoted to the Sophists), but there is also, for instance, an extensive section devoted to "philosophies and philosophers" in comedy and tragedy.

Moreover, this relocation of texts and doctrines (and the addition of a good number of new monographs on single Presocratic authors) has gone hand in hand with a more properly historiographic reflection on the validity and limits of the definition of "Presocratic" thought, together with a consideration of the vastness and variety of the "intellectual endeavor" that took place in the period before Socrates. Laks himself undertook the latter path with a series of studies that eventually fed into a book with an eloquent title, whose

English translation has been published by Princeton University Press: *The Concept of Presocratic Philosophy: Its Origin, Development, and Significance* (2018). I have moved in the same direction with the present book. Here I have not tried to delineate a "history" of the doctrines of single Presocratic authors, nor did I aim to illustrate cameos of strong intellectual personalities such as Anaximander, Heraclitus, Xenophanes, Parmenides, or Empedocles— even though in certain sections of the book I ended up tracing an overview of these thinkers. Rather, I have tried to answer a fundamental question: To what extent are we able to trace the birth of the particular form of knowledge, which today we call philosophy, back to these thinkers, as well as to other more- and less-well-known ones, and also to poets such as Hesiod, or to personalities that are traditionally classified as sages, such as Pherecydes?

It is no longer possible today to accept more or less passively the image of Thales as the "first philosopher" that the ancient sources (starting with Plato and Aristotle) have handed down to us. We have known for a long time that this is not a historical fact but rather, the fruit of a representation stemming from a retrospective projection of a "philosophical ideal of life" that is a product of a time much later than that of Thales. As Werner Jaeger demonstrated in a memorable study (Jaeger 1928), the ideal of the superiority of contemplative life originated and developed in the Academy and the Lyceum in the wake of inquiries started by their respective founders, and it immediately accompanied (for promotional purposes, we might say) an elaboration of exemplary images and stories of prior sages that was as rich as the available documentation was lacking (especially in the case of Thales).

Another fundamental landmark in the scholarship on the Presocratics was Harold Cherniss's acute and painstaking analysis of the wealth of references in Aristotle's writings, which enabled him to draw conclusions that are of paramount importance for any subsequent interpretation. In fact, not only is Aristotle the most generous source on Presocratic doctrines but he also inaugurated in his school a process of gathering and arranging the "opinions" (*doxai*) of the preceding philosophical tradition. This activity marked the beginning of ancient doxographical literature, still an indispensable tool for our knowledge of that tradition. (It is well known that no text by these thinkers has come down to us, with the exception of two great discoveries of the second half of the twentieth century, both included as new entries in Laks and Most's edition: the Strasbourg papyrus, containing more than seventy lines of a poem by Empedocles, and the Derveni papyrus, containing an allegorical commentary to a writing attributed to Orpheus, interspersed with references to Preplatonic cosmological doctrines.) Now, Cherniss has demonstrated that Aristotle's goal is not to write a *history* of the preceding theories (nor, after all, should we expect that of him) but rather, to identify single pieces of the puzzle and relocate them in different places of his reflection, at times to appreciate them and at other times to denounce their insufficiency in light of *his* _own_ theoretical apparatus; the terms and concepts that Aristotle attributes to the Presocratics, then, are mostly the result of his reformulation (Cherniss 1935). This "discovery" has been the foundation for a long series of studies that has emphasized the broader, general panorama of ancient historiography on the Presocratics, sounding out the particular modalities that govern the selection and classification of philosophical _doxai_ in ancient doxographical texts, from Plato to Diogenes Laertius to the Christian authors (Cambiano 1986, Osborne 1987b, and Mansfeld 1990 are just a few examples). At the same time, scholars have expressed strong doubts regarding the validity of what was, since the beginning of the twentieth century, the essential research tool for studying Presocratic thought: Hermann Diels's arrangement of texts by and on these authors in _Vorsokratiker_, one of the most influential products of nineteenth century _Altertumswissenschaft_ (Diels 1903, after Diels 1879), a mature fruit of the "positivistic" confidence of being able to reconstruct "what the Presocratics really said," based on careful philological analysis of the sources that mention them, in the form of direct testimony or a more or less literal citation.

On the other hand, this framework was shaken by the long wave of an anthropological approach to Greek culture that owes much to the pioneering studies of Eric R. Dodds (1951) and Francis M. Cornford (1952), among others. The second half of the twentieth century saw a burgeoning interest in the great themes of myth and the irrational, which had remained in the background of a classicist perception of Greek culture described in terms of balance and rationality. Thus scholars gradually broke free of that dichotomy between rationality and irrationality (inherited from Aristotle, on one hand, and from the Enlightenment on the other) that had, until then, dominated a history of ancient thought seen as a history of the advances of reason. In the new perspective, the knowledge of the Presocratic period too has revealed new fields, such as the exposure to magic, the vitality of the mythical unconscious, soteriological aspirations—consider Walker Burkert's "shaman" Pythagoras (1972) or Peter Kingsley's "magician" Empedocles (1995). It is also remarkably important, from this perspective, that more and more attention is finally being paid to the historical, sociological, and anthropological conditions of the Presocratics' intellectual activities. These factors have brought about an extraordinary widening of the horizons that has enabled scholars to align or, better yet, to interweave Presocratic thought with other manifestations of the broad "intellectual endeavor" of the period before Plato; an endeavor that involved not only natural philosophers but also doctors and mathematicians, geographers and historians (Lloyd throughout his career, but especially 2002c; Gemelli Marciano 2002).

The new panorama, brought to light by historical and comparative studies, is undoubtedly rich and well suited to the antihistoricist trend in contemporary culture. Yet I take issue with the fact that a great part of it is constructed not only *without* resorting to the information contained in the Aristotelian tradition but also, often, *against* Aristotle and his "falsifications" (among the most malicious, the identification of *phusis* as the exclusive object of philosophical inquiry, from Thales onward). In other words, some interpreters seem to believe that in order to free ourselves from the historiographic patterns of Aristotle and other ancient sources, we should deny any validity to their writings, or perhaps systematically turn them around—and this seems to me to be a new form of slavery. Let us consider, for instance, how Andrea Nightingale developed (not without remarkable insights) her thesis that philosophy is a construction intimately connected with Plato's and Aristotle's speculations on the notion of contemplation (*theōria*) as the goal of the philosopher. Her argument hinges on the observation that the term *philosophia*, in its first attestations toward the end of the fifth century BCE, denotes generic intellectual activity, without referring to a specific discipline; and here Nightingale sees the proof that the earliest thinkers were not philosophers, since they did not give a specific definition of their own intellectual activity but instead aspired to be perceived as "wise men" (*sophoi*), engaging themselves more in the performance of a practical and political wisdom than in the knowledge of nature (Nightingale 1995, 2001, 2004). Yet Nightingale is not the only scholar to deny the philosophical intent of the Presocratics' intellectual pursuits. Geoffrey Lloyd and Laura Gemelli Marciano, for instance, take somewhat similar positions, although they have very different perspectives. They too insist on the fact, undeniable in itself, that a characterization (and more importantly a *self*-characterization) of philosophy as an autonomous activity does not exist before Plato.

My approach is in stark opposition to the one I just described, which I would call "revisionist." In this introduction I will limit myself to raising two rather general objections. First, I observe that the absence of the noun for and/or the awareness of performing a certain activity does not prevent us from admitting that some significant elements of that activity are at work. Second, I should say that a hermeneutical process is always influenced by certain preconceptions, and in this sense the position of those who reject a priori the possibility of attributing to the Presocratics an activity comparable to what we call "philosophy" shows as much prejudice as the position of those who (like myself), on the contrary, admit the possibility. Thus, my argument in this book is also driven by a certain preconception about the nature of philosophy (which I preliminarily take as the elaboration of a *critical* stance toward received opinions). Yet the precision of a hermeneutical process may be aided by a responsible illustration of its premises, such as the one that I am trying to offer in these pages.

I should add that I have tried in any way I could to avoid the risks of a predetermined construction. First of all, as is evident from the title, I prefer to speak of a *plurality* of beginnings of philosophy in Greece, and I trace its various beginnings in different contexts and different periods: in a study of nature centered upon the problem of cosmic order (chapters 1 and 2), in matters of cultural polemics (chapter 3), in the elaboration of a discourse on the soul (chapter 4), and in the formulation of principles of reasoning (chapter 5). Moreover, I have avoided seeking a teleological structure with a beginning and development that were too defined, opting instead to give my exposition a different design from the one normally followed in the histories of philosophy (which tends to be a progressive one, Aristotelian and Hegelian in character). To this end, I have tried to situate various authors, with their particular conceptions and even their respective critical stances, in their specific contexts, by which I mean not only the political environment but also the context of communication in which their intellectual activity took place before being circulated more broadly, thanks to the medium of writing. By applying the most specific and updated historical research on archaic Greece, I believe I was able to avoid a twofold temptation: either glorifying the birth of philosophy as the product of a Greek "miracle" (according to Renan's famous formulation) or aligning it with other intellectual "revolutions" that might have taken place in response to similar environmental or political transformations in distant societies such as Israel (with the Prophets), India (with Buddha), China (with Confucius and Lao-Tze), or Persia (with Zoroaster), in a phase that lasted six hundred years (800–200 BCE, the so-called "axial age" in Karl Jaspers's other famous formulation; see Eisenstadt 1986).

In the first chapter, I first dwell on the theories of great interpreters such as Francis M. Cornford and Walter Burkert; both were interested in finding— though via different channels—the origin of Greek philosophy in the background of Eastern civilizations, and insisted on the similarities rather than the differences between the cosmological doctrines of the Ionians and the Mesopotamian creation accounts. With all due respect and admiration for this approach, which has been an ever-beneficial antidote to a rationalistic reading of Greek thought as a *logos* born and developed in stark opposition to *muthos*, I argue that the search for the *archē* started by Thales and continued by the other Ionians represents a truly *new* contribution to the understanding of the nature of things, basing my thesis on the claim that Aristotle's exposition is fundamentally correct. In general, I believe (as should be clear by now) that any attempt to reconstruct Presocratic thought should utilize not only the *ipsissima verba* of the Presocratics but also the data of indirect tradition. Philology offers excellent tools for grasping pertinent information, through the filters of theoretical stratification and anecdote, even from highly personal testimonies such as Plato's and Aristotle's; these data often facilitate our understanding of textual references and enable us to reconstruct, more or less, their hypothetical context. The alternative approach—regarding the ancient accounts as the product of not only a retrospective projection but also an inexorably falsifying reconstruction—is like throwing out the baby with the bathwater. This is why in the first chapter I opted for an unbiased reading and a "strong" interpretation of Presocratic thought like the one offered by Aristotle in the first book of *Metaphysics*, and found within it various signs of the problematic tension in Aristotle's construction, as well as still viable and interesting reflections on the character of the new wisdom of the naturalists (whose forefather is Thales), in its relationship with the knowledge of nature that arose from the mythological tradition.

 In the second chapter, I found it appropriate to identify at least one common trait that allows us to call an intellectual activity "philosophical," and I defined this trait as a *critical* intent directed toward traditional, or at any rate established, points of view. This definition should be understood in a minimal sense, that is, it does not require that a determined theoretical stance be accompanied by an explicit and explicitly polemic explanation against the points of view that have been rejected. It is enough that an idea is put forth knowingly, as innovation and as *fact*. This can already be said of endeavors such as Hesiod's in the *Theogony* and Pherecydes of Syros's (an occasion to discuss the relationships with a tradition between cosmology and "theology") and is even more true for the cosmic frameworks that Ionian thought began to construct, elaborating an idea of cosmic order that marks, in itself, an epochal break from the structure of the mythical cosmogonies.

 In the third chapter, after dealing with the link between the rise of the *polis* and the beginnings of philosophy (by considering in detail the theses of Jean-Pierre Vernant and Geoffrey Lloyd), I turn my attention to the role that writing—or rather, the authors' specific and well-aimed expressive choices—played in the modalities of philosophical formulation. Convinced that the different types of writing contain very specific clues about the author's relationship with his or her original audiences (who receive the texts aurally), I tried to understand Anaximander in Miletus, engaged in discussions regarding the political choices of the time, Heraclitus before his fellow citizens in his attitude as a prophet, and Xenophanes in the far-flung places he visited as a professional rhapsode.

 The fourth chapter reprises a thematic concern, focusing on the discourse on the soul that develops in this period and is intertwined with the discourse on the cosmos in diverse ways. Here, again, places matter—and I was pleased to see that a collective volume on *La sagesse présocratique* published a few years ago was organized according to the geographical location of the various Presocratic thinkers (Desclos-Fronterotta 2013). We meet Empedocles of Akragas immersed in an Italian scene that is agitated by problems of immortality and spiritual salvation. Not far from Sicily, we find the followers of Orphic religion as well as Pythagoras and his first pupils. Against this backdrop we observe the cognitive experience of Parmenides of Elea, who, in the proem of his writing, presents it as the result of a religious revelation and initiation. Both Parmenides and Empedocles authored a poem in hexameters, the epic meter, and the fifth chapter revolves around this fact: the adoption of poetry, which may seem problematic according to modern canons of philosophical communication, is on the contrary illuminating, because it confirms that these authors certainly did not think of themselves as philosophers; rather, they placed their activity within a recognized literary tradition, that of epic poetry, in order to give authority to their message, knowing full well how *innovative* their ideas were. At the same time, prose writing began to emerge among other authors whom I discuss, and I will show how, during the second half of the fifth century BCE, prose would become the medium of rational argumentation par excellence.

In conclusion, I have tried to represent Presocratic thought in all its variety and different directions, because so many of these were sacrificed in later philosophy, especially after the Aristotelian delimitation of a precise terrain of competence in philosophical reasoning. And I hope to have succeeded in putting together a narrative that is not blocked by a retrospective glance but rather takes a "perspectival" one, to use Michael Frede's hopeful term: a story that I have reconstructed while trying as much as possible to walk in the shoes of its protagonists, as it were, who knew where they were departing from and the new paths they wanted to open, but could not predict the twists and forks in the road or the obstacles that would appear later along the way.

CHRONOLOGICAL CHART

THIS CHART LISTS on the left a rather select number of Greek historical events contemporaneous with certain intellectual developments, and on the right the names of philosophers, poets, historians, mathematicians, and sculptors who are mentioned in this book on account of their more or less direct influence on the beginnings of Greek thought. Given the difficulty of ascertaining exact dates of birth and death, and for reasons of simplification, I chose to associate each name with only one date (BCE, of course) indicating the "flourishing" (*akmē* in ancient Greek) period, that is, the high point in an author's life and work, which the ancients normally placed around his fortieth year. Of course, most of these dates are wide approximations, especially in the case of authors such as Xenophanes or Euripides, whose activity spanned several decades.

Historical Events		Cultural Developments	
First Olympic games	776		
		750–725 (?)	Homeric poems
		700	Hesiod
		650	Archilochus
		630	Alcman
			Epimenides
Draconian laws in Athens	620		
Thrasybulus tyrant of Miletus	610		
		600	Thales
			Sappho
			Alcaeus
Archonship of Solon in Athens	594		
Three governments of Peisistratus in Athens	561–528	555	Anaximander Pherecydes; temple of Hera at Samos; temple of Artemis at Ephesus
Persian conquest of Asia Minor	545	545	Anaximenes
		530	Xenophanes
		525	Pythagoras
Hippias and Hipparchus, tyrants of Athens	527–510		
Death of Polycrates of Samos	523		
Darius king of Persia	521–486	520	

Historical Events		Cultural Developments	
War between Sybaris and Croton; anti-Pythagorean revolts in Magna Graecia	510		
Cleisthenic reforms in Athens	508		
		500	Hippasus of Metapontum; Alcmaeon
			Acusilaus of Argos
Ionian Revolt		499	Hecataeus of Miletus; Heraclitus
Destruction of Miletus	494		
Persian Wars	490–480	490–480	Parmenides; Pindar; Aeschylus
		455	Zeno
		450	Empedocles; Polycleitus
Age of Pericles	440–430	440–430	Anaxagoras Herodotus; Sophocles; Phidias; Hippodamus of Miletus; Melissus; Ion of Chios; Hippocrates of Kos; Protagoras; Gorgias
Peloponnesian War	431–404	431–404	Antiphon; Hippias; Leucippus; Euripides; Hippocrates of Chios; Diogenes of Apollonia; Philolaus; Oenopides of Chios
		427	birth of Plato (d. 347)
		420	Derveni papyrus; earliest golden tablets
Athenian expedition to Sicily	415–413	415–413	Democritus; Thucydides; Aristophanes
Athenian democracy restored	403		
		399	Death of Socrates
		398	Plato's first trip to Sicily; Archytas; Philistion of Locri

THE BEGINNINGS OF PHILOSOPHY IN GREECE

CHAPTER ONE

Thales, Father of Philosophy?

Before the Presocratics

"Presocratic" refers to a long phase of Greek thought that stretches over two centuries (the sixth and fifth BCE). This label, still in use, first appeared in a handbook of universal philosophy published toward the end of the eighteenth century, during a period of "reorganization of historical consciousness," which "was also one of new periodization."[1] And the demarcation has repeatedly been questioned over the past few decades, in the wake of a generalized anti-historicizing trend that has left its mark on the study of the ancient world.

Indeed, such a category as "Presocratics" may sound reductive in and of itself, since it groups under the same umbrella authors who differ greatly in intents, interests, and writing styles. Paradoxically, the main trait shared by these thinkers is that their works have come down to us as fragments, or through ancient testimonies or citations in the works of others. Other reasons to question the "Presocratic" categorization could easily be listed here, but first it will be more useful to reflect on the lasting fortune of the term.

Now, it is clear that the use of such a term identifies Socrates as the turning point at the end of a determined line of development within Greek thought. In this historiographical framework, the Athenian philosopher acts as the founder of ethical inquiry, thus marking a crucial break from a tradition that was mainly focused on the observation and analysis of the physical world. The ancient authors themselves have made vivid contributions to this picture. Socrates's devoted pupil Xenophon, for instance, emphasizes his mentor's lack of interest in the "nature of all things." Conversely, he stresses his attention to the "human" condition and the elaboration of moral notions such as wisdom and courage (*Memorabilia* I, 1, 11–12, and 16). But Plato insists more than others on Socrates's detachment from natural inquiry. In his *Apology* (19d),

---

[1] I am referring to Johann Augustus Eberhard's *Allgemeine Geschichte der Philosophie* (1788), as quoted by Laks (2001c, 293). See also Laks 2018 [2006], 19–20.

we see a Socrates on trial who is busy defending himself against the charge of having formulated dangerous cosmological doctrines. Again, in the still more dramatic setting of the *Phaedo* (96aff), Socrates devotes part of his final conversation with his disciples to explaining the reasons for his dissatisfaction with an inquiry into the natural world (*peri phuseōs historia*) like the one carried out by Anaxagoras, though he had initially been drawn to it. Moreover, throughout the first phase of Plato's production, the character Socrates elaborates countless variations on the problem of defining certain moral concepts.

In the first book of *Metaphysics*, Aristotle builds on this preexisting framework to trace a powerful outline of the philosophical tradition that preceded him. Here, too, the backdrop is dominated by natural inquiry until Socrates intervenes, isolating the field of ethics and investigating it with a specific method (the search for universals and definitions: *Metaphysics* I, 6, 987b 1; *Parts of Animals* I, 1, 642a 28). According to this view, Socrates represents a rupture between an earlier phase of philosophy, where an interest for nature prevails, and a later and more complete one, characterized by dialectic, starting with Plato's inquiry on the Forms (*Metaphysics* 1, 3, 983b 7; 1, 6, 987b 31). The sequence leading from the Presocratics to Socrates and then to Plato thus overlaps with a division of philosophy into physics, ethics, and dialectics. This combination will later be perfected (in particular by the Stoics) and make its way into the main text of Hellenistic historiography, Diogenes Laertius's *Lives of the Philosophers* (I, 14; II, 16; III, 56).

Plato's dialogues would have sufficed to present subsequent generations with the idea of Socrates as the *primus inventor* and discoverer of a new world—the one closest to man, to be sure, but never before glimpsed. And Cicero admirably condensed this depiction by describing Socrates as "the first one to call philosophy down from the sky and place it in cities and even into our homes" (*Tusculanae*, V, 4, 10). Yet it was thanks to Aristotle (though popularized by Diogenes Laertius)—and to the powerful organization of Aristotle's philosophical construction—that this shift of the philosophical gaze came to be embedded in a strong evolutionary framework that was destined to reemerge in eighteenth- and nineteenth-century Germany, where it would serve the periodization needs of philosophical historiography. In fact, the utility of the Presocratic category can be explained through this process of refunctionalizing Aristotle's outline, and Hegel's *Lectures on the History of Philosophy* (1833) and Zeller's *Philosophie der Griechen* (1844ff) offer the most illustrious and emphatic arguments for this reading of Aristotle. And its fall from grace, after all, is relative.[2]

---

[2] See Beall (1993) for a brilliant study of the relationship between Hegel's *Lessons*, in their various editorial stages, and their Aristotelian source. On the relationship between Zeller's and Hegel's constructions, see Leszl 1989 and 2011. Brancacci 2002 acutely notes other reasons for the deserved success of the notion of "Presocratic."

It is true that the definition of Socrates as the _after_ of the Presocratic period has encountered a growing number of objections. Is it not the case, for
instance, that signs of ethical and anthropological interests are already present before Socrates? Consider the concern for the vicissitudes of the soul that
pervades the Orphic and Pythagorean traditions, as well as the writings of
Heraclitus and Empedocles. Some of the authors that we call "Presocratics"
are contemporary with Socrates (e.g., Democritus), and where should we place
the Sophists?[3] However, these are relatively simple questions, and in asking
them we are still moving along a predefined path. In fact, the majority of
scholars may continue to use the current terminology for the sake of practi-
cality, while others circumvent the problem by talking about "Preplatonic"
thinkers (thus leaving Socrates in splendid isolation). The _after_ of the Presocratics seems to posit a preliminary problem of definition, with little bearing
on the evaluation of specific authors and contexts. But can we say the same
about their _before_?

Another familiar formulation describes Thales as the "father of philosophy." It is worth remembering that this, too, stems from an image created in
antiquity. Thales is the first thinker from whom we have been handed down
insights on nature, hints of geometrical demonstrations, as well as astronomical and meteorological interests; the sources report his opinions on problems
that would become topical, such as the causes of earthquakes and of over-
flows of the Nile. His activity can be traced in Miletus between the second half
of the seventh century BCE and the first decades of the sixth (among other
things, he reportedly predicted a famous eclipse in 585 BCE, but this information must be taken with a grain of salt). A port city on the coast of Ionia
and a congested crossroads between East and West, Miletus at this time was
particularly prosperous and lively, as shown by the numerous foundations of
new colonies across the Mediterranean and along the coastlines of the Black
Sea. It is not by chance that, in the sixth century, the city will be home to
Anaximander and Anaximenes (who, together with Thales, form the renowned
triad of "Ionian scientists"), as well as Hecataeus. The last authored the first
geographical treatise in Greek (_Journey around the World_), as well as a
mythographical writing (_Genealogies_) wherein mythical tales are subjected to
a systematic and rationalistic critique in order to retrieve their historical core

---

[3] Walther Kranz, in the _Vorrede_ to his fifth edition of Diels's _Fragmente der Vorsokra-
tiker_ (1934–37), observed that "Presocratic" should be used strictly to indicate those who
preceded the "Socratics," by analogy with the practice of calling "Postsocratics" only those
who came after them (we'll remember that Nestle's influential 1923 work is titled _Nach-
sokratiker_). But Kranz's main insight was that the _Vorsokratiker_ featured many a contemporary of Socrates (some of whom even outlived him), and that the edition as a whole was
nevertheless tied together by the panorama of thought outlined in it, which, while not
strictly "Presocratic," was certainly _not_ Socratic, since those authors represented a line of
thought that was influenced by neither Socrates nor Plato.

from beneath the contradictory elaborations of legend. The exchange with different cultures (from both the East and the colonies) on one hand, and the needs of maritime trade on the other, trigger the elaboration of new theories geared toward understanding atmospheric phenomena, exploring new territories, and reflecting on Greek traditional knowledge.

Starting from the Hellenistic period, Thales is reported as the author of several writings, including a poem titled *Nautical Astronomy*. However, it is more likely that he did not leave behind any written work: the earliest sources that mention his doctrines, such as Herodotus and Aristotle, depend on an oral tradition. It is no wonder, then, that his image was soon surrounded by an aura of legend, imbued with the allure of the archetype.[4] In a famous digression in Plato's *Theaetetus* (164a–b), Thales is the name of the philosopher who, distracted while observing the stars, falls into a well, thus provoking the scorn of a Thracian servant girl—a memorable prefiguration, in the dramatic setting of the dialogue, of the tragic end that the city of Athens has in store for Socrates. This image will later enjoy widespread popularity as a metaphor for the failure of philosophical contemplation in the "life-world."[5] Conversely, Aristotle invokes Thales as grounds for rehabilitating the practical value of philosophy. He tells how, thanks to his knowledge in matters of astronomy, Thales was once able to predict an abundant olive harvest. He then bought all the oil mills in the region, only to sell them again when the right time came. He reportedly did this not so that he could make a sizable profit but in order to discredit those who, citing his humble lifestyle, had accused philosophy of being worthless (*Politics* 1, 11, 1259a 7–22). It is clear that for both Plato and Aristotle, Thales is "good to think with"; that is, he serves as an early figure upon whom to project that philosophical ideal of life that developed much later, between the Academy and the Peripatos.[6] It must be noted, however, that both Plato's and Aristotle's accounts pivot around Thales's meteorological and astronomical knowledge: neither author, in other words, has any doubt that the "first philosopher" concentrated his scrutiny on the natural world.

It is again Aristotle who, in the first book of *Metaphysics*, interprets this interest in natural inquiry as a turning point marking a new epoch. According to him, Thales's role is as decisive as that of Socrates, and symmetrical to it. In

---

[4] On the figure and activity of Thales, see the extensive treatment by O'Grady 2002, rich in materials though weakened somewhat by the author's excessive confidence in the possibility of reconstructing "what Thales really said." For a critical use of the sources on Thales, see instead Gemelli Marciano 2007b.

[5] For the meaning of this Platonic image, whose history is masterfully described by Blumenberg (1987), see also Butti de Lima 2002, 27ff.

[6] It was Jaeger (1928) who proposed this reconstruction of the manifold tradition of anecdotes, in which the most ancient thinkers (including the Seven Sages) are chosen as representatives of an ideal of life, whether it be contemplative, practical, or political. On Thales's "metamorphoses" in the ancient tradition, see also Mogyoródi 2000.

fact, since Thales identified water as the principle of all things, he is seen as the "inaugurator" of the study of material causes that started the investigation of nature and, consequently, philosophy itself. In Aristotle's view, philosophy then evolved into an understanding of *all* things (*Metaphysics* I, 3, 983b 20).[7]

This was another crucial move on the part of Aristotle. Admittedly, it was soon opposed by a tendency to trace the beginnings of philosophy to the East. Herodotus and Plato had already shown admiration for the lore accumulated by the Egyptians long before the Greeks appeared on the horizon. Plato knows something about Zoroaster (*Alcibiades I*, 122a), and Aristotle himself mentions with great interest the dualistic conceptions of Persian magi (*On Philosophy*, frag. 6 Ross; *Metaphysics* XIV, 1091b 10). But a number of other Greek authors, especially from the fourth century onward, assert the philosophical precedence of Persians, Chaldeans, Indian gymnosophists, and the Druids. Diogenes Laertius will vigorously argue against this position in the proem of his *Lives of the Philosophers*. According to an authoritative hypothesis, this work was written in an anti-Christian vein and its main purpose was to reclaim the Greek character of philosophy.[8] The claim of a pre-Greek barbarian philosophy, resurrected within the framework of the new Christian one, will nevertheless prevail (thanks in particular to Clement of Alexandria's *Stromata*, from the beginning of the third century CE) and make its way through modern historiographical philosophy until Brucker—that is, until the detour caused at the turn of the nineteenth century by the aforementioned "rebirth" of Aristotle's historiographical paradigm. Once again, a triangulation took place (Aristotle-Hegel-Zeller), sanctioning the removal of the East from the history of philosophy and reinstalling Thales in his pioneering position. As we know, this endeavor was rather successful: until very recently, the majority of school textbooks started off inevitably, and unproblematically, in Greece with Thales.

In recent years, however, even this schematization has met increasing criticism. Giorgio Colli's *La sapienza greca* is representative of the situation in Italy. Inspired by the desire to rewrite Herman Diels's classic edition of the fragments of the Presocratics—to this day the reference work for the studies in the field (in the edition revised by Walther Kranz)—Colli's project originally called for eleven volumes, but after the author's death it was left incomplete at the third tome (devoted to Heraclitus). Nevertheless, its overall design is fairly clear, thanks in particular to the fact that Colli's musings on the subject had already been expressed elsewhere. The reasons behind the project's structure are especially evident: while the first book treats religious lore predating Presocratic thought, the second features the Ionians, preceded (as in

---

[7] See Frede 2004 for an attentive analysis of the complex strategy executed by Aristotle in the first book of *Metaphysics*.

[8] See Momigliano 1986.

the Diels-Kranz edition) by the semimythical figures of Epimenides and Pherecydes. In this overtly Nietzschean endeavor, Colli proposed a global reorganization of the approach to ancient thought, pinpointing the source of philosophy or, better yet, the source of "wisdom"—as opposed to "knowledge," intended as an expression of decadent rationalism, and initiated as such by Socrates and Plato—and identifying it with ecstatic experience, in a ritual context dominated by Apollo and Dionysus. This hypothesis was developed at the price of many a forced interpretation, but it should nevertheless (or perhaps for this very reason) be credited with bringing to the fore a central hermeneutical problem, namely, the inseparability of the issue of the *beginning* of philosophy and that of the *nature* of philosophy itself.[9]

In fact, the identification of a specific starting point of philosophy tends to be tied to a specific choice concerning its objects, modalities, and purposes. The more convinced we are that philosophical activity has to do with a positive curiosity about the outside world, the keener we will be to accept Aristotle's portrayal of Thales. This is what happened, for instance, in those positivistic accounts of authors endowed with great historical acumen such as Burnet and Gomperz, for whom the history of early Greek thought became a history of acquisitions—possibly seen as anticipations of modern science. Conversely, we will be prone to opposing that same portrayal if we tend to identify philosophy with the wise men's quest for the origins of being, as Colli unambiguously did—but he was not and is not the only one.

In my view, a problem like the one we are dealing with here requires more nuanced answers. But first I would like to reformulate it in terms that are just as clear-cut: we may ask ourselves whether philosophy was born as an autonomous exercise of critical reasoning bursting into an arena governed by religious and mythical wisdom, or whether this very wisdom was its deeper and more propelling source. Or rather, in other (Greek) words: does philosophy start as a *logos* that interrupts and unhinges the monopoly of *muthos*, or is philosophy itself a *muthos*?

The stakes are undoubtedly high, and the problem cannot be circumvented with some easy terminological sleight of hand, such as the one we adopt when we speak of "Preplatonic" thinkers in order to avoid the hurdle represented by Socrates. In this case, we have to venture into, and take soundings from, the background Thales might have drawn from for his beliefs on the cosmos and its origin. We cannot overlook the fact that an appreciation of water as a natural principle can already be traced to the earliest text of Greek literature, the Homeric epics, where the sea (*Okeanos*) is called "origin of the gods" and "of all things." Represented as a river that encircles Earth (seen as a flat disk), Okeanos is the source of all waters, fresh or salty. Moreover, Hesiod, in his

[9] Cf. Colli 1977, 1978, and 1980, with the various objections of Graf and Barnes 1979, Cambiano 1980, and Voelke 1985.

Theogony, points out that the union of Okeanos and Tethys—both born of Sky (*Ouranos*) and Earth (*Gaia*)—results in abundant aqueous offspring: three thousand Oceanids (who, scattered across the earth, keep watch over it and the depths of the sea) and as many river gods.[10] But we can dig even deeper and go even further back in time, given the possibility that these representations are derived, in turn, from non-Greek beliefs. In fact, water plays the role of a cosmological principle in the great fluvial civilizations of Egypt and Mesopotamia. Numerous Egyptian texts speak of a primordial aqueous mass (referred to as Nun in the *Book of the Dead*, toward the end of the second millennium) from which the world emerged. Furthermore, the fertilizing power of the primordial principle was generally recognized in the annual flooding of the Nile. As for Mesopotamia, Apsû designates the realm of cosmic water in Sumerian and Akkadian mythology. The *Enuma Elish* (or *Enûma Eliš*), the most renowned Mesopotamian poem "of creation," was written in Akkadian toward the end of the second millennium BCE (the title corresponds to the first two words of the text, meaning "when up high"). It postulates a primordial mingling of waters (Apsû, male, and Tiamat, female) that generates a series of sky and earth divinities that are Marduk's forebears; in the present world, Apsû still appears, this time as the cosmic region under the earth.[11] Thales, who himself posited that the earth floats on water, may have been aware of some of these conceptions.

We are also informed of his travels to Egypt. It is true that the land of Egypt, admired and revered for its wisdom, was an almost mandatory travel destination for the first *sophoi* in the biographical tradition. After all, it was thanks to the merchants coming from Miletus, Chios, and Samos, under the auspices of Pharaoh Psammetichus I, that the port of Naucratis was founded (620 BCE) in order to facilitate the exchange between Egypt and Ionia. And we cannot rule out the possibility that curious seafarers may have traveled to Egypt or elsewhere together with Greek human and material resources, and that Thales may well have been among them.[12] At any rate, Miletus's preeminent

---

[10] See Homer, *Iliad*, 14, 201, 246, and 302; 18, 607; 21, 195; Hesiod, *Theogony*, 133 and 337–70. Herodotus (IV, 8) comments that the idea of an Okeanos encircling Earth is rather common among the Greeks, even though they do not provide a demonstration of it.

[11] The pioneering collection of essays by Frankfort, Frankfort, Wilson, Jacobsen, and Irwin 1946 remains an indispensable source of information on the Eastern and Middle Eastern roots of Greek cosmogonical knowledge. On Mesopotamian cosmology, see also Bottéro and Krämer 1989 and, more recently, an up-to-date assessment by Rochberg 2005. On the *Enuma Elish* in particular, see Maul 2015.

[12] Van Dongen 2007 stresses the importance of Naucratis in his prudent analysis of a vast group of archaeological and historical data pertaining to the relations between preclassical Greece and the Near East. It should be noted that, unlike Egypt, Mesopotamian cultures cannot be proved, with the documentation we possess, to have had a *direct* influence on preclassical Greece.

geographical position amid these commercial routes is likely to have promoted, across Middle Eastern as well as Mediterranean inlands, a familiarization with other cultures.

To conclude, the picture becomes rather complicated if we try to go back beyond Thales—in other words, if we ask ourselves whose "son" this controversial "father" of philosophy was—for this kind of question compels us to venture into the grueling territory of traditional wisdom and lore, preserved by myth. In particular, it forces us to explore the cosmogonic myths, whose ramifications will stretch out well beyond the phase of the Ionian cosmologies and whose roots are, after all, rather remote. So remote, in fact, that we must look for them *elsewhere,* be it in Egypt or in the Near East. When it comes to philosophy, the question of *when* is intertwined with that of *where,* and the exploration of the philosophical contents of myth undermines the very foundations of the paradigm of a Greek origin of philosophical reasoning.

Ex Oriente Lux?

When touching upon the problem of the cognitive status of myth in Greek thought, we cannot overlook the history of scholarship on the subject, which is one of the richest and presents some of the roughest terrain. So, before delving deeper into our argument, it will be worth exploring some of its pivotal moments.[13] As we know, ancient thought had expressed a firm devaluation of the repertoire of classical mythology as a hodgepodge of fictions and errors, which made its way through to the eighteenth century and found the most fertile ground in the rationalism of the Enlightenment. However, in the pre-Romantic climate of the last decades of the eighteenth century, philosophers such as Herder and innovative classicists such as Heyne initiated a rehabilitation of the intellectual contents of myth that has carried on to the present day, with an alternation of leaps forward, pauses, and resistances. Another decisive step was taken during the second half of the following century by the philologist and historian of religions Hermann Usener, whose lesson has been reprised not only in the context of *Altertumswissenschaft,* by scholars such as Rhode or Diels but also—outside this context—by Warburg and Cassirer. From then on, the development of a history of religions that was keen on anthropological comparativism and, conversely, the attention to the modalities of symbolical expression has struck progressively harsher blows at the divide between myth and philosophy. Nor can we forget the role played by Nietzsche in the retrieval of myth's power of truth and vitality, to be played against the rigidity and false optimism of scientific rationalism, symbolized in the eyes of the philosopher by Socrates. In this same critical perspective,

[13] For a more detailed treatment of the episodes mentioned hereafter, see Bodei 1982, Sassi 1982a and 1986, Borsche 1985, and Most 1995.

Nietzsche was brought to the equally influential discovery of the peculiarity of Presocratic thought, whose primeval authenticity he highly praised.

Of course, there have also been opposite strategies, which were even partially successful in revamping the idea of a teleological development from mythical imagination to logical thinking. Consider for instance the fortune of Wilhelm Nestle's *Vom Mythos zum Logos* (1940), whose title served for a long time to label Greek culture as the one that, as early as the archaic period, made the neat and triumphant transition "from myth to reason."[14] In general, however, the most careful scholars have proven less and less prone to speak in terms of a stark polarity between *muthos* and *logos*, and at the same time have gradually turned their attention to the relationships between East and West. Concurrently, the problem of the beginnings of philosophy had been brought to the fore, but—the milestone represented by the myth/reason opposition having been lost—it grew more complicated. We shall see how this happened by focusing on two exemplary cases.

During the first half of the last century, Francis MacDonald Cornford chose the very "beginning of knowledge" as his main object of reflection. Cornford was once called "an imaginative man with a rare ability to challenge the mind of his reader."[15] Indeed, more than fifty years after the publication of *Principium Sapientiae* (and more than sixty years since the author's death), this book remains persuasive, the fruit of a perfect combination of intuition, clear argumentation, and effective writing.[16] A shrewd and sensitive scholar, Cornford studied with the enthusiastic guidance of Jane Harrison, and his earlier works are heavily influenced by the anthropological approach to ancient culture (with a particular focus on ritual aspects and the manifestations of the primitive) that is a trademark of the group of the so-called Cambridge ritualists (among whom Gilbert Murray is usually listed, despite his being at Oxford). Harrison led the group for some years, but her influence did not prevent the intellectual autonomy of its members from emerging freely.[17] In fact, after more than a decade of collaborative work, at the outbreak of World War I the members of the group parted ways and Cornford began increasingly to cultivate the philosophical penchant that always characterized him.[18]

---

[14] Most 1999a has shown the noninnocence of Nestle's endeavor. In the first pages (and note the time and the place), the author declares that this intellectual maturation seems to be a prerogative of the "Aryan" people alone.

[15] Vlastos 1955, 65.

[16] See Cornford 1952, published posthumously (Cornford died in 1943, leaving an incomplete manuscript) and edited by William K. C. Guthrie.

[17] Beard 2000 has shown that the idea of a proper "group" is largely the product of a later mythicizing process.

[18] Perhaps for this reason Cornford appears rather seldom in the otherwise rich and often excellent literature on the ritualists; see Bonanate 1974, Ackerman 1991, Calder III

The problem of the beginning of philosophy had already attracted Cornford's attention. His 1907 monograph *Thucydides mythistoricus* offers a reading of Thucydides that reveals a tragic, at times Aeschylean vision of human nature, one that invites the reader to interpret the *History* as a full-fledged tragedy, the tragedy of Athens. While this thesis is still stimulating for Thucydides scholars,[19] I am more interested in pointing out how it goes hand in hand with a more general reflection, well summarized in the following passage:

> In every age the common interpretation of the world of things is controlled by some scheme of unchallenged and unsuspected presupposition; and the mind of any individual, however little he may think himself to be in sympathy with his contemporaries, is not an insulated compartment, but more like a pool in one continuous medium—the circumambient atmosphere of his place and time.[20]

Thus, according to Cornford, the mind of the individual is unwittingly influenced by the tacit premises of the world he or she inhabits. Just as Dante could not guess that his design of redemption would appear unconvincing within an astronomical framework that was no longer geocentric, and Cornford—as he himself notes—would not be able to determine to what extent his vision of the world and that of his contemporaries was "colored" by Darwinian biology, so too the Greek historians, Thucydides included, cannot be fully understood without taking into account the products of contemporary poetry. Moreover, when studying any author (philosophers included), one must take into account that "mythological phase of thought," that "background of glistening chaos" from which the Greek spirit emerged in seemingly beautiful harmony. This mythological background, however, is usually neglected in classical scholarship. In particular:

> The history of philosophy is written as if Thales had suddenly dropped from the sky, and, as he bumped the earth, ejaculated, 'Everything must be made of water!'[21]

In *From Religion to Philosophy*, a work published a few years later, Cornford combined the notion of collective representation (elaborated after Durkheim and Mauss) with the need to establish continuity between the mythical-religious tradition and the Presocratics. This allowed him to trace an anticipation of later element-based cosmological models to an ancient "to-

---

1991, and Schlesier 1994. And then there is that magnificent exercise in intellectual biography, Guthrie 1950.

[19] It was reprised by Vidal-Naquet (2000). See also Chambers 1991.
[20] Cornford 1907, viii.
[21] Ibid., x.

temic" tendency to classify things. Within this framework, the job of philosophy is presented as a mere clarification of themes that are already focused in the collective consciousness of a tribal society no longer satisfied by the ritual plane: even the concept of *phusis*, one of the core tenets of Presocratic thought, is connected by Cornford to the notion of *mana* of a tribal group (a connection that has been widely criticized).[22]

In fact, Cornford later abandoned this research path, which was admittedly as fascinating as it was speculative. He similarly abandoned the reference to the Jungian theory of a collective unconscious, even though at some point he had used it to substantiate the notion of "inexplicit suppositions."[23] He preferred to seek confirmation of his intuitions within his own field of inquiry. And there he was, at an inaugural lecture in 1931, reinstating his conviction that philosophical discourse is driven by "premises that are rarely or never expressed" (in that they are shared by all people of a particular culture and taken for granted) and arguing that the approach of ancient science to the problem of motion is oriented more by maxims that belong to a most ancient popular wisdom (such as "like acts on like") than it is by the observation of nature.[24] Thus the ancient philosophers' frames of thought, projected onto the background of a prephilosophical knowledge, fall under the rubric of dogmatism, one that precludes the discovery of the scientific laws of motion and change. The relationship between the Greek philosophical tradition and a preexisting one, already glimpsed twenty years earlier, is exemplified here for the first time within a broader framework. But an even more comprehensive picture is presented in the last great book, whose title is a declaration of its central problem: *Principium Sapientiae.*

In the first part of the book, Cornford identifies and contrasts two dominating tendencies within the earliest phases of Greek philosophy: on one hand, the study of nature started by the Ionians, and on the other the configuration of a level of truth underlying the phenomena, advanced by philosophers such as Pythagoras, Parmenides, and Empedocles (and Plato, who in this respect followed in their footsteps), who chose to deliver their message using prophetic and inspired tones. It must be noted that Cornford combines his insistence on this precious "inspired" current with the intriguing statement that it is the continuation of ancient shamanic traditions. From this we first glimpse an idea of philosophy as religious wisdom, and it is not by chance that the title of the book is taken from a famous line in Proverbs: *Timor Domini principium sapientiae.* But let us leave aside the problem of what constitutes

---

[22] See Cornford 1912, in particular chapters 1 and 2. Bréhier's reaction (1913) is noteworthy for its mixture of serious attention and no less serious perplexities regarding Cornford's approach.

[23] See Cornford 1921, 6 and passim.

[24] Cornford 1931, 12. Along the same lines, see Cornford 1934 and 1936.

wisdom in Presocratic thought,[25] and focus for a moment on the second part of the work, "Philosophical Cosmogony and Its Origins in Myth and Ritual." It is evident at once that Cornford, whose argument does not appear to be new, is intent on diminishing the innovative character of the Ionian cosmologies:

> If we give up the idea that philosophy or science is a motherless Athena, an entirely new discipline breaking in from nowhere upon a culture hitherto dominated by poetical and mystical theologians, we shall see that the process of rationalization had been at work for some considerable time before Thales was born.[26]

In the following pages, Cornford tenaciously and coherently realizes his declared purpose: to examine the doctrines of the Ionians and separate the elements that derive from the observation of nature from those inherited from tradition.[27] In particular, he focuses on Anaximander, whose ideas appear to be more complex than those of Thales (and we have more information on them, in any case). He revisits them in the light of an array of images and problems that he believes were previously developed—though on a mythopoeic level—in the context of religious tradition. We shall come back to the details later, but it should be noted that for Anaximander the origin and formation of the cosmos take place by means of a differentiation from an original state, which he calls *apeiron* (that is, "unlimited," with respect to both quantity and quality). This prompts Cornford to pinpoint a series of analogies (which are undeniable in and of themselves) between Anaximander's ideas and a variety of cosmogonic tales, attested not only in Greek culture predating Anaximander himself but also in the ancient Near East, India, China, and the traditional cultures of Oceania. With insight, Cornford observes that, in all of these tales, creation is represented as an act of *separation* from an original state of *indifferentiation*.

Consider, to start with, the cosmogonic section in Hesiod's *Theogony* (lines 116ff), the first phase of which consists in the separation of Sky and Earth. According to Cornford, this act of separation is again represented in the gory tale that unravels without interruption from the cosmogony. This is a reference to the famous episode of Kronos rebelling against his father, Ouranos (who, fearing the sons Gaia bore him, had pushed them all back inside their mother's womb), and severing his genitals with a pruning hook made by Gaia herself, in a rage (lines 176ff; then, as we know, the story repeats itself: Kronos will devour his sons by Rhea, until Zeus, the youngest, dethrones him:

---

[25] This will be dealt with in detail in chapter 5.

[26] Cornford 1952, 188.

[27] Ibid., 187. The notion of collective unconscious is not brought into question here, but it could have been; we might suppose that it was absorbed by the more generic but still effective notion of "inheritance."

lines 453ff). Cornford recognizes the Babylonian epic poem *Enuma Elish* as the direct precedent of this story. Here Marduk, the god of creation, kills Tiamat, primordial water divinity, "splits her in half like stockfish," and builds the firmament out of the upper half. Similarly, Egyptian mythology contains the story of the separation of Earth (the god Geb floating on abyssal waters) and Sky (the goddess Nut) at the hands of Shu, the god of air. Analogously, at the beginning of Genesis, God moves along an indefinite aqueous mass before the creation of light, after which he divides it into waters above and below the firmament. Cornford also notes in a Maori tale, which is the most well known version among Polynesian creation myths, a mechanism of separation between Sky (Rangi) and Earth (Papa), the two entities from which gods, men, and things originate.

The comparative material collected by Cornford is impressive for the evidence it gathers and for its quality. It is also remarkable that soon after his death another text was added to this list of parallels, namely, the Hittite-Hurrian *Song of Kumarbi*, published in 1943. This text predates Hesiod's *Theogony* by five hundred years and contains, like Hesiod's poem, a story of violent usurpations that alludes to a sequence of cosmic disorder and order. Alau, the first god of the sky, is overthrown by Anu during the ninth year of his reign, and Anu is in turn overthrown and castrated by Kumarbi after the same amount of time. We may recall that Ouranos receives a similar treatment from Kronos; moreover, Kumarbi bites and swallows Anu's genitalia, producing offspring. Among these is a storm god, who will dethrone Kumarbi just as Zeus did Kronos. The hypothesis that Hesiod's *Theogony* contains an adaptation of this Babylonian myth, perhaps purged of the goriest details, has found strong confirmation in the aforementioned text, which provided proof of a Hittite mediation.[28] More generally, as we will note again later, after Cornford one cannot overlook how indebted Greek culture is to the East. Within this framework, however, Cornford comes to a conclusion regarding the Ionian cosmologies that is not easy to accept: they should be considered, under this new light, as the result of a trimming of the mythical repertoire, made poorer and poorer through a process of rationalization. According to Cornford, this process reached its most extreme phase with Anaximander but started long before him. This would explain why Anaximander's cosmogony is anything but "a free construction of the intellect reasoning from direct observation of the existing world."[29]

But Cornford does not stop here; he dedicates a few pages to a close comparison between Hesiod's *Theogony*, reinterpreted as a hymn to Zeus for gaining sovereignty over the other gods, and the Babylonian epic *Enuma Elish*, a hymn to the victory of Marduk over Tiamat, cosmic deity of disorder, and his

[28] See Dodds's footnote to Cornford 1952, 249n1.
[29] Ibid., 201.

reestablishment of an order that is at once natural and political. The scholar is particularly interested in reminding us that the text of *Enuma Elish* was tied to a rather specific ceremony. In fact, it was normally recited (presumably from the end of the second millennium BCE) during the festival for the Babylonian New Year, in a context of a ritual celebrating the regularity of the seasons and, at the same time—in a kind of osmosis between natural and political order—a ritual of sovereignty: the creation myth must therefore be read, like any other myth, as the narrative version of a ritual. Cornford applies here a sort of axiom (even if a controversial one)[30] of the Cambridge ritualists, and goes on to add that even when myth is transposed onto a different cultural terrain and the link with ritual is lost, the original meaning of this link continues to be perceived "obscurely" and lingers on; but it does so at the expense of a process of rationalization that is mistaken for a reasoned reflection on nature, while it is nothing other than the purification of a cluster of inherited images.[31] It is with Hesiod that the myth of Marduk is revived in a now prosaic form, one that is no longer authentically mythical and can barely be told apart from "early Greek systems which historians still innocently treat as purely rational constructions."[32] Ultimately, the general lines of this creation myth do not depend on the observation of natural phenomena (only a "lunatic under the influence of hashish" would, from the mere sight of the starry sky and the earth beneath his feet, elaborate the strange theory that they derive from a monstrous deity being torn in half!).[33] In fact, those lines have been traced in the context of extremely ancient rituals.

> The primary factor is the thing *done*. It is also the proper starting point for inquiry. Instead of picturing a hypothetical horde of savages, at no particular time or place, sitting round a camp-fire and speculating on the origin of the world, we can take as our point of departure a set of rites which we know to have been performed in the cities of Mesopotamia at the date of the earliest records we possess. As we have remarked, the rites are already extremely elaborate; behind them must lie a very long prehistoric period of development through simpler phases of society, leading back into the palaeolithic and terminating, no one knows when or where, in something that might be called "primitive."[34]

In the field of ancient studies, Cornford's comparatist perspective helped pave the way for an anticlassicistic trend that has become mandatory: it is impossible to deny that Greek culture is greatly indebted to mythical thinking and

---

[30] According to Lambert (1968) (who should be read also for a detailed description of the ceremony), the link between mythology and ritual in Mesopotamia was actually the product of a later construction of the priests.

[31] Cornford 1952, 225ff, in particular p. 238. See also Cornford 1941.

[32] Cornford 1941, 100.

[33] Ibid., 111.

[34] Cornford 1952, 230.

to Eastern cultures when it comes to one of its most acclaimed achievements, namely, the area of rational thought. However, it is also undeniable that a biased inquiry that focuses on similarities rather than differences is more likely to miss the peculiar characteristics of one culture or the other. For what concerns the Greeks, we should ask ourselves how they *transformed* the materials coming from the East and articulated them into constellations of thought wherein the borrowed elements may have taken on a new meaning.

As a case in point, let us consider Marduk and the Zeus of Hesiod. Both gods are chosen as leaders of the other deities and as perpetrators of a cosmic order based on the distribution of the different areas of power among the gods. Beyond this similarity, there is indeed a significant difference to be noted: while none of the other gods is related to Marduk, the organization under Zeus follows the lines of his familial ties. Now, this familial structure serves to systematize the cosmic picture, and it also contributes to dramatize the ever-conflicted relationship between the power of Zeus and that of the other gods. At any rate, while Hesiod derived single elements from Eastern traditions, it is noteworthy that he adapted them into a coherent whole aimed at symbolizing Zeus's supremacy over the divine and human order, which established a narrative model that had a lasting influence on Greek culture.[35]

Cornford's approach to the Ionian cosmologies lends itself a fortiori to the same objection. The scholar, as if obsessed with the need to push as far back as possible the infancy of philosophy, to the point of causing philosophy to "disappear" into myth (or even of causing both to disappear into ritual), traces Anaximander's system (reduced to the pattern of undifferentiation/nonseparation) to a nonspeculative, most ancient origin that is lost in the dawn of time. Thus his argument overshadows the real significance and innovation of Ionian thought, which started with the removal of divine personas: when it comes to the conflict of opposites such as hot and cold, dry and wet that is central in Ionian thought, Cornford prefers to emphasize the legacy of the mythical figures Gaia and Okeanos rather than stressing the elaboration of a notion of *nature* that pivots around the idea of an internal regularity independent of the intervention of supernatural forces. By doing this, he prevents himself from appreciating the starting phase of a reflection on the idea of natural *order* in the context of the Ionian cosmologies: an idea that was later appreciated by scholars who considered religious tradition as one of many factors to be evaluated against the political and social context of the Greek world.[36]

Some of the best comparative studies on the problem of myth/philosophy still move along the lines of Cornford's work. As a matter of fact, the steadily

---

[35] See Allan 2006, 30–31.

[36] See at least Vlastos (1955), for a review of *Principium Sapientiae* showing all the reasons that sparked Vlastos's interest in this theme, and Vernant (1957), who takes a clear position regarding Cornford. The theme of cosmic order will be the core of chapter 2.

mounting evidence on the East has allowed us to discover a growing number of analogies with Presocratic cosmology, confirming that the problem of the Eastern background absolutely cannot be avoided.[37] Nonetheless, the evaluation of the relationship between documentary evidence and the features of archaic Greek thought does not yet seem to meet well-defined criteria, in the sense that the necessary acknowledgment of the debts to other cultures has been paired with a problematic—to say the least—assessment of the Greeks' own specific contribution to the beginning of philosophy. This is the case (the second, and last, that I have chosen to illustrate my argument) of a scholar of philosophy and ancient religion such as Walter Burkert.

Walter Burkert is still today, like Jean-Pierre Vernant is in a different field, a prominent representative of an anthropological approach to the ancient world. His work, like Vernant's, is dominated by an interest in the history of religions. However, while Vernant studied the most specific and innovative aspects of Greek culture and society, Burkert preferred to insist—in the wake of Konrad Lorenz—on the psychobiological constants of humankind. For him, then, anthropological comparativism was not just an antidote against the humanistic temptation to idealize the Greeks but also a paramount instrument for reading the Greek evidence, seen as a "mirror" of the deepest roots of culture (singular), reaching all the way through the Paleolithic period. While Vernant focused on the elements of discontinuity that characterize the origins of Greek thought, Burkert always shared with Cornford (to whom he significantly referred more than once) what we might dare to call an obsession with continuity.[38] There is, however, an important difference: according to Burkert, Greek philosophy has religious, mythic, and ritual roots, but he—unlike Cornford—does not explain myth exclusively in connection with religious ritual. Rather, myth itself becomes a locus of speculation from its very beginnings—except that these beginnings are not to be found in Greece.

Let us start with some methodological considerations in the introduction to a book where Burkert reconstructed the pronounced presence of foreign images, myths, and rituals on Greek soil, advancing the thesis that in the period between 750 and 650 BCE, Greek religion and literature were deeply influenced by Eastern models, in a way that also influenced the following developments:

> The studies presented in this book may still run up against a final and perhaps insuperable line of defense, the tendency of modern cultural theories to approach culture as a system evolving through its own processes of internal economic and social dynamic, which reduces all out-

---

[37] Cf. Hölscher 1953, Schwabl 1962, and West 1971.

[38] A clear outline of Burkert's argument can be found in Schlesier (1994, 321–28). Vernant's theoretical premises have been studied in depth by Laks (1998 and 2008); some aspects of Vernant's arguments on the birth of Greek thought will be analyzed directly in chapter 3.

ward influences to negligible parameters. There is no denying the intellectual acumen and achievement of such theories. But they may still represent just one side of the coin. It is equally valid to see culture as a complex of communication with continuing opportunities for learning afresh, with conventional yet penetrable frontiers, in a world open to change and expansion. The impact of written as opposed to oral culture is perhaps the most dramatic example of transformation wrought from the outside, through borrowing. It may still be true that the mere fact of borrowing should only provide a starting point for closer interpretation, that the form of selection and adaptation, of reworking and refitting to a new system is revealing and interesting in each case. But the "creative transformation" by the Greeks, however important, should not obscure the sheer fact of borrowing: this would amount to yet another strategy of immunization designed to cloud what is foreign and disquieting.[39]

Here Burkert tried to formulate a theoretical model for approaching Greek culture that aimed on one hand to preserve its internal autonomy, and on the other to project it onto a world interspersed with "penetrable frontiers": this way, the process of "creative transformation" brought about by the Greeks[40] will not be underestimated, and at the same time their debts to other civilizations will not be obscured. So far so good, in principle. In reality, throughout the book the attention falls on the indebtedness of the archaic world to the Semitic East in the most disparate fields, from technology to medicine to mythology. This is not surprising, since Burkert was always more interested in exploring the background rather than in identifying the characterizing traits of the earliest phases of Greek thought. His reflection on this subject has nevertheless been a tormented one, and this is important in its own right.

Let us compare two other writings by Burkert composed within ten years of each other. In a 1987 work, devoted to the many parallels between Greek mythology (read: Hesiod) and Near Eastern mythologies (regarding which he mentioned Cornford's pioneering contribution), the scholar backdated "the origin of Greek philosophy ... to the Sumerians, the Babylonians and the Hittites, not to mention the Egyptians."[41] (Coincidentally, that same year Erik Hornung, an influential Egyptologist, claimed that "already the Egyptians set in motion the process of philosophy," seeing the first formulation of questions on being, death, and the cosmos in Egyptian texts such as the *Book of What Is in the Underworld*.)[42] Later, however (1996), in concluding a lecture on

---

[39] Burkert 1992, 7.

[40] As we know, this notion is an example of autorepresentation by the Greeks, the most famous attestation of which is found in *Epinomis*, 987d.

[41] Burkert 1987, 21–23.

[42] Hornung 1987, 125.

Greek and Eastern cosmogonies that he had opened, once again, with an appreciation of Cornford, Burkert revisited his position by identifying the distinctive trait of Greek philosophy with rational *argumentation*, which started with Parmenides. This meant granting the Ionian cosmologies the privilege of a close relationship with the mythical sphere, which he ascribed (together with Hittite, Babylonian, and Egyptian cosmologies) to the genre of the "just so story." In all of these texts, he noted, the origin and the first events of the cosmos are presented in the form of an ordered story: it is this particular form that makes all of these stories myths.[43] This point is the result of a long journey of reflection, which deserves a great deal of attention: mythical discourse is qualified as such—and it differs from philosophical discourse—because of its imaginative and narrative *form*.

Cornford was loath to recognize that myth has an autonomous *speculative content*, because he still remained bound—beyond his intentions, no doubt—by a rationalistic stance. Burkert, on the other hand, having assimilated Usener's and Cassirer's message, did not hesitate to recognize myth's power to organize and represent experience, which in some cases reaches high levels of abstraction: as he incisively wrote not so long ago, "there is *logos* in cosmogonic myth from the start."[44] Hence the need to introduce a notion of *form* to separate the two: mythic *logos* is written in fictional form, philosophical *logos* in an argumentative one. This is an interesting reevaluation of the thesis, once championed by Burkert himself, that the beginning of philosophy should be sought in the mythical sphere. However, the identification of argumentative form as a distinctive criterion of philosophy does not seem to solve our problem, for it corresponds to an idea of philosophy as logical-deductive reasoning that appears reductive, not only on a general level of definition but especially if we consider the notable diversity of thought patterns in the Presocratic period. Let us limit ourselves to the case of Parmenides: if we focus on his role as "inventor" of logic, what should we make of the proem in which he tells us, in inspired tones, of the journey that led him to a goddess who revealed to him the truth about Being? A similar objection can be put forward against Jaap Mansfeld's proposal to limit Thales's founding role to the area of science, given that science *today* would not be a branch of philosophy; thus philosophy began rather with Heraclitus or Parmenides. This thesis, too, stemmed from a reductive definition of philosophy (intended in this case as epistemological and ontological speculation) brought about by a critical preconception that does not take into account the philosophical character of the Ionians' inquiry on nature, which preceded Heraclitus and Parmenides.[45]

Another limitation of the picture brought forth by Burkert (and developed along the same lines by Mansfeld) is that the Ionian cosmogonies, if set

---

[43] Burkert 1999a, 35ff, and Burkert 1999b.

[44] Burkert 1999b, 104.

[45] See Mansfeld 1984, and Leszl's response (1985), with which I fully agree.

aside because uninteresting, are confined to a no-man's-land, with the other important consequence that, in this perspective, Parmenides or Heraclitus steps into the picture as an unexpected flower in the desert, similar—to use Cornford's words—to "a motherless Athena." Instead, we need to go back to the Ionian cosmogonies if we want to outline a picture of the *beginning* of Greek philosophy that on one hand takes into account the complexity of all its components, and on the other preserves its continuity with the mythical background. To this end, it will not suffice to dissolve the classic pairing *mythos/ logos* and reformulate it in terms of an opposition between mythical and philosophical *logos* differing only with regard to the presence of imagination and/or abstraction. We will need to combine this move with others: rather surprisingly, Aristotle will be the first to point us in this direction.

Back to Aristotle

Let us start by noting that the Greek term *muthos* is a typical "false friend," in that it does not have the generally depreciative meaning of "false story," endowed at best with symbolic meaning, that inevitably accompanies the word *myth* in modern Western languages. Rather, the majority of the many instances of *muthos* in Homer designate speech uttered in public, from a position of authority, by leaders in the assembly or heroes on the battlefield: it is the discourse of power, one that enforces obedience toward the prestige of the orator. Conversely, *logos* (in its few Homeric instances) tends to designate well-organized, but also potentially deceptive, discourse. After the Homeric Age, the respective frequency of the two terms gradually shifts, and so do their respective connotations. *Logos* gains more and more importance as the designation of speech that does not depend on tradition but only needs to be evaluated with respect to its internal organization, while *muthos*, on account of the fact that its significance stems from the prestige of the speaker, takes up the meaning of speech that cannot be verified. This causes *muthos* to indicate preferably (but not always) speech that lacks credibility in the context of argumentative strategies, particularly those of historians or philosophers who use *muthos* to refer to the positions of *others*, which they intend to discredit.

This semantic development would be too complex to deal with at length here.[46] But we must at least mention Thucydides, who, in the so-called *Archaiologia* of Book I, reconstructs the earliest phase of Greek history based on a tradition of earlier stories. In dealing with this tradition, the historian is concerned with separating the most-plausible facts from those elements that became patently fictional (*to muthōdes*: I, 21, 1) in the long run. Then we must dwell on Plato. As shown by Luc Brisson, *muthos* is for Plato any speech that aims at persuading and uses to this end more or less effective images instead

---

★ [46] I refer the reader to the illuminating treatments in Lloyd 1990 (1ff), Lincoln 1999 (8ff, 37ff), and Cozzo 2001 (25ff, 85ff).

of argumentative mechanisms designed to reach well-thought-out theoretical truths.[47] After all, Plato's judgment of myth is not always a negative one, and it varies from context to context based on ethical considerations. On one hand, the often "immoral" stories in the poetic tradition (first and foremost the episode of Ouranos and Kronos, which contains one of the goriest depictions of the world of the gods) should absolutely be banned from the educational horizon of the city of the *Republic*; on the other hand, Plato himself employs the patterns of mythical discourse (thus competing with the poets) in contexts where he would rather try to persuade than conquer rational certainties, on such topics as the essence of the soul or the origin of the universe, which cannot, by their own nature, be experienced. Myths are also contained—and articulated vividly and with grandeur—in the depictions of the afterlife outlined in the *Phaedo*, the *Gorgias*, and the last book of *Republic*, aimed at providing an effective picture of the vicissitudes of the soul after death, its transmigrations into bodies of superior or inferior nature, and the rewards or punishments awaiting the individual depending on his moral conduct.

Even the description of the creation of the cosmos by a divine demiurge, presented by Timaeus in the dialogue of the same name, is called *muthos* (but also, with an equivalent meaning, *logos*) and declared, if not indisputable, at least "plausible." From a different angle, on the other hand, the depreciative connotation of *muthos* may be brought to the fore again to qualify *other* cosmological speeches, considered incapable of dealing with a specific problem being discussed. In a well-known passage of *Sophist* (242b–243c) Plato outlines—through the words of the Eleatic Stranger—the history of those who discussed Being before him. Now, each and every one of these predecessors seems to want to "tell us a story, as if we were children." Someone said that Being is made of three entities, which are sometimes in conflict and sometimes mutually well disposed, to the point of marrying and bearing children (this is a possible allusion to Pherecydes's theogony, focused on *Chthoniē*, *Zas*, and *Chronos*). There have also been some who said that the entities are two (hot and cold, or dry and wet) and united them in marriage. The Eleatic school maintained the unity of Being, "thus forging their own personal myth," while still others argued that Being is one and many at the same time (the "Ionian Muses" of Heraclitus are stricter, Empedocles's Sicilian ones more lax). None of them, at any rate, was concerned with the intelligibility of their speech; on the contrary, "they could not care less about us, the mass they despise," and did not pause to clarify what is meant by "Being." Thus, Plato relegates all previous philosophical tradition on Being to the area of myth—even the reflection of the Eleatics—in order to better consolidate his dominion over the terrain of metaphysical inquiry. This is made possible precisely by the malleability that the notions of *muthos* and *logos* have for him, and by

[47] Cf. Brisson 1982, Murray 1999, and Morgan 2000.

their magmatic interplay: in the passage from *Sophist*, *muthos* is, after all, almost a kind of *logos*, characterized not so much by falsehood or by a lack of rationality as by inadequacy on methodological and dialectical levels.[48]

We shall now ascertain that Aristotle's position regarding myth is just as flexible by dwelling precisely on that first book of *Metaphysics*, where Thales is presented as the first "of those before us who embarked upon the study of the things that are and philosophized about the truth" (I, 3, 983b 1–3). In this book, intended as an introduction to the problem of substance that runs through the treatise, Aristotle attempts a general outline of the preceding philosophical tradition, revised in the light of his own reflections on the four causes (material, efficient, formal, and final). As is well known, Aristotle presents the doctrines of his predecessors as anticipations—more and more complex, but inadvertent—of a theory that he believes he has finally brought to its full fruition. The markedly teleological perspective that determined the fortune of this framework in the historicist climate of the nineteenth century also marks the beginning of its disrepute, and it has only fallen lower over the course of the last century. However, it may be time to recuperate some of its elements. Granted, we will need to carefully analyze Aristotle's account, which is not intended as an objective historical reconstruction but as a retrospective construction serving to illustrate a personal theory.[49] Yet we can read between the lines and detect elements of internal tension indicating an attitude toward tradition that is anything but dogmatic or simplistic.

In reflecting upon the origin of the philosophical enterprise, Aristotle seems even more willing than Plato to grant cognitive significance to myth. He believes that men began to philosophize, that is, to seek knowledge, out of a feeling of ignorance brought about by their marveling at problems not immediately understandable, such as those arising from the origin of the cosmos and the astral phenomena. So the contents of myth are an expression of this marvel, and "he who loves myth is a philosopher, in a way" (*ho philomuthos philosophos pōs estin*: I, 2, 982b 18). Nor does Aristotle limit himself to making this basic statement, as demonstrated by the two references to Hesiod's *Theogony* that appear shortly afterward. The first reference occurs during the discussion of efficient cause, which thinkers like Empedocles and Anaxagoras realized indirectly, for both revealed the need to track down a principle of movement that is fundamental to the order and good of the cosmos: the former by introducing the forces of Love and Strife, the latter Nous. In doing so, they came close to glimpsing—albeit unwittingly and imprecisely—the role of finality in determining becoming (by focusing on the final cause, which

---

[48] See Adomenas (2006) for an illuminating reading of Platonic passages showing particular formal traits (primarily the mythic setting and a hermeneutical obscurity) that according to Plato characterize the philosophical discourse of the Presocratics.

[49] I have dealt elsewhere with this delicate problem (Sassi 1996).

includes a focus on the formal cause of things, Aristotle believes he made his most relevant contribution, thus completing the reflection on causality). Now, according to Aristotle, "one might suspect that Hesiod was the first to look for such a factor, he or anyone who posited love or desire as the origin of beings, such as Parmenides" (I, 4, 984b 23; followed by a quotation from Parmenides frag. 13, then the beginning of the cosmogonic passage in *Theogony*, lines 116ff, which is actually quoted in a slightly incorrect and rather abbreviated form: "First of all things was Chaos, then broad-breasted Earth, then Love, distinguished among the Immortals").[50] Hesiod is mentioned again later as an eminent proponent of the idea that the earth is generated before all other elements: an idea, shared by the majority of men, which the philosophers disdain but which deserves to be considered for its antiquity and diffusion alone (I, 8, 989a 10).

This appreciation of the mythical knowledge underlying the poetical tradition is fairly frequent in Aristotle. Elsewhere, he formulates the hypothesis that all myths preserve the "remains" (often hidden under increasingly heavy structural layers) of a most ancient wisdom that was periodically lost in a catastrophe but later rediscovered (because the loss had been partial). An instance of these "ruins" of an "ancient philosophy" is represented by proverbs, which survived tremendous destructions of humanity thanks to their characteristic concision and sharpness (according to the lost dialogue *On Philosophy* [frag. 8 Ross]). In book XII of *Metaphysics*, Aristotle also recognizes that the men of very ancient times were able to grasp the divine nature of the stars. Such an intuition was later passed on "in mythical form" (*en muthou schemati*), after having been veiled with a representation of the gods in human or animal guise in order to persuade the population to follow the laws. But those who are able to "separate" these additions from the rest, after all, may also be able to "grasp" a still valid doctrinal core: indeed, Aristotle sees ancient divinization of the astral bodies (which he calls "first substances") as a predecessor of his own concept of unmoved divine mover (XII, 8, 1074a 38–b 14).[51]

Thus myth, when the deformations it underwent over time have been properly pruned away, reveals the traces of most ancient philosophical truths. Moreover, as documented by the aforementioned Hesiodic references, Aristotle admits that the poetic medium is capable of hosting philosophical concepts. In other words, not even in Aristotle is the opposition between *logos*

---

[50] As a matter of fact, the pairing of Hesiod's and Parmenides's texts was already in Plato; in the *Symposium* (178a–b), Phaedrus cites them as "proof" of the antiquity of Eros. We should also consider the possibility that Parmenides, by calling Eros "first" of all gods, was trying to correct Hesiod, who placed Eros in a primordial triad with Chaos and Gaia; see below, 59n44.

[51] For a thorough treatment of these themes and for further textual references, see Verdenius 1960, Verbeke 1961, Casertano 2007 (55ff), Johansen 1999, Palmer 2000 (in particular 192–203), and Cambiano 2002.

and *muthos* that stark: we might even say that already for him "there is *logos* in *muthos*," were it not for the fact that his way of decoding mythical discourse follows a fully rationalistic pattern. But this is not the only surprising turn emerging from the Aristotelian text, considering the reading approach we have been proposing. If we now go back to the passage indicating that the beginning of philosophy can be discovered in Thales, and examine it more closely, we will find that, in order to separate the new terrain of knowledge from the mythical one, Aristotle has pulled off a rather complex feat, not only precociously applying the hermeneutical principle of the opposition between the abstract character of philosophical reasoning and the fictional character of myth but also understanding the need to combine this insight with further distinguishing criteria (I, 3, 983b 6–984a 2):

> Most of those who first philosophized thought that the principles of all things were exclusively of the material kind. That of which all beings consist, from which they first come to be and into which they are destroyed in the end, persisting as an underlying substance but changing in its affections—this they call an element and principle of beings.... However, they do not all agree as to the number and kind of such a principle. Thales, the founder of this sort of philosophy, says that it [this principle] is water (therefore he also claimed that the earth rests on water), perhaps deriving this assumption from the observation that the nutriment of all things is moist, and that warmth itself comes from this and lives by it (and that from which they come to be is the principle of all things). He then derived this assumption from this consideration and also from the fact that the seeds of all things have a moist nature and water is the principle of the nature of moist things. There are in fact some people who think that those who first spoke about the gods in ancient times, living long before the present generation, had the same conception about nature. For they made Okeanos and Tethys the parents of becoming and water, which they called Styx, the oath of the gods. For what is most ancient is most honoured, and what is most honoured is an oath. Yet it is unclear whether what seems to be an ancient and venerable opinion was actually (formulated) about nature; what is certain is that Thales is said to have expressed himself precisely in this way about the first cause.[52]

The first part of this passage clearly shows how Aristotle filters earlier philosophical accounts, selecting and recombining, based on personal coordinates,

---

[52] The second part of this passage is quoted in its entirety in Laks and Most's edition as a reconstruction (R32) of Thales's argument, whereas in Diels and Kranz's edition (11 A 12) it was cut after the reference to the divine oaths, thus obscuring the meticulousness of Aristotelian discourse.

the doctrinal elements gathered from tradition (which, in the case of Thales, is exclusively an oral tradition, and rather scant). Moreover, it is not impossible for the modern reader to extrapolate elements useful for historical reconstruction from a theoretical grid that is as powerful as it is legible.[53]

In this case we see that Aristotle ascribes to "those who first philosophized" an interest in the "principle" (*archē*) of things, the idea that this is unique, and the tendency to recognize it in the material world (which is to say, in Aristotelian terms, in the "material cause"). But there is more: this principle, in line with the Aristotelian system, is something that exists beneath the qualitative variations of things. Now, the notion of a material substratum characterized by stability and permanence is an Aristotelian invention, and to project it onto the beginnings of natural philosophy would be patently anachronistic. Moreover, in this phase the term *archē* would not have been employed[54] to mean "basic principle": in archaic Greek literature, the term appears with the meaning of "command" or temporal "beginning"; in the context of natural philosophy, it may have conveyed the idea of a principle—chosen based on various considerations about priority—from which all things originated. It is unlikely that Thales's water was meant to establish a qualitative connection between all things and a principle intended as their unitary *essence*. It is more likely that he reflected on the *origin* of things, and water seemed suitable to explain, to some extent, a state of becoming.

We are pointed in this direction a few lines later by Aristotle himself, and it must be noted that the author, after mentioning Thales, does not refer to any lingering on his part about the requisites of material cause and prefers to ascribe his ideas to more concrete data. On one hand, the appreciation of water in Thales is connected with the idea that the earth is kept afloat by a cosmic aqueous mass; on the other hand, according to Aristotle, Thales derived his theory from the observation of the role played by moisture and heat in biological phenomena. Aristotle points out that "perhaps" (*isōs*) Thales started from this observation, and clarifies that he did not receive it from the existing tradition (as he did with the doctrine on the position of the earth):[55] this confirms that Aristotle is proceeding in his account in such a way as to enable the reader to formulate his personal opinion on the proposed hypoth-

[53] At least after Cherniss's (1935) detailed analysis of the mechanisms of Aristotelian discourse.

[54] If it was indeed used; we are not sure it ever was, even by Anaximander. The interpretation of the meaning of *archē* proposed here, which has been made possible by Cherniss's studies, prompts us to see the Milesians as the theorists of a "generative substance" (in the terms discussed by Graham [2006]) rather than as proponents of a rigorous material monism.

[55] Aristotle refers again elsewhere to the idea that the earth "lies on water" as an opinion that must certainly be ascribed to Thales, and discusses it closely (*On the Heavens*, II, 13, 294a 28, in 11 A 14 DK).

eses. And indeed it is plausible that Thales may have been led to choose water as the "vital" element for the whole sensible universe by an assessment of its role in the generation and growth of all living things, through a process of inference entirely justified in an era that lacked a clear distinction between biological and geological phenomena.[56]

But Aristotle makes a further remark regarding Thales's pivotal role. He mentions "some" who ascribe a speculation on nature even to the "men of very ancient times" who "first spoke about the gods," indicating Okeanos and Tethys as "parents of generation," or stating that the gods swear upon the water of the river Styx (which demonstrates the sacral aspect of this element). Aristotle is thinking here of a few Homeric passages that refer to Okeanos and Tethys as the "parents" of all the gods (*Iliad* 14, lines 201, 246, and 302) and to the Styx as "dread river of oath" (*Iliad* 2, line 755; 14, line 271, and 15, lines 37–38; a most ancient river, since Styx is the eldest daughter of Okeanos in Hesiod's *Theogony*, lines 400 and 775–806). These texts are part of the evidence used by modern scholars who point out remnants of Eastern wisdom that may invite us to backdate the beginning of philosophy. Now Aristotle is telling us that even in antiquity there were one or more commentators convinced that it was possible, thanks to an allegorical reading, to extrapolate speculative elements from theogonic poetry. It is not important to identify Hippias and/or Plato, to whom Aristotle refers without naming names, as supporters of this position.[57] However, it is interesting to note that Aristotle knows and reflects on a reading method, elaborated by others, that was aimed at finding philosophical *doxai* in poetic texts by decoding their expressive structure: in other words, a method based on the assumption that the difference between *muthos* and *logos* is essentially a *formal* one.

In short, form matters. But from this shared observation Aristotle comes to conclusions different from Burkert's. Regarding the representation of Okeanos and Tethys and the swearing on the river Styx, he states that it is "*not clear* whether this opinion, a somehow venerable and ancient one, happened to be made concerning nature."[58] In other words, it may well be possible to glean a certain vision of nature beneath the fictional structure of the Homeric text,

[56] See, for instance, Hankinson 1998a, 11–12.

[57] The problem has given rise to rich and interesting scholarship; cf. Snell 1944, Classen 1965, Mansfeld 1983 and 1985, Patzer 1986, and Balaudé 2006.

[58] I support Mansfeld's (1985) criticism of the standard translation of this passage, although I propose a partially different interpretation. I am also going to depart from a translation I proposed elsewhere (Sassi 2002, 69), and I do not think I have yet come to terms with the particular difficulty of this phrase. In any event, it confirms the striking *caution* underlying Aristotle's account (see also Laks 2004). Moreover, there is no doubt that, in counteracting the mythical account, Aristotle is intent on emphasizing the "theoretical precision" of Thales's explanation; Hussey also insists on this important point (2006, 7ff).

but the close hermeneutical work needed to reach this point indicates that the text was unclear from the start. Conversely, "it is said that Thales's opinion concerning the first cause was precisely this." "It is said," because we have no direct information regarding Thales's opinions; if this information is true, however, it reveals anything but a remote intuition covered by names of divine figures full of symbolical resonances. To paraphrase Aristotle, we might say that Thales called things "by their names" when he sought an explanation for them in water, the stuff of daily life. The *clarity* of Thales's formulation presupposes new content: in gazing at nature without resorting to the divine, he did not act as a passive recipient of the picture of the world inherited from myth.

The other important criterion that guides Aristotle in the separation of poetical and philosophical knowledge is clarified and confirmed by a further passage in *Metaphysics* (III, 4, 1000a 9–20). In discussing a major *aporia* (do corruptible and incorruptible entities have the same principles?), Aristotle notes: "the followers of Hesiod and all theologians have only been concerned with what seemed plausible to them, and could not care less about us."[59] In fact, they have said that the gods are the principles of things, but also told us that they are immortals thanks to the nectar and the ambrosia they eat. ... But how can the gods be eternal, if they need nourishment? Nectar and ambrosia are nothing but "mythical devices" that need not be taken seriously, unlike the opinions of those who provide the "demonstration" and the "cause" of the things they say. If we now reformulate the problem of Thales in light of this argument, we might say that the poets who speak of Okeanos and Tethys feed us with unfounded stories, while Thales, with his observation of the power of moisture and heat, has (perhaps!) provided some proof for his statements.

Finally, I would like to propose giving more credit to Aristotle's reasons for naming Thales the "father of philosophy": the clarity of expression combined with a limitation of the role of the divine in nature, and the possible (though embryonic) application of an empirical procedure. These indications might prove fruitful for the modern scholar.

Knowledge Has Many Faces

One last remark should be made, however: the Presocratics were not interested only in nature. Aristotle, who chose to write a history of *physiologia* aimed at emphasizing the turning point represented by Socrates, ended up

---

[59] I have chosen a "strong" translation of the Greek verb *oligoreō*—"to hold someone or something in low esteem"—in order to facilitate comparison with the passage in *Sophist* where Plato laments, with very similar wording, the argumentative negligence of earlier philosophers (see above, 20–21). For this connection see Frede 2004, in particular 30–33 and 43.

normalizing an intellectual landscape that had been far richer than the one emerging from the first book of *Metaphysics*. The figure of Thales himself is thrust into this picture, which showcases his interest in the physical world while sacrificing other aspects of his thought that were nevertheless present in the tradition known to Aristotle.

As already mentioned, Thales might also appear as the herald of a kind of socially useful practical wisdom, a role with which Aristotle seems to be familiar when he cites the episode of the olive mills in *Politics*. Thales was also constantly present in the various ancient lists of the Seven Sages and thus chosen—together with a series of personalities from the first decades of the sixth century—as a representative of an intellectual context where moral wisdom is intertwined with practical sense, political ability, and poetic talent, or at any rate with a good dose of verbal and gestural eloquence. In fact, according to some sources (Diogenes Laertius I, 22, who attributes the anecdote to Demetrius of Phaleron, a pupil of Aristotle and an important political figure), Thales was proclaimed "the first" *sophos* by the city of Athens in a decree dated to 582 BCE. These lists also include politicians such as Solon and Pittacus, a tyrant (Periander), and a seer (Epimenides). It would be pointless to look for single elements of truth behind the many anecdotes about this or that sage: as Bruno Snell has shown, the tradition of the Seven Sages is largely the product of a construction that began in the fifth century BCE.[60] This tradition nevertheless shows traces of an idea of wisdom aimed not so much at the acquisition of scientific notions as at a practical and moral reflection. Such an approach characterized Greek culture in the period between the seventh and the sixth centuries BCE, a phase that saw the toiled establishment of the institutions of the polis after a series of harsh economical and social conflicts perceived as a consequence of the crisis of aristocratic values. Solon, the least legendary among the Seven Sages, famously personifies this approach. Archon of Athens from 594 to 593 BCE, Solon is the author of a complex legislation aimed at saving the city from a political and moral crisis whose main cause he saw in the greed of the rich and their abuse of power at the expense of the poor. His reforms consistently aim at mediating social conflict and are inspired by an ideal of moderation memorably propagandized in his elegies.

The tradition of the Seven Sages was of course well known to Aristotle, and he probably centered on it, on at least one occasion, a picture of the beginnings and developments of knowledge intended as an alternative to the one he would provide in the first book of *Metaphysics* (which shows a different agenda, a higher level of elaboration and systematization, and was incomparably more successful). As documented by a long passage by Johannes

---

[60] Snell 1938.

Philoponus (frag. 8 Ross),[61] the Aristotelian writing *On Philosophy* must have featured a description of the civilization of those who survived the Flood thanks to the subsequent discoveries of useful *technai*, the fine arts, the "civic virtues" that coexist—with the Seven Sages—with the invention of the laws and all that favors cohabitation in the polis, and finally on the emerging interest in the natural bodies (*phusikē theōria*) and in the knowledge of divine truths. The last are defined as the object of the highest form of *sophia*, but *all* the preceding phases are seen as manifestations of *sophia* (the term is used here in the polyvalent if unitary sense, typical in the archaic period, of a cognitive and practical ability in the context of a specific area of competence). As in the first book of *Metaphysics*, what we are dealing with here is a history of knowledge that is teleologically oriented: but here the exposition starts from the *technai* and the political wisdom of the Seven Sages, then moves to the theoretical sciences.[62] This different choice may be explained with the specific contents of *On Philosophy*, where Aristotle investigates the intrinsic nature of philosophical activity by examining the different faces of *sophia* depending on the context. Thus the highest level of knowledge (represented, one might suppose, by Plato) would be connoted as such because it deals with ontologically supreme entities. Conversely, in *Metaphysics* Aristotle shows a specific interest for theoretical knowledge, the highest level of which is reached by fulfilling the understanding of the causal principles of reality.

That is why Thales attracts Aristotle's attention within the framework of *Metaphysics* 1: not as one of the Seven Sages (although he was one of them), but for the contribution he made to natural science, in Aristotle's estimation, that is, his intuition of the material cause; here, his contributions to technical and practical thought remain in the background. Later on in the same context (*Metaphysics* I, 6, which we have already mentioned) Socrates holds a parallel position, having launched a journey of reflection—ethics—that had never been explored before. His position is, however, also reduced due to the prominent role that Aristotle assigns to concept analysis in his discourse on virtue. In fact, however, Socrates' teaching did make use of a few central aspects of the tradition of the Seven Sages: we must think not only of his sententious use of moral (especially Delphic) maxims, but also of his embracing not so much an exposition of theories as a *performance* of wisdom, which he realized in the practice of the dialogue and in his *exemplum*. This relationship between the Socratic experience and the earlier practice of moral dis-

[61] The hypothesis that the passage by Johannes Philoponus (*Introduction to Nichomachus'* Arithmetics, I, 1) belonged to the writing *On Philosophy* is not universally acknowledged; in any case it is imbued with Aristotelian elements. Berti (1997, 263–66) provided some starting points for the reading I propose here.

[62] It must be noted that Plato grants Solon the title of *philosophos*, which he then bequeathed to his heirs (*Charmides*, 154e–155a).

course, long overshadowed by the reception of the agenda of *Metaphysics*, is a remarkable phenomenon that has been rediscovered in recent scholarship.[63]

In fact, the most characteristic feature of the intellectual landscape of the period preceding Plato is the very coexistence and intersection of a plurality of intellectual trends, which overlap and compete with respect to their methods, approaches, and areas of interest.[64] Rather soon, for instance, we encounter poets (Hesiod and perhaps Alcman, as we shall see) interested in cosmogonic and cosmological themes, or a writer of history like Hecataeus, whom we might compare, in light of his critical position against traditional stories, to Xenophanes (for whom, however, the appellation of philosopher may not be entirely appropriate).

On the other hand, nature is not the only field of philosophical interest in the sixth century BCE. In this regard we must again emphasize the role of the Seven Sages, and Solon in particular, whose reflections on the prerequisites of lawfulness and justice necessary for keeping a city together are rightly seen as the beginning of ethical and political thought; on the basis of this consideration, and rightly so, Solon has been instated as a thinker on par with the other Presocratics.[65] Conversely, the *phusiologoi* often branch out into fields other than that of natural inquiry. Mathematics was one of these, probably since Thales, then with Pythagoras and his school; it is also possible that Zeno of Elea's arguments were directed toward the procedures of contemporary mathematicians. Moreover, medicine was a full-fledged field of inquiry that interested those who studied nature.[66] This observation is valid first and foremost for Alcmaeon of Croton but also for thinkers known mostly for their complex explanations of being and becoming, such as Parmenides, Empedocles, or Anaxagoras. It might seem striking, in particular, that we possess a sizable number of *doxai* from all these thinkers in the area of embryology, showing a range of explanations of the role played by either parent with regard to generation, sexual differentiation, and fetal development. The amount of information on this subject may have been determined by the preferences of the doxographers (which, we might further hypothesize, may have been determined in turn by the interest Aristotle focuses on more ancient explorations of this problem in *On the Generation of Animals*). However, this consideration does not completely diminish the value of the doxographical tradition, and we may take comfort from the fact that a source external to the line of philosophical doxography, the lexicographer Pollux, attributes the formulation

---

[63] See Martin 1993. Sharp 2006 has some interesting observations about the modalities of interpersonal communication in the relationship between Croesus and Solon as portrayed by Herodotus.

[64] See Cambiano 1997; Lloyd 2002c and 2005, 11–16.

[65] See Lewis 2006, 8.

[66] For this reason we might even suggest (with Frede [1986]) that the theoretical side of Greek medicine started among the philosophers.

of embryological doctrines even to the Sophist Antiphon (87 B 34–39 DK). In conclusion, there is no doubt that in the Presocratic period the terrain of embryology, far from being the sole prerogative of professional physicians, was open for discussion to anyone who chose it as his field of inquiry.

Other similar situations will gradually emerge from these pages. However, we have yet to mention a specific category of authors, namely, those who wrote treatises on their own *technē*.[67] By far the most famous among these is Polycleitus's *Canon*, devoted to the description of the rules applied in carving the well-known *Doryphorus*. Moreover, the centrality of the notion of symmetry in this writing (and in the sculptor's practice) has been linked to Pythagorean theories, which garnered Polycleitus a place among Diels's *Vorsokratiker* (number 40) and, as a direct consequence, a peculiar interest on the part of historians of ancient philosophy.[68] An analogous case is provided by the work of the architect Hippodamus of Miletus, who lived during the first half of the fifth century BCE and was known for the urban planning of the Piraeus and (perhaps) of Thurii, and remembered by Aristotle for his views on the best form of political organization, connected with the problem of an equal distribution of the civic body across the urban territory, as well as for the lavish robes he wore in layers even during the summer, as a rather obvious way of showing off an expertise that covered "the whole of nature" (*Politics*, II, 7, 1267b 22–1268b 25: this testimony is partially reprised in 39 A 1 DK).[69]

We may leave aside the fundamentally nominalistic problem of whether Polycleitus or Hippodamus may be welcomed or not among the Presocratic thinkers, accepting or refusing Diels's attempts at categorization. What I would like to stress—in the light of the significant number of "technicians" who reflect on their own activity (from cooking to nutrition, from wrestling to horse riding, from medicine to painting), sometimes with intents and outcomes of remarkable theoretical interest—is the pluralism of knowledge and styles of reasoning that characterize the intellectual enterprise of the sixth and fifth centuries BCE. On the other hand, if after these necessary preliminary clarifications we try to outline a field of strictly philosophical knowledge, we shall not sacrifice the extraordinary complexity of this situation nor stiffen the elasticity of its internal articulations. It will be possible to populate this field with personalities that differ greatly in approach and sets of problems, thanks

---

[67] Festugière (1948, 32) provides a useful outline of the *Technai*, although in some cases his postulation of full-fledged treatises is a stretch and is not supported by the ancient sources. And to Festugière's list we must add the treatise of musical theory by Lasus of Hermione, Pindar's music teacher.

[68] Huffman 2002 is rightly skeptical concerning the link with Pythagoric doctrines. In any case, Polycleitus is described since the first phases of the doxographical tradition as an eminent figure of the *doctus*-artist (see Settis 1973).

[69] Hence the late characterization of Hippodamus as *meteōrologos* (Hesychius, in 39 A 3 DK).

to a series of important elements they have in common. A first element—accepting a suggestion from Anthony Long—may be recognized in the interest for "all things."[70] Such a formulation, more than that of the "study of nature" championed in the first book of Aristotle's *Metaphysics*, belongs to a scientific agenda that is not aimed solely at the physical world but also at that other great set of problems concerning the soul and the nature of knowledge. It is also true that "the intellectual ambition to return the world to a state of order, to elaborate an all-encompassing discourse" has interested the poets, too, since the time of Homer:[71] on this particular point the philosophers eventually differ by referring to different sources of authority (a theme that will be developed in chapter 5). Another distinctive trait of philosophical discourse that we shall emphasize frequently in the course of subsequent chapters is represented by a particular critical attitude, which is applied both "vertically," with respect to the mythical tradition or prior formulations of the same problem, and "horizontally," with respect to those who profess a different kind of knowledge and champion different approaches. Of course, criticism is not the prerogative of the philosophers alone (it is equally important, for instance, to the historians), but it ends up being such in connection with the problem of "all things." We can see this immediately, starting with the Ionian cosmologies.

[70] Long 1999a.
[71] Miralles 1996, 873.

CHAPTER TWO

Philosophy in the Cosmogonies

Hesiod: Cosmic Masses and Divine Personas

While Homer is the first author of Greek literature, Hesiod, who flourished around 700 BCE, is the first to talk about himself in the first person. In one of his two great poems, *Works and Days*, he tells how he once went to Chalcis in Euboea, where the funeral games in honor of Amphidamas were taking place, and won a prize for poetry in a competition by singing a "hymn." Among the many prizes established by the sons of the noble warrior, he carried off a two-handled tripod, which he then dedicated to the Muses of Helicon, "on the spot where they first set me upon the path of clear-sounding song" (lines 650–662). Helicon is a mountain in Boeotia (Hesiod's native region) where the poet received his initiation, as he explains in detail in the proem of the *Theogony*. It has been speculated that the hymn with which he won at Chalcis was the *Theogony* itself.

We may consider Hesiod's two poems as a diptych.[1] In the guise of a handbook on how to achieve success through a life of virtuous work, intertwining its moral stance with practical instructions pertaining to various contexts, *Works and Days* advances a view of the human condition characterized by suffering and injustice. The roots of today's evils are traced to the baleful creation of Pandora (Zeus's punishment for humanity after Prometheus's theft of fire) and in the notion that the world is in progressive degeneration from a long-gone primordial age when a "golden race" lived, with the result that in the current era, the Iron Age, the only redemption for humanity is offered by honest labor. By contrast, the *Theogony* (composed before the *Works and Days*, as proven by the internal retrospective references in the latter) paints a picture of the relationships between the gods (or repaints it through an idiosyncratic rearrangement of the mythic repertoire, not only of the Greek tradition). After the preliminary invocation to the Muses, the poet focuses on the

---

[1] This image is central in Strauss Clay 2003; see in particular p. 6.

vicissitudes of the succession Ouranos, Kronos, and Zeus and of Zeus's rise to power. The latter establishes a reign of order promptly threatened—but later reinstated—by the terrible fight with the rebel sons of Ouranos, the Titans, and the monster Typhon. The overall outcome of the story (which continues with the various unions of Zeus, followed by copious divine offspring) is the reestablishment of order in the human world, backed by guarantee through the power relationships in the divine world.

There is no doubt that Hesiod's *Theogony* was a successful endeavor. Its pivotal role in the organization of the Greek pantheon—which, incidentally, makes it the favorite target of a line of criticism going from Xenophanes to Plato—is famously recognized by Herodotus in the second book of his *Histories*, which is dedicated to Egypt. After noting that the Greek names of the gods (imported from Egypt by the Pelasgians) are relatively recent, Herodotus adds that before Homer and Hesiod (who, he believed, preceded him by four hundred years), people did not know the genealogies of the gods or their outward forms. It was Homer and Hesiod, and not other, later poets (the allusion is to Orpheus and Musaeus), who composed a "theogony" for the Greeks, attributing epithets to the gods and determining their honors and prerogatives (*Histories*, II, 53). The general tone of the passage indicates that Herodotus—who claims that this opinion is his own and not derived from others—understands the effectiveness of the genealogical paradigm as an organizational system for the gods' respective spheres of influence. Even modern scholars recognize this novel use of genealogy as Hesiod's fundamental contribution to the shaping of Greek religious culture.

Of course, several elements in Hesiod's framework seem to have been borrowed from Eastern lore, and we are reminded again that the sequence from Ouranos through Zeus to Kronos is closely reminiscent of the articulation of primordial divinities described in the Hittite *Song of Kumarbi* and in the Babylonian myth of Marduk. Moreover, the power struggle between the gods, in both Hesiod and his models, represents an outline of the cosmos. So Hesiod is not the first to resort to genealogy and familial ties as the tools best suited for delineating a picture of the origin of the cosmos. But he remains the first to use it on Greek soil, exhibiting unprecedented, encyclopedic ambition, with the aim of presenting his own arrangement as *the right one*. His innovative awareness emerges clearly in the proem of the *Theogony*, where Hesiod describes his initiation as a poet (lines 1–115). One day, while he was grazing his flock on Helicon, the Muses came to him and vehemently reproached him.[2] Then they cut off a laurel branch, gave it to him as a scepter, and awoke in him a divine voice with which to sing both future and past events. They finished by ordering him to celebrate the ancestry of the gods at the beginning and at the end of every one of his songs. This invitation is

---

[2] On the contents of this rebuke, not easy to interpret, see below, 143–44.

reprised in the final invocation of the proem, when Hesiod makes a specific and articulated request to the Muses (lines 104ff): he begs them not only to grant him a pleasant song but also to tell him "how in the beginning the gods, the earth and the rivers were born, and the boundless sea seething with its swell, and the bright stars and the broad sky above." The Muses will have to tell him "from the beginning ... which of these first came to be" (line 115).

At this point, after much insistence on the novelty of his agenda and contents, Hesiod begins his account of the generation of the gods. One aspect of Hesiod's innovation is that this theogonic framework, which aims to start from the very beginning, first presents (lines 116–138) the more abstract forms of the entities in the cosmology that will later unfold with the actions of divine personas equipped with complex psychologies and strong emotions (Ouranos's fear of being usurped, Gaia's anguish for Ouranos's persecution of their children, Kronos's hatred for his father):

> And so first of all Chaos came to be, then
> broad-breasted Gaia, always a safe abode for all
> the immortals who dwell on the peak of snow-clad Olympus,
> and cloudy Tartaros in the recesses of the broad-pathed earth,
> and Eros, who is the most beautiful among the immortal gods,
> the limb-melter, and of all the gods and men
> overpowers the mind and wise counsel in their breasts.
> From Chaos Erebus and black Night came to be,
> and then from Night Aether and Day came forth,
> whom she bore and conceived having mingled in love with Erebus.
> Gaia first of all generated starry Ouranos, equal to herself,
> so that he may cover her all around,
> and so that she may be the ever-safe dwelling place of the blessed
> gods.
> Then she bore great mountains, graceful haunts of the Nymph
> goddesses,
> who dwell on the woody mountains,
> and then she bore the barren sea, seething with its swell,
> Pontus, all of them without delightful love. But then,
> having lain with Ouranos, she bore deep-eddying Okeanos,
> and Coeus and Crius and Hyperion and Iapetus,
> and Theia and Rhea and Themis and Mnemosyne
> and golden-crowned Phoebe, and lovely Tethys.
> After these Kronos was born, youngest of all, crooked of counsel,
> the most terrible of all her children, and he hated his powerful father.

This very famous passage can be interpreted on several levels. What strikes one first is the intersection of multiple generational sequences, outlining the framework within which the divine presences inhabiting the human world will proliferate. These include not only the most familiar of Greek deities, such as Zeus and Aphrodite, but also personalities that belong rather to mythology than to cult, such as the Titans, as well as deeds and personifications of abstract notions, both positive and negative, such as *Nikē* (Victory) and *Pseudos* (Falsehood). A closer look at the text reveals some structural processes that, while not immediately apparent, surely reflect a precise operation of rationalization on the traditional repertoire.

First, the choice to posit a primeval *chaos* is significant. We should not translate this term as "confusion" or "disorder" (a much later semantic development), but rather as "abyss" or "chasm," for it entertains a strong etymological relationship with the Indo-European root **cha*, designating something that "gapes" (the Greek verb *chainō/chaskō*, "to open one's mouth," to yawn— often figuratively—derives from the same root). Cornford argued, based on this etymology, that the first act of Hesiod's theogony consists of the separation of Ouranos (Sky) and Gaia (Earth).[3] If we stick to our text, Gaia is born after Chaos, and Ouranos even later, the offspring of Gaia. Thus it seems preferable to think that the author is postulating the opening of an indefinite and immense empty space; elsewhere in the poem, murky Tartarus (which may be a duplicate representation of Chaos) is described as an abyss (*chasma*) containing "the springs and boundaries" of all things, of the earth and of Tartarus itself, of the sea, of the sky, and of the night (lines 736ff). If this interpretation is correct, we are dealing here with a primordial state, characterized mainly by shapelessness, prior to the separation of Sky and Earth. In any case, Hesiod not only hews to his Eastern models[4] in this respect but also acts as an important link from those precursors to Anaximander's *apeiron*.[5]

Note that Hesiod, when he states that *chaos* comes before everything else, says that it "comes to be," whereas Anaximander will express the need to establish the eternity of the *apeiron* in order to account for its being a principle. We should be open to the possibility that the *Theogony* alludes to a preexisting condition and that *chaos* itself might be a modification. But this would be a rather obscure allusion; it is more likely that Hesiod felt "compelled" to use this expression because of the genealogical pattern he had inherited. Moreover, using images of human generation to describe physical processes will have a long afterlife in the Presocratics' reflections on the cosmos. And if we want to look for signs of development, Hesiod may appear as a forerunner (or at least a middleman) in this kind of reflection, inasmuch as his Eros, a cosmic

---

[3] See Cornford 1952, 194–95; see also above, 12–14.

[4] We might also recall the Ginnungagap, the primordial "abyss" in ancient Norse cosmogony that separates the frozen region of Niflheim from fiery Muspell.

[5] See Solmsen 1950 and Vlastos 1955. Miller (1977; reprised in Miller 2001) thinks that the first phase of Hesiod's cosmogony is the separation of Earth and Tartarus, though he does not deny the important role of the idea of a primordial indifferentiation.

force whose role is to accompany the union of Night and Erebus or Gaia and Ouranos, is born after Chaos and at the same time as Gaia and Tartarus. In fact, Parmenides will give Eros an analogous role in the second part of his poem (considering what emerges from frag. 13), and Empedocles will play with the opposition of Love and Strife as the two forces governing the aggregation and disaggregation of the four elements. Unsurprisingly, Aristotle insists on this continuity in his treatment of the development of the theories of causality.[6]

Other elements indicate that Hesiod, while working within the genealogical paradigm, makes a significant effort to arrange his materials to form a framework of complex relationships between the various parts of the cosmos. After the preliminary phase, when Chaos, then Gaia (as well as Tartarus and Eros) are born, two different and parallel generations spring from Chaos and Gaia. By way of a principle of analogy, from Chaos derive amorphous entities such as Erebus (which designates darkness in general) and Night; subsequently, and through a mechanism of opposition, the union of Erebus and Night generates Ether (diffused brightness) and Day. This progeny does not have a "history," in the sense that it does not continue in a series of altercations and conflicts between anthropomorphic individuals, for this is instead the arena of the descendants of Gaia.[7] She generates Ouranos (as her specific opposite) by parthenogenesis, then the Mountains and the Sea (through a process of self-speciation). After the separation of Gaia and Ouranos, their integration can take place through mating, resulting in the birth of Okeanos (a symbol of unity in differentiation, since he connects his parents on the line of the horizon) and of the other Titans. The birth of their last son, Kronos, inaugurates the period when the cosmic forces famously take up gradually personal physiognomies, and the order of Zeus is established. Thus we can glean a general itinerary, from the shapeless to the completely formed (from Chaos to Zeus), that incorporates several subitineraries, from the negative to the positive (from darkness to light), from the formed (Gaia) to its subsequent specific forms (everything that springs from Gaia).

There is a logic in this cosmogony. Rather than the product of a mythopoeic process, it appears to be the result of a series of systematic choices stemming from an original reflection. This observation fully justifies the view of Hesiod as a "prolific thinker" and a "speculative personality" to be "included in the prehistory of Greek philosophy," which was independently formulated by two great scholars of early and classical Greek thought.[8] By contrast, in

---

[6] See above, 21–22.

[7] As observed by Most (2006, xxxi).

[8] Fränkel (1973 [1962], 96–98) and Diller (1946, 140), respectively. In the wake of the illuminating study by Philippson 1936 on Hesiod's use of genealogy, Diller and Fränkel

dealing with the problem of the *principium sapientiae* around the same years, Cornford preferred to place Hesiod against the backdrop of the Near Eastern mythic repertoire: as we saw in the previous chapter, using this framework he devalued the filter of Hesiod's rationalism as a superficial veneer incapable of hiding a perennially vivid mythical legacy. Clearly, two such disparate assessments are only possible because they both measure Hesiod's philosophical relevance in terms of the level of abstraction he applies: and in this respect the glass will always be either half full or half empty, depending on one's point of view. But—as I anticipated earlier—other criteria should be used to identify the moment when the "glass" of philosophy begins to fill up.

Anaximander in a World "without Gods"

According to ancient sources, Anaximander of Miletus reached his prime (what the ancients called *akmē*, or "flourishing") less than forty years after Thales, toward the middle of the sixth century BCE. The flourishing of the third famous Milesian, Anaximenes, may have fallen shortly thereafter, between 550 and 540 BCE. The Hellenistic biographical tradition puts these three thinkers in a clear sequence of discipleship: Anaximander was an "auditor" and pupil of Thales, while Anaximenes was Anaximander's. The existence of a collegial affiliation is not attested before the Hellenistic period, let alone in the few extant fragments of Anaximander and Anaximenes: thus it is surely the product of an erudite construction based on the observation that these three thinkers shared a common homeland and an interest in cosmology. We might surmise that, in a communication network difficult to reconstruct today, one of them was aware of the ideas of the other and took them into close consideration in formulating his own. In any case, the modalities of this process, which we shall try to clarify later, do not seem to presuppose "institutional" transmission of knowledge.

The most favorable point of departure for our analysis will be Anaximander, whose ideas we can reconstruct with some degree of certainty by combining the information provided by the indirect tradition with an analysis of the longest extant fragment of his work. It is rather doubtful that Anaximander used the term *archē* as a formal designation of the "principle." In any case, it seems certain that he ascribed the origin of the cosmos to an entity called *apeiron*, a term formed by privative *a-* and *peras* ("limit"), thus indicating something "boundless" (with regard to both its temporal and spatial extension) and at the same time qualitatively undetermined. In the beginning,

---

proposed different but equally valuable readings of his cosmogony and of the cosmological traits emerging from the rest of the poem. See also Miller 1977 and the acute analysis of the general structure of the *Theogony* offered more recently by Strauss Clay (2003, 12–30).

according to Anaximander, a nucleus generating hot and cold was separated from the *apeiron*, and from this nucleus the different masses that occupied a specific place in the cosmos were progressively distinguished. The earth, imagined as a cylindrical drum (with a base diameter equivalent to three times its height) is located at the center of the cosmos and there it rests in equipoise because, thanks to its being "equidistant from all things," "it is not governed" by any factor that might push it in one direction or the other. We might deduce that while the *apeiron* spreads out in all directions ad infinitum, the universe is spherical in shape, with the earth at the center. The solution offered by Anaximander to the problem of the stability of the earth is rather interesting in its own right (we might see in it the application of a physical principle of sufficient reason), and it may have benefited from Thales's idea that the earth floats on water and on the fundamental objection that this idea might encounter: if the earth is floating on water, then what is supporting water itself?[9]

Anaximander's theory of celestial bodies is also a circumstantial and ingenious one. It must have served to explain the main astronomical problems of the time (eclipses, the definition of solstices and equinoxes, the lunar phases). His astronomical interests are reflected in the *Suda*, where he is reported to have introduced in Greece a fundamental instrument, the gnomon (the vertical shaft used to indicate the direction and height of the sun). Now, according to Anaximander's description, during the cosmogonic process a layer of the atmosphere adheres to the earth, surrounding it; around this layer—like bark around a tree—is a layer of fire, which, from the pressure of the air, is divided into several circles enclosed within rings of mist. The stars, moon, and sun correspond to different openings in the atmosphere, through which fire shows as "through the mouthpiece of a bellows" (frag. 4). Curiously, the stars, moon, and sun are located in a precise sequence, at increasing distance from the earth. Such a sequence does not have parallels in other Greek astronomical systems but has been noted by Walter Burkert in the documents of an Iranian religious tradition, shamanic in character, where the stars, moon, and sun feature as the consecutive stops in the soul's journey toward Paradise. At the time, Burkert saw value in this hint of dependence from the East, and while admitting that the foreign religious framework is "translated" by Anaximander into

---

[9] The general lines of this cosmogony are described in [Plutarch], *Stromata* or *Miscellanea*, 2, and Hippolytus, *Refutation of All Heresies*, I, 6 (=12 A 10 and 11 DK). The connection between the central position of the earth and a principle of sufficient reason was established by Aristotle (*On the Heavens*, II, 13, 295 b 10 = 12 A 26 DK), but it should be taken with a grain of salt, since the Aristotelian formulation closely resembles a passage in Plato's *Phaedo* (108e–109a) where Socrates refers to the idea (not specifying whose idea it is) that the earth is at the center of the cosmos thanks to a "perfect equilibrium," but here the earth has a spherical shape that justifies this theory much better than the drum shape imagined by Anaximander.

a new language, he used it to claim that Greek philosophy began as a "religion of nature."[10] Yet nothing compels us to think that the sequence in Anaximander's framework of stars, moon, and sun retained the mystical significance that it may have had originally, and elsewhere. In principle, nothing prevents a single derived element from taking up a completely different meaning within a new structure, especially a complex one.[11] Concerning the specific locations of the celestial bodies, we should consider another important piece of information; according to some sources, Anaximander specified that the distance separating the earth from the circles of stars, moon, and sun is nine, eighteen, and twenty-seven times the diameter of the earth, respectively. Of course, this idea lacks any empirical foundation, but it points to an intriguing interest in symmetry and cosmic balance. We have already seen this interest at work in Anaximander's approach to the problem of the shape and position of the earth, and we shall now see it confirmed in the impressive formulation of frag. 1:

> Whence is the coming-to-be of the things that are, there too their destruction happens, according to obligation; for they pay the penalty and retribution to each other for their injustice according to the ordering of time.

The image of judicial dispute is highly effective in representing the conflicted relationships between the things arising from the *apeiron*. Anaximander does not seem to have elaborated an abstract notion of opposites such as hot and cold, dry and wet—certainly not in the sense that will become canonical in the Aristotelian explanation of physical processes. The "things" mentioned in the fragment are probably natural substances that combine aspects of matter, force, and physical quality.[12] They are substances such as wind or water, or mist, or fire, that turn out to be in incessant competition: one may at times prevail over the others, but this prevalence represents an act of injustice that

[10] Cf. Burkert 1963, followed by West 1971, 87ff. In keeping with the scholar's critical and autocritical acumen is Burkert 1994–95 where, after identifying further oriental forerunners of Anaximander's cosmogony, he concludes by stressing the specific contribution of Anaximander and Anaximenes to a new idea of "nature."

[11] This and other principles of exegetical caution are brought up by Lloyd (1982 and 1996b) as far as the scientific cosmologies are concerned. This principle is also valid, as we saw before (34ff), for an assessment of Hesiod's construction.

[12] von Fritz (1971, 16–17) is very clear on this point. For a general treatment of the discussion on Anaximander, essentially unchanged since then, see Sassi 1980. But for a recent, broader treatment, see Gregory (2007), who successfully brings to the fore (in particular on pp. 13–25) some features distinguishing philosophical cosmogonies from creation myths (including Hesiod's): the presence of supporting arguments, an economical treatment of causal principles, and removal of the arbitrary intervention of divine personalities, all supplanted by "invariant" principles aimed at explaining the regularity of the cosmos.

must be redeemed within a certain time. This forced alternation of imbalances and penalties manifests itself, for instance, in the regular change of seasons, in the alternation of day and night, or in the cycle of water evaporating from the sea and returning to the earth as precipitation. Thus we may read Anaximander's words as the first statement of a cosmic law based on a principle of dynamic balance.

Returning to Anaximander's cosmogony, we note that it does not result in a fight among gods but in the birth of animals and humans. This alone can be interpreted as going beyond the mythical accounts. Simply put, there is no Prometheus here, and no Deucalion and Pyrrha surviving a flood. Along a gradual itinerary from the origins of the world to its present state, the birth of mankind takes place without a break and without divine creators; instead it is presented as the extension of those same interactions between physical factors that have articulated the changes of the cosmos since its very beginnings. It is also noteworthy that the indirect tradition preserves traces of the role assigned to time in regulating the process of becoming. According to Anaximander, the first animals were born from moisture heated by the sun; wrapped in thorny bark, "as their age increased" they moved onto dry land (perhaps also following a gradual desiccation of the surface of the earth), but they survived only "for a short time" due to the bark "breaking off" in the new environment. This implies that other animals came into being that were more suitable to live in the new habitat. Following this, men developed inside the belly of a certain type of fish, which protected and nurtured them until the moment when they were able to find nourishment on land.[13]

The balance of things and species does not appear to be entirely immanent in the universe. After causing the first movements of the cosmic masses, the *apeiron* continues to regulate their transformations in the present world. In other words, the *apeiron* is a principle not only because it gave rise to an ordered cosmos but also because it continues to "surround all things and govern them all" (Aristotle, *Physics*, III, 4, 203 b 6 = A 15 DK).[14] It wields its sovereign power to guarantee that none of the constituent parts of the

---

[13] The testimonies pertaining to Anaximander's anthropogony and zoogony are found in 12 A 10 and A 30 DK. According to Plutarch, Anaximander discussed *galeoi* in detail. *Galeus levis* is a kind of shark whose female is equipped with a pouch where the young are kept for a certain period after the eggs have hatched. It is possible that Anaximander knew about viviparous fish and used them as an example to explain through a mutation the development of an animal incapable of providing for itself at birth, like humans. A comparison with Darwin would be anachronistic, but the interest and originality of this theory are undeniable.

[14] The term conveying the meaning of "to surround" in the Aristotelian text (*periechein*) might derive from Anaximander. However, in frag. 2 of Anaximenes, it appears as air that "surrounds" the cosmos. "To govern" (*kubernan*) is used to describe the action of the first principle in Heraclitus, Parmenides, and Diogenes of Apollonia; see Jaeger 1947, 58n39.

world exceeds the limits of a temporary predominance to the extent that it overpowers the others; this role has been compared to that of the Hippocratic doctor, a grantor and/or restorer of the body's balance of powers, which constitutes the health of the individual and is under constant threat of one power prevailing over the others.[15] Thus, while the *apeiron* is indebted to Hesiod's *chaos*, it breaks from it in one fundamental respect; its supremacy is not replaced nor replaceable, while *chaos*, as we have seen, is followed by Zeus's current dominion (and the plot of the *Theogony* serves precisely to reconstruct its troubled antecedents).

The *apeiron* lacks any personal connotations, and the elements participating in the events of becoming are likewise impersonal, purged of any anthropomorphic characteristics. As we already saw in the case of Thales's water, the elements for understanding the world surrounding us are sought in the material world and objectified data and are stripped of the trappings of divine personifications. But, unlike Thales's water (and Anaximenes's air), the *apeiron* is not a substance immediately ascribable to the phenomenal world, nor does it exist as a constitutive principle of things. Rather, its nature is inferred theoretically, from the necessity of postulating an entity that is something "other" than the pairs of opposites and thus purely neutral with respect to the cosmic conflict. Moreover, this conflict is given a reductive explanation; whereas Hesiod's world is teeming with divine figures, Anaximander ascribes the variety of phenomena to the interaction of a limited number of factors (essentially two, hot and cold), thus bringing the workings of their relationship to the fore.

Ultimately, Anaximander simply talked about the stars, the sun, and the moon, just as he spoke of "the unlimited" and of "things that are." The use of expressions such as *to apeiron* ("the unlimited") and *ta onta* ("the things that are" of frag. 1), substantive forms of an adjective and a participle respectively, is significant. Substantivation through use of the definite article represents a peculiar feature of ancient Greek, a language keen on processes of abstraction and conceptualization.[16] The deanthropomorphization of nature takes place also through a search for linguistic transparency; a search for "clarity" that (as Aristotle clearly understood regarding Thales) is not a merely formal endeavor; on the contrary, it (quite literally) gives substance to the elaboration of new content. And the fundamental originality of Anaximander's cosmological account is that, unlike the Homeric and Hesiodic views of the world, it

---

[15] See Freudenthal 1986, in contrast with Vlastos 1947, who argues that maintaining the balance of opposites does not require the action of the *apeiron*.

[16] This is an acute and conclusive observation by Snell (1953 [1947], 220), who already remarked Thales's use of a common noun, *water*, instead of a mythic name. Hölscher (1953) aptly developed these observations in arguing for the "Greek" and scientific character of the Ionian cosmologies.

pivots around a philosophical notion that does not depend on the presence and/or intervention of divine figures.

This development reflects and is part of a broader process of "secularization" of archaic Greek society. During the formation and consolidation of the fabric of the polis, with the need for complex procedural techniques and decisions and for careful legislative regulation of the economic and power relations between the classes, the mechanisms for maintaining the social order increasingly break away from references to the supernatural.[17] This situation is well represented in the works of Solon, whose writings demonstrate full awareness that the life of a political community has its own internal logic. In frag. 11, for instance, Solon deplores those among his fellow citizens who enslaved themselves to Pisistratus and reminds them that it is not the gods but men who are responsible for their own misfortune: "if you have suffered grieves because of your own wickedness, do not hold the gods accountable for it" (lines 1–2). Particularly in the long elegy *On Good Government* (*Eunomia*), Solon insists that it is men's arrogance and oppression that ruin the city (frag. 4, lines 1–8):

> Our city shall never be destroyed through the dispensation of Zeus or the will of the blessed immortals, for such a greathearted guardian, Pallas Athena, born of a mighty father, holds her hands over us. It is the citizens who, foolishly bribed by money, want to destroy a great city, and the mind of the people's leaders is unjust. They are surely going to suffer much pain on account of their insolence.

Solon is a religious man who continues to honor Athena as the patron goddess of the city. Nevertheless, she does not protect the citizens from themselves. Solon denies precisely those aspects of the gods' presence, namely intentionality and responsibility, that were central in Homer and Hesiod's worlds. For him, Athens can be saved only through a government held together by justice, one that limits the hubris of the wealthy. He was inspired in his reforms by this vision of the polis as an ordered structure whose preservation or destruction lies in the hands of its citizens, who are not influenced by external powers. The choice of an *internal* diagnosis of the city's evils, with the subsequent identification of the remedies that need to be applied, is what makes Solon a *political thinker*.[18] What I want to stress here is the affinity between this approach to the issues of the polis and Anaximander's perspective "without gods," during the same years, in his explanation of the cosmos. Though distant from Athens, Miletus is still a Greek city, experiencing similar upheavals. We can legitimately guess that the pressing issue of rationality and

[17] See Humphreys 1986.
[18] See Lewis 2006, 11–22, not forgetting Solmsen 1949, 107–23.

regularity in the social order contributed to the development of a new view of the natural world, one centered upon notions of balance and symmetry.

To clarify, the Presocratics' attitude toward the presence of the divine element in the natural world is far from being a rationalistic rebuttal. This is well demonstrated by the fact that if we scan the indexes of Diels and Kranz's *Vorsokratiker*, few words appear more frequently than *theos*, "god." Aristotle attributes to Thales the saying that "everything is full of gods," connecting it with the idea that the whole universe is intermingled with the soul, intended here as a principle of movement. He is doubtful about this connection, as indicated again by *isōs*, "perhaps," which seems to be a sort of leitmotif in Aristotle's approach to the works of the "first philosopher" (*On the Soul*, I, 5, 411 a 7 = 11 A 22 DK).[19] Evidently, in the fourth century this opinion was already being handed down without a context for understanding it. It would not be surprising if Thales chose those words to express the observation that the moving force of the universe manifests itself as something divine because it contains some sort of immortal *psuchē*. At any rate, the position of the two other Milesians is less uncertain. For Anaximander, the *apeiron* took up typically divine attributes such as agelessness, immortality, and indestructibility (frags. 2 and 3), and we might surmise that Anaximenes too attributed a divine character to the element that he identifies as the *archē* or origin of all existing things, namely, air. Breath and air surround the world in the same way that the soul, which is made of air, holds us together (frag. 2).

The frequent statements supporting the divinity of the original principle in Presocratic thought led Werner Jaeger to put forth a famous thesis, that the first Greek thinkers were constructing—some of them with the zeal of religious reformers—a sort of "theology" of nature. A few remarks should be made regarding this idea.[20] First, we can justifiably speak of "theology" when dealing with reflections on the nature of the gods or on the validity of certain beliefs. In this sense, several Presocratics can be grouped under the category of "theological thinkers": Xenophanes, for instance, on account of his criticism of the representation of the gods in myth; Heraclitus and Empedocles, for the numerous references to contemporary ritual practices made—by both of them—in the context of personal reflections on the idea of the divine; and perhaps Parmenides too, if we consider that he presents his account under

[19] See above, 24.

[20] See Jaeger (1947); his fine readings on several points remain unequaled, along with the critical considerations of Vlastos (1952); more recently on these themes see Adomenas 1999 (in particular for Heraclitus), Broadie 1999, Most 2007, and Gregory (2013; his treatment notably also includes the Hippocratic writings *On the Sacred Disease* and *On Regimen*). Drozdek (2007), apparently ignoring the discussion developed around Jaeger's theses, proposes a reconstruction of the Presocratics' "theology" in which the very search for the *archē* is part and parcel of an investigation of the essence of the divine.

the aegis of a religious epiphany. It is a different matter in a discourse on nature (even one elaborated under a theistic, or pantheistic, light), if the divine is featured there not as a direct object of inquiry but as one of its "side effects." This distinction helps us understand why Plato, in the tenth book of the *Laws* (888e–889b), ignores the various divine characterizations of the principles in the natural philosophers and proclaims an anathema on his predecessors for having seen only chance and the material elements at work in nature, which in his eyes amounts to a denial of the existence of the gods. Similarly, Aristotle defines the inquiry of Thales and his successors as *phusiologia*, that is, a "discourse on nature" (*phusis*), clearly distinguishing it from the *theologia* that, before Aristotle himself and his foundation of a rational science of the divine, is simply the "discourse on the gods" of poets such as Homer and Hesiod. Significantly, Aristotle does not take issue with the role that the reference to the divine has for those same thinkers; on the contrary, he informs us, in discussing Anaximander's *apeiron*, that "the majority of the *phusiologoi*" attribute features of immortality and indestructibility to the principle from which things originate and into which they perish, and this is the same as identifying it with 'the divine'" (*Physics*, III, 4, 203b 10–15).

Plato and Aristotle have gleaned in their assessments a crucial feature of the philosophical tradition that precedes them. Indeed, the *explanatory horizon* of the study of nature had a tendency to exclude the action of divine personas. Consider earthquakes, which because of their rarity and violence were traditionally associated with supernatural actions (for example, Poseidon brandishing his trident in Homer). We know that Thales saw earthquakes as sudden movements of the earth floating on water (11 A 15 DK), while Anaximenes explained them as fractures produced by an abrupt drying up of the earth's crust (13 A 21 DK; see also A 7, 8 DK). Within the notion of nature that starts being formulated from Thales onward, one need not look elsewhere to explain natural events; nature itself, pervaded by some divine power, inspires a reverence traditionally reserved for the gods.

The Invention of the Cosmos

Some years later, around 500 BCE, Heraclitus declared that, beyond the shadow of a doubt (frag. 30),

> this cosmic order, the same for all of us, no god or man made it; but it always was and is and will be an everlasting fire, in measures kindled and in measures quenched.

For Heraclitus, fire is the substance of all things, a physical element capable, thanks to its lightness and mobility, of passing through an incessant process of becoming, where it is lit and quenched in interactions with the other elements. But fire also guarantees that the components of the universe remain the same in quality and quantity, establishing itself as the "reason" (*logos*) and "measure" (*metron*) of all change. The idea of an "everlasting" fire allows Heraclitus to make an unprecedented move; his cosmology does not need a cosmogony, since the measure of becoming—fire—is eternal, and the world has always been the ordered whole that we know. What is even more noteworthy is the fact that the universe is described here, probably for the first time, as a *kosmos*; an ancient Greek term that, ever since Homer, had the primary meaning of "order" and "good arrangement" in an ethical and aesthetic sense (it can sometimes be translated as "ornament," with a connotation that is preserved in our modern term "cosmetics") and does not show an immediate correlation with the realm of nature; such a correlation, according to our sources, seems to have been established by Heraclitus.[21]

As we saw, we owe to Anaximander the identification of the order of the universe as its intrinsic quality. Yet Heraclitus's text is remarkable for its unambiguousness on this point and for its pointedly polemic character. Similar tones will later be used, not by chance, by those Hippocratic physicians who harshly attack religious and magical medicine in the name of a new approach toward disease. Consider how the author of the treatise *On the Sacred Disease*, written between the fifth and fourth centuries BCE, denigrates those representatives of a magical medicine ("magicians, purifiers, quacks and frauds") who ascribe epilepsy to a divine punishment and prescribe purifications and incantations to treat it (the most ancient antecedent of this explanatory scheme is in the *Iliad*, where Apollo sends a plague upon the Achaean camp). Conversely, the Hippocratic physician claims that this disease "has a natural cause like the other diseases" (specifically an obstruction of the cerebral vessels, mainly affecting individuals with a phlegmatic constitution) and is not more divine than the others; or, rather, all diseases are divine inasmuch as nature itself is divine in all its manifestations (chapters 1 and 2).

More or less in the same period, the author of *Airs, Waters, Places* (the well-known work concerning the influence of the environment on psychophysical traits of the peoples of Asia and Europe) deals in a similar way with the problem of impotence among the Scythians. This condition was traditionally thought to be caused by Aphrodite's wrath following the destruction of one of her temples; on the contrary, the physician claims that "no disease is more divine or more human than another, but they are all equally divine," and "they all have their own natural traits." Moreover, effeminacy does not affect all Scythians, but only the noblest among them, due to the swelling of the articulations caused by horseback riding (chapter 22).

We see that in these texts the mention of divine entities is rejected because it implies the recognition of an obscure and supernatural intervention, which the healer thinks he must either propitiate (through prayer) or enforce (through

[21] See Vlastos 1975, along with the remarks of Leszl (1982, 68ff).

various magical acts). Moreover, the manifestations of nature itself are declared divine in that they reveal nature's extremely regular structure and, therefore, its comprehensibility; the Hippocratic physician proclaims his ability to identify the causes of the disease and to suggest the most suitable remedies in purely physical and physiological terms.[22] Upon closer inspection, the general traits of such a vision of nature had already been outlined in the Ionian cosmologies. The well-known Hippocratic passages just quoted show the most mature elaboration of an idea central to Greek thought, to which the natural philosophers also contributed since the beginning, though not in such an explicit form—namely, the general idea of "nature" (*phusis*) as a sphere comprising all phenomena in the world around us—and its explanation is sought in material processes characterized by an internal regularity, without referring to the external action of a divine personality.

However, the idea of nature was not simply lying there waiting to be discovered. On the contrary, it was *constructed* as a pawn within a specific cultural strategy. As Geoffrey Lloyd rightly observed,

> Some of those who insisted on the category of the natural used it to demarcate and justify their style of inquiry, in contrast to those rivals whom they were hoping to put out of business ... some Hippocratic authors used nature to rule out any possibility of any *super*natural interference in diseases. The concept of the natural had its attractions for them precisely because it enabled a wedge to be driven between *their* medical practice and that of the competition.[23]

Undoubtedly, around the end of the fifth century BCE, the term *nature* fully covered that field of inquiry, defined by the reference to a model of regularity, which "the naturalists, the *phusikoi*, made their own."[24] The initial phases of such a process of appropriation are less certain. According to Lloyd, the workings of an intellectual debate can be identified and studied only where explicit stances of the participants are preserved (as in the case of the aforementioned Hippocratic writings). On the other hand, omissions count, too (when they are not simply fortuitous). It is relevant in this respect that the unanimous tradition on Anaximander does not mention interventions of gods in the physical world, for, as conceived by Anaximander, the world does not need the gods (or at least the Olympians; we will explore the sovereign status of the *apeiron* in the following pages). Anaximander must have been already *consciously* formulating a notion of natural order, the same natural

[22] On this particular point see Hankinson 1998b. For a broader, thus more complex, treatment of the different approaches to diseases and cures in Greek medicine, see Lloyd 2003, 14–83.

[23] Lloyd 1992, 422. See also Lloyd 1979 and 1987, 11ff.

[24] Lloyd 2002b, 506.

order that would be claimed shortly afterward by Heraclitus. Of course, if we compare this with a diatribe between physicians that can be explained in terms of professional rivalry, we will have to admit that it is not quite clear what role an Anaximander or a Heraclitus might have been able to claim *for himself.* Let us put this question on hold for now and stress that through their theories they were certainly speaking *against others*; against Hesiod, for instance, and in general against a cosmogonic tradition based on religious assumptions.

The Horizon of the Theogonies

Let us remind ourselves once again that Hesiod's *Theogony* serves to sanction the Olympic pantheon, whose order—governed by Zeus, who won first against Kronos and then against the monstrous force of Typhon and the Titans—is presented as a projection of the cosmic order. In this view, the *Theogony* could be interpreted as a hymn to Zeus. There is no evidence enabling us to establish a formal link between Hesiod's poem and ritual practice as in the case of the *Enuma Elish*, where Marduk, the hero and ruler of the gods, who defeated the primeval monster Tiamat, is responsible for an ordering of time and space periodically sung and reenacted during the Mesopotamian ritual celebrating the New Year. On the other hand, we cannot rule out that the *Theogony* may have been composed in connection with the funeral games of Amphidamas, that is, in a ceremonial context; in archaic Greece, religious festivals still constituted the occasions most suitable for hosting recitations with theogonic contents. In any case, an important element shared by the cosmogonic sections of the two texts (and also characteristic, for instance, of the creation described in *Genesis*) is the idea of the primordial state as an indeterminate mixture needing to be organized. Moreover, both treatments give central importance to the identification of an ordering principle that intervenes at a later time and has the traits of a sovereign deity. Thus, the story of the hardships encountered by the divine agent of the order is instrumental to the legitimization of his power.

In a memorable essay, Jean-Pierre Vernant saw in these cosmogonies the elaboration of myths "of sovereignty." According to Vernant, the structure of the Babylonian epos of creation (as well as of other theogonies documented in Phoenician and Hittite contexts) can be explained with its dependence on a social and political organization governed by a regal figure homologous to the divine ruler. Similarly, in Hesiod's theogony we see the survival of a strong idea of sovereignty as a guarantee of the cosmic and social order that dates back to the Mycenaean period; after the Mycenaean period, however, the memory and meaning of this idea faded, together with the sovereignty rituals holding them together. Moreover, detaching myth from ritual affords Hesiod a relative autonomy in treating his materials; in particular, it encourages the "naturalistic" tendency of his cosmogony that we mentioned above. However, "despite the attempt at conceptual delineation it represents, Hesiod's thought remained the prisoner of its mythic framework."[25] According to Vernant, Hesiod would have been able to step out of the framework of divine genealogies only if he had had the ability to represent the world as a *kosmos* governed by a law of balance and symmetry. On the other hand, Anaximander seems to have had this ability because (a) he eschews the "monarchic" character of myth, and (b) he develops the idea that the principle regulating the universe is present since the beginning, thus merging into the *apeiron* the temporal principle and the principle of the order of the universe. "Indeed, for the natural philosopher the world's order could no longer have been established at a given moment by a single agent; the great law that ruled the universe, immanent in *phusis*, had to be already present in some way in the original element from which, little by little, the world emerged."[26]

This interpretation had the merit of introducing, by referring to a specific historical framework, an important distinction between mythical and philosophical cosmogonies; while the former appear to be modeled after a social order governed by a sovereign figure, the latter are guided by a new idea of balance that, according to Vernant, emanated directly from the experience of the emerging Greek city. In this framework, philosophy starts as cosmogony and is a daughter of the polis. It will be useful to make a few remarks regarding this fundamental thesis, to which we shall return again.

We are encouraged to make these remarks by a passage in the fourteenth book of *Metaphysics*, where Aristotle points out a common stance of philosophers and theologians regarding the problem of the cosmic order (Vernant himself uses this passage for his argument, but he only cites it in passing). Let us remember that in the twelfth book of *Metaphysics*, in reflecting upon nature and the first motor of the universe, Aristotle claims that this first motor has always been at work for, if it had ever been in a state of potentiality, passing from potentiality to actuality at a given moment, it would have been possible for movement never to come into being (whereas the world cannot be a contingent product). According to Aristotle this difficulty has been overlooked by both the *theologoi*, who generate everything from Night, and by the *phusikoi*, who (like Anaxagoras) posit an initial phase of confusion in which "all things were together"; neither of these groups posited an actual cause that enabled them to explain the beginning of movement (XII, 6, 1071 b 23).

[25] Vernant 1982 [1962], 117. Here, and only concerning Hesiod, Vernant follows Cornford's reading to the point that he interprets the images of kingship as mere "*souvenirs*"; a reductive consideration, all things considered, for an account that delineates what will remain, for centuries, the "official" traits of Hellenic religion.

[26] Ibid., 114–15. See also Vernant 1996, 202ff. The following remarks are part of a general reassessment of Vernant's interpretation of the origins of Greek thought that I have undertaken elsewhere (Sassi 2007).

Throughout book XIV the problem is dealt with in essentially analogous terms, but because of the different aim (a critique of the idea of the Good in "some present-day thinkers," including the Academic Speusippus) the tone shifts, and the tirade against Speusippus is redirected against the "theologians" (while the natural philosophers, as we shall see, escape the attack). Here Aristotle's formulation becomes particularly interesting, for he brings up the problem of the relationship between the principle of generation and that of the Good (whether they coincide, or whether the Good appears only later) and notes that those "ancient poets," "the theologians," appear to agree with those among his contemporaries for whom "the Good and the Beautiful appear only after some development of the nature of beings." Indeed, they claim that "to rule and govern are not those[27] who were first in time (*basileuein kai archein . . . ou tous prōtous*) such as Night, Ouranos, Chaos or Okeanos, but Zeus; they are nonetheless led to affirm this on the grounds of the changing of the rulers of beings (*dia to metaballein tous archontas tōn ontōn)*" (XIV, 4, 1091 a 33–b 8).

Aristotle, then, groups under the same category of "theologians" various authors who posit at the start of their cosmogonic accounts a principle that, while first in time, is destined to be replaced. The generation of the universe from Okeanos, as we know, was maintained in the Homeric text, while Chaos was the original principle in Hesiod. Night (*Nux*) is a primordial and supreme force in Orphic contexts,[28] but also in a *Theogony* attributed to Musaeus and in one written by Epimenides of Crete. It is worth pausing here for a moment. Epimenides is a semilegendary figure to whom the tradition attributes prophetic and miraculous powers, together with shamanic experiences (detachment from the body and a decade-long slumber in the cave of Dyctean Zeus on Crete). A historical event of which he is reported to be the protagonist (the purification of Athens after a sacrilege) indicates that he lived during the seventh century BCE.[29] Judging from the extant fragments, his poem was in continuity with Hesiod on one hand and with the Orphic tradition on the

[27] Aristotle's use of the masculine adjective *prōtous* implies that he is talking about gods (*theous*), for such are the figures included in the list that follows. On this point, see also below, 51.

[28] In the so-called "Eudemian" theogony (from Aristotle's pupil, who mentions it in his *History of Theology*, frag. 150 Wehrli), Night is the first principle of all things. Pierris (2007, 17–20) notes that this is the only text to properly configure that "nocturnal monism" that Aristotle has in mind, since both Musaeus and Epimenides pair Night with Tartarus and Air respectively, making a dual choice that would imply, in Aristotelian terms, the recognition of a double causality (material and formal). We may add that even in the Orphic theogony commented upon in the Derveni papyrus, Night (a feminine noun) is paired with Ether (a masculine noun), which acts as its opposite. In all these cases, however, Night belongs to the first cosmic generation, and Tartarus and Ether, at least, do not seem to have a much stronger structuring power than their partner.

[29] See Arrighetti 2001.

other. Indeed, a primary position was given to a pairing made by Air (*Aēr*, masculine in Greek) and Night (*Nux*, feminine); from Night are born Tartarus and two Titans, and their union creates an egg from which comes the next generation. Ouranos and Gaia likely entered the scene at this point, followed by their son Kronos, and lastly by Zeus; this *Theogony* may have also featured the Cretan legend of the Kouretes secretly rearing Zeus in a cave on Mount Ida.

It is difficult to read Epimenides's Air as an anticipation of the physical element that, according to Anaximenes, generates all things through condensation and rarefaction. Rather, Epimenides's Air is "haze, the dark and gloomy part of the atmosphere," and with Night and Tartarus it contributes to the depiction of a "nocturnal and dark primeval reality." In Epimenides, too, we see in action that "primacy of darkness," of which we have already seen variations in Hesiod and in Orphic contexts.[30] Moreover, in Epimenides too the power of the cosmic forces gives way to the power of personal deities, the genealogic model dominates, and high turnover among the gods overshadows and conceals natural events. Aristotle, then, gleaned an important point when he saw in the privileged role of Night or other principles a unifying trait in the discourses of the "theologians." Indeed, giving primordial importance to forces such as Night or Chaos may appear to be a "theological" answer to the problem of the origins, at least insofar as this answer is partial on its own and requires as a corollary the action of a god belonging to the sphere of light, capable of guaranteeing—as a ruler—the present order.

On one hand, the close reading of the passage from *Metaphysics* that we have just proposed may confirm the general traits of Vernant's interpretation. On the other, it authorizes us to rectify one of its particular implications. In Aristotle's view, the distinguishing feature of the theologians' cosmogonies is indeed the fact that an ordering function is attributed only to the combatant who emerges as victor at a later time and after a power upheaval. However, the element of kingship does not play any role in the distinction between theologians and *phusikoi*. In fact, Anaximander's "unlimited" and the cosmic principles of other Presocratics are all but free of traits of sovereignty.[31] Aristotle himself gives the *apeiron* the role of "enveloping" and "governing" all things in terms that leave no doubt that the image of sovereignty continues to be at work in the argument for the supremacy of the principle, even in a theory like Anaximander's, where the principle of order is present since the beginning (*Physics*, III, 4, 203b 7).

---

[30] See Mele 2001, in particular p. 247, and Breglia Pulci Doria 2001. Bernabé (2001), on the other hand, tries to associate Epimenides with Ionian naturalism.

[31] Valeri (1995) pointed this out in a discussion of Vernant's theses. See Laks 2008 for other observations on the role of the *apeiron* that contradict Vernant's "nondynastical" interpretation.

In conclusion, Anaximander's innovation does not seem to lie as much in the first point made by Vernant (the repudiation of a "monarchic" principle, which is more apparent than real) as in the second, namely, that it goes beyond the logic of an alternation of disorder and imposed order (reflected in the violent conflicts between deities) and instead promotes a notion of order whose premises are inscribed, *ab origine*, in nature itself. Once again the justification for stressing this aspect lies in Aristotle's text, where—not by chance—masculine terms (*tous prōtous, tous archontas*) are used to describe the principles posited by the theologians, precisely because the theologians insist on the actions of divine personas. What makes Hesiod a *theologos* and distinguishes him from a *phusiologos* like Anaximander is not the mere narrative and figurative form of his thought, through which one can still glimpse features of rationality (or even, as we have seen, rationalism); conversely, Anaximander is not at all unwilling to use images and personifications (as seen in the mechanisms of prevarication and punishment regulating the relationships between things and in the supremacy of the *apeiron*). The point is, once again, that Hesiod's account presents itself as the commemoration of a history of the gods aimed at justifying their prerogatives within the official religion, whereas this problem is altogether absent from the conceptual horizon of the natural philosophers, absorbed as they are in the description of *phusis* as an area that can be and deserves to be studied in its own right.

Pherecydes's "Mixed Theology"

Pherecydes of Syros, like Epimenides (and Abaris and Aristeas), is a characteristic figure of archaic wisdom to whom the biographical tradition attributes miraculous powers and educational travels to the East. He is of interest as the author of a cosmogonic writing, though it is only fragmentarily preserved and hard to read (even its title, *On the Five* [or *Seven*] *Recesses*, is uncertain and of dubious interpretation).[32] It is noteworthy that such a work, which is more or less contemporaneous with that of Anaximander, is written in prose, and an elevated prose at that, suitable for a lofty theme such as the birth of the gods and the creation of the cosmos. This theme may, however, indicate an aspiration to appeal to a narrower context and a select audience that, while not a match for the multitudes gathered for a religious celebration, was perhaps chosen from them. In any case, the mode of expression was accompanied

---

[32] Schibli 1990 is a valuable guide for reconstructing this work. West 1971 devotes a large section to Pherecydes, but provides a global assessment, one that unilaterally devaluates Pherecydes's speculative merit. The fragments pertaining to Pherecydes are collected under number 7 in the section of the *Vorsokratiker* dedicated to "Archaic Cosmologic and Gnomic Prose."

by a search for new contents, as demonstrated in the vigorous claim for the timelessness of the main cosmic divinities that likely constituted the *incipit* of the writing:

> So *Zas* and *Chronos* and *Chthoniē* always were; but *Chthoniē* came to be named Earth (*Gē*) after *Zas* gave her the earth (*gēn*) as a gift.

These divinities only partially correspond to Hesiod's Zeus, Chronos, and Gaia. In order to bring to the fore their deepest cosmological meaning, Pherecydes uses etymology as an effective gnoseological tool. He elevates Zeus, now named *Zas*, to an unrivaled holder of vital power (the Greek verb *zēn/zan* means "to live"), while *Kronos* becomes *Chronos*, or Time, which by its very nature has always coexisted with the other divinities, and always will (*Chronos*'s seed generates fire, air, and water, distributed into five recesses where a second generation of gods is born). In the case of Earth, the etymological play is even more complex; at the beginning she is *Chthoniē* (a name that refers to its deeper and more ancestral regions), but then becomes *Gē* (a normal variant of *Gaia*) thanks to a gift from *Zas*. We learn from frag. 2, a long description of the wedding of *Gē* and *Zas*, that said gift is a wedding present, a "large and beautiful shroud" embroidered with images of *Gē* herself and *Ogēnos* (Okeanos), with which *Zas* "honors" the bride on the third day, inviting her to unite with him, and she unveils herself. On one hand, this representation has an etiological meaning, as it is aimed at describing the origin of the "festivals of unveiling" or *anakalupteria*, ceremonies that took place on the third day of wedding rituals (during which the groom presented the bride with a gift); on the other hand, it is also a clear allegory of creation; the fertilizing power of the Sky transforms *Chthoniē* into Earth as we know it, and envelops her in the sumptuous array of her visible traits.

By asserting that the divine powers are timeless, Pherecydes amends the Hesiodic model, which postulates that all the gods are born or generated (as is Chaos), and he appears to be moving along a line of thought offered first by Anaximander, then by Anaximenes, Heraclitus, and the sharp-witted comic Epicharmus (frag. 1 DK). Moreover, *Zas* and *Chronos* are equal "cocreators" from the very beginning, as is *Chthoniē*, from the moment she became *Gē*. Furthermore, the creation of the universe does not take place by forceful imposition of a state of order over one of disorder and violence. As Vernant would put it, for Pherecydes the original principle is also the principle of order, and in this respect he is closer to Anaximander than he is to the mythical cosmogonies. Aristotle was already well aware of the peculiarity of Pherecydes's stance in this respect. In fact, in the same passage of *Metaphysics* where he sees the distinction between "primeval" and "governing" divinities as a trademark of the mythical cosmogonies, he goes on to clarify that among the ancient poets there are some who "used a mixed style ... in the sense that they did not express everything in mythical form, like Pherecydes and some others, who refer to the first principle of generation as the best one" (XIV, 1091b 8).

Yet Pherecydes's representation does not go beyond the limits of the divine world. Moreover, it features the detailed description of a battle between two factions, led by *Chronos* (who reprises the name of *Kronos* here and the traits of the sovereign god) and the snake-god *Ophiōn* (or *Ophioneus*). This *Ophiōn* is rather similar to Typhoeus, the monstrous, rebellious son of Earth and Tartarus who is banished back into Tartarus by Zeus's thunder (Hesiod, *Theogony*, lines 821ff). Furthermore, if we think of the battles between Marduk and Tiamat or between Horus-Osiris and Seth, we cannot help but notice the influence of Eastern models in Pherecydes's account. The fact that the battle probably takes place when order has already been established may signal an attempt to break away from those models. At any rate, Pherecydes seems to posit that processes of birth and ordering necessarily require that there be conflict at some point in time; thus he still follows the logic of a succession of order and disorder that we have recognized, from Aristotle to Vernant, as a useful criterion for differentiating the mythical cosmogonies from the scientific ones.

We may ultimately call Pherecydes a "theologian," since he is more interested in investigating the histories of the gods than in studying nature, but he deserves the title of "mixed" theologian, since he combines traditional elements with personal reflections on the problem of the origin of the cosmos. The validity of Aristotle's argument is strengthened by a close examination of the preserved fragments of this *Theogony*, whose author stands out as a significant transitional figure.

A Cosmogony in the Temple of Thetis?

In 1957, the scholarly community reacted with understandable surprise to the publication of a papyrus dating between the first and second centuries CE, which contains a commentary on a text by Alcman, a lyric poet from Sparta who lived during the second half of the seventh century BCE and wrote choral songs (known as *partheneia*) destined to be sung mainly by female choruses in religious festivals.[33] The commentator, after reminding his readers that young maidens led these choruses, notes that the poet "speaks as" or is "a philosopher of nature" (*phusiologei* or *phusikos esti*). We can surmise from what follows (a paraphrase of the poem, interspersed with a few words quoted directly from the original text, and clearly shaped by the patterns of Aristotelian and Stoic philosophy) that the poem painted a picture of primordial confusion of "all things" in which, thanks to the intervention of the Nereid Thetis,

[33] For the most recent edition of the text (POxy 2390, frag. 2) with ample bibliography, see Funghi and Most 1995.

a *poros* (a "way" or "passage") came to be, followed by a *tekmōr* (a "boundary line" or simply "limit"). These "thresholds" presumably start a process of differentiation that causes the ordering of the world into its distinct features. In the first phase of this process, the day and the moon emerge, "glimmering" against a backdrop of primordial "darkness."

A somewhat more obvious element in this picture is the primeval position of "darkness," which, as we have seen, is a distinctive trait of various archaic cosmogonies. Yet other elements are perplexing. For example, the notion of an indeterminate original mass from which the cosmos is born through a process of differentiation seems to anticipate even Anaximander's explanation, in a context where the terms *poros* and *tekmōr*, the two principles responsible for the ordering of the cosmos, take on a strongly abstract flavor. And in Anaximander's model (and in the Ionian cosmologies in general), becoming takes place independently of "supernatural" interventions, whereas in Alcman's fragment, *poros* and *tekmōr* are presented as instruments of a divine personality, namely Thetis. This Thetis should not be confused with Tethys, the Titanide married to Okeanos, that we encounter at the beginning of Hesiod's *Theogony*. We are dealing instead with the niece of Pontus and daughter of Nereus, wife of Peleus and mother of Achilles. Here she is given a demiurgic role unprecedented in cosmogonic thought, a role so striking that the commentator (who certainly had in mind the figure of the Demiurge in Plato's *Timaeus*) compares her action to that of a craftsman.

These issues were put to rest by Martin West, through two valuable observations. First, West pointed to a passage by Pausanias (III, 14, 4) that refers to a temple erected at Sparta in honor of Thetis, precisely during Alcman's time. Second, he insisted on the etymology of the name *Thetis*, which can be read as a feminine *nomen agentis* of the verb *tithēmi* ("to put" or "to establish"); thus Thetis would be "she who orders." The historical and cultic coordinates, together with the discovery of the etymological play (a practice already frequent in the archaic period, from Homer to Hesiod to Pherecydes) established Thetis in her capacity as divine guarantor of order. Following this trend, scholars have granted "Alcman's cosmogony" a crucial position in the transition from *muthos* to *logos*.[34] In what seems like a consecration of this reading, the fragment (Oxyrhynchus papyrus no. 2390) was included in the second edition (1983) of Kirk, Raven, and Schofield's *Presocratic Philosophers* (in the first chapter, dedicated to "The Forerunners of Philosophical Cosmogony"); what is more, it appears here next to the work of Pherecydes, as another "mixed theogony."

A few years later, however, this interpretation was closely examined by Glenn Most, who argued with good reasons that Alcman's song must have

---

[34] After West 1963, see for instance Vernant 1970, Voelke 1981 and 1984, and Calame 1983, 437ff.

consisted in the simple re-evocation of a story of gods; it was the commentator, an expert in the Stoic model of allegorical reading of myths, who forced his cosmological interpretation onto the text. Alcman's *partheneia* normally feature an invocation to the Muses, followed by a mythical narration, followed in turn by gnomic observations and specific references to ceremonial circumstances. According to Most, then, it is more likely that Alcman sang the mythical events of the amorous dalliances between Peleus and his future bride, who wanted to escape a mortal's courting by using a shape-shifting ability typical of a marine deity. According to this hypothesis, *poros* would be the "expedient" used by Peleus in order to be able to seduce Thetis, and *tekmōr* would be the "goal" of his actions.[35]

It is not possible here to delve deeper into such a complex issue.[36] But it is well worth reflecting, if not on Alcman's *cosmogony*, then at least on the *possibility of a cosmogonic section* in one of his writings. Glenn Most challenges this possibility on the basis of a lack of ancient references to a cosmogony by Alcman; he thinks it odd that there is no mention of such a cosmogony, either by Aristotle, in the first book of *Metaphysics*, or in the doxographical tradition. Moreover, according to Most, Alcman's poetry is very much tied to Spartan religious ceremonies, and it would be curious for the poet to take the liberty of inserting a cosmogonic treatment into a ritual context; this would be possible only if we were to attribute social implications to such a treatment that are not attested. On this point, at least, I disagree; there is nothing to prevent us from thinking that the exaltation of the cosmogonic role of a female deity—in the context of a poem sung by young maidens, in a city where that divinity is honored—took on a paradigmatic function, in the same way as a commemorative myth would have. Besides, Hesiod's *Theogony* is proof that a poet's cosmogonic speculations may have relevance in cultic and social life, and the reference to Thetis as an ordering deity could confirm an analogous ritual tie, albeit in a rather localized version.

What is more, elsewhere Alcman shows that he is capable of rising above the more immediate level of ceremonial occasions. The famous Louvre Partheneion, for instance, features the notions of *Aisa* ("one's lot") and *Poros* itself (the "way" that humans can go) in the form of divinized principles; the context is a reflection on the limits of the human condition, nestled between the reference to the Spartan saga of the sons of Hippocoön and praise of the gleaming beauty of the choristers. This and other elements authorized Hermann Fränkel to think that Alcman has a remarkable penchant for "abstract philosophical speculation."[37] Of course, the ancients' silence regarding

---

[35] See Most 1987.

[36] Elsewhere I have dealt with this theme using detailed philological arguments and more textual and bibliographical references (Sassi 2005).

[37] Fränkel 1973 [1962], 164.

a possible cosmogony by Alcman may seem striking if we think of Hesiod's philosophical fortune. We might, however, see this cosmogonic effort as an isolated case in Alcman's work, and as such overshadowed by a poetic production whose general character is lyrical, not philosophical.

Undoubtedly, specific traits of Alcman's framework remain problematic. Reacting to the interpretation current at the time, Most rightly observed that "what is astonishing here is not so much that it is Thetis who plays the role of a demiurge, but rather that there is a demiurge at all."[38] Indeed, Greek cosmological thought, from Anaximander to Plato's *Timaeus*, does not further elaborate on the notion of an intelligent creation carried out by external powers that are driven by conscious intents. There is no trace of such a notion even in the poets. In Hesiod's *Theogony*, the first phase of creation takes place according to a dynamic of parental relations between cosmic masses, which, though divine in nature, act blindly. Only in a second phase does a dominant figure emerge, Zeus, but he is not omnipotent; indeed, his culminating act, the ordering of the cosmos, is far from effortless. This concept has been associated with a fundamental tenet of Greek religion: that the gods, too deeply anthropomorphic, are not powerful enough to create the world.[39] And if the power of Hesiod's Zeus is inadequate for such an endeavor, should we not assume that the same holds true for Alcman's Thetis?

Let us try to defend the traditional interpretation one more time. We may recall Alcman's Lydian origins. In his hometown, Sardis, he may have learned those stories, which are common in Near Eastern mythology and are centered on the idea of a creator-god. These included Marduk splitting Tiamat (the primordial aqueous mass) in half, as well as the God of Judaism creating light before everything else, distinguishing it from the darkness of the waters. On the other hand, in Greece we find Pherecydes of Syros, who, probably inspired by Eastern models, grants Zeus an especially preeminent position. But with Pherecydes we are dealing with a project of rationalization of the traditional repertoire, and his originality earned him Aristotle's appreciation. Frankly, it seems difficult to imagine that Alcman was attempting such an operation, which would have sounded rather bold to a Greek ear in a poetic context. It is even harder to imagine that the main actor of that cosmogony might have been an admittedly minor divinity like Thetis. In Pherecydes's account, after all, Zeus—the ruler of the Olympic pantheon—is invested with a power comparable to that of his Babylonian counterpart, Marduk. Even if we emphasize the fact that Thetis had her own honorific cult in Sparta, this information is not enough to give her such a significant role in a city whose relationship with the sea, real or symbolic, was practically nonexistent. In sum, it seems unlikely that Alcman was using a "weak" mythological figure to import a "strong"

---

[38] Most 1987, 4.

[39] See Classen 1962, in particular p. 11.

cosmogony—based on a model of divine sovereignty characteristic of Near Eastern religions—into the rather particular context of a Greek city.

It is still possible, however, that Alcman was outlining a "soft" cosmology, suitable for the occasion and context of his poem. In fact, there is ample evidence through comparative analysis to justify a hypothesis that in his framework a divine figure knows and/or establishes the "way" (the "course," we might say) of "all things" in relation to a given "end" or "result." Time and again, archaic Greek literature features the exaltation of the power of the gods (usually Zeus) over the "course" and "result" of the events, sometimes even over the movements of the stars (Hesiod, *Works and Days*, line 565; Semonides, frag. 1 West, lines 1ff; Archilochus, frag. 298b West; Solon, frag. 12 W²; Pindar, *Pythian* IX, lines 44ff; *Olympian* II, lines 15ff). According to this view, the gods are endowed, if not with cosmogonic powers, at least with the ability to guarantee the regularity of natural rhythms that is brightly manifest in the itineraries of the stars. This may be the *soft* cosmological outlook—completely acceptable for the lyric genre and for the taste of the poet and his public—that we have been looking for. It is plausible to think that in this text Alcman presented a divine figure endowed with conscious control of the "ways" (*poroi*) of the cosmos, and that the separation of the day and the moon from darkness is the tangible result and manifestation (*tekmōr*) of this. And we might concede that a feat like the one just described could have been attributed, in a specific event for praising the goddess, to the figure of Thetis. Nothing more, but also nothing less.

A New, Self-Conscious Knowledge

> Hesiod, Alcman, Epimenides, Xenophanes, and others show us that
> cosmology was not the private preserve of a select academy of
> "Presocratics": in any Greek town, in any generation, there must have been
> rhapsodes, seers, and amateur sages who were at the ready to give an
> account of the origin of the world. They are nameless, and for the most
> part, no doubt, unoriginal. But it was among them that ideas slowly
> evolved and basic assumptions hardened, and if we forget them, we shall
> exaggerate the originality of our Presocratics.[40]

We have to agree with West's statement (and note that his opening list might be extended to Pherecydes), but we will need a few clarifications in order to make the most of it in terms of understanding the Presocratic cosmologies.

Let us go back to the knot that binds philosophy and myth and observe an important fact that is too often neglected in the treatments of the subject. The mythical sphere harbors stories that show enormous variation, depending on

---

[40] West 1967, 1.

several possible models of generation of the cosmos and of man, and these different narratives coexist for a very long time. The *Enuma Elish*, often cited in this chapter, is by no means the only cosmogonic representation in Mesopotamia. Other texts from the same area, rather than focusing on an original separation of sky and earth, present a "gemination" model in which the sky produces the earth, the earth produces the rivers, the rivers produce mud, and so on (see, for example, the cosmological incantation *The Worm and the Toothache*). Others offer an image of heaven fertilizing the earth with rain (an obvious analogy with the birth of humans; see the prologue of the *Dispute between the Tree and the Reed*). To use Jean Bottéro's felicitous wording, we are in the realm of "calculated imaginings"; representations aimed at providing a *plausible* picture of reality in a cosmos that pivots around the central axis of man-god relations. In such a realm, differing representations can be perceived as compatible.[41] At the same time, the earliest Greek philosophers seem to be inspired by the conviction, albeit implicit, that "the various theories and explanations they propose *are* directly competing with one another" and "their urge is toward finding the best explanation, the most adequate theory,"[42] which implies some level of critical discussion.

Undoubtedly, Hesiod has one foot planted firmly in the realm of "calculated imaginings." In the *Theogony*, Tartarus sometimes appears after Chaos, sometimes as its murky double; similarly, Ouranos can be both the sky above us and the god of the same name, equipped with emotions, who inflicts and suffers tremendous violence. In *Works and Days*, the myths of Prometheus and Pandora and the Five Races are juxtaposed with the same intention (to explain the wretched human condition). These examples, to which we could easily add more, indicate that Hesiod admits "multiple approaches" to a single problem, because he is less intent on a causal inquiry about nature than on pressing his existential and moral views. Christopher Rowe successfully used the criterion of "multiple approaches" to argue for the nonscientific character of Hesiod's reflection. The scholar rightly noted that:

> If we assume that Hesiod is in competition with an Anaximander or a Herodotus (or a Thucydides), then he comes off badly; but though there is some overlapping, as for example in Hesiod's description of the birth of the world, he is really playing a different game, under different rules. Philosophers and historians are in the business of giving precise and systematic accounts of causes; Hesiod is not. Where we do find system and consistency is in his moral attitudes.[43]

[41] See Bottéro and Kramer 1989, 79ff, and Bottéro 2000, 36ff.
[42] Lloyd 1970, 12. See also Furley 1987, 17.
[43] Rowe 1983, 134.

However, we have seen that Hesiod's treatment of the birth and constitution of the world expresses a personal point of view that contradicts other existing accounts. And this approach is of interest for the history of philosophy, not only because some of its most innovative elements (from the notion of *chaos* to that of a cosmic *erōs*) will later spark the interest of philosophers but also because it shows that Hesiod's endeavor is itself the product of a critical attitude.

The considerations invited by Pherecydes's *Theogony* are only partially similar. Here, too, we can sense the author's critical outlook. In both theme (the claim that the gods are timeless) and form (the choice to write in prose), Pherecydes seems to want to break away from the tradition started by Hesiod and followed by other authors of theogonies, such as Epimenides. But Pherecydes's account remained an isolated effort, and as far as we know it was not reprised or developed. Admittedly, we know of an Acusilaus of Argos who wrote a theogony in prose toward the end of the sixth and beginning of the fifth centuries BCE (it is mentioned in the *Vorsokratiker* in a note). From the fragments we have, however, Acusilaus seems to follow Hesiod's structure. He too posits that Chaos comes first, and from it come Erebus and Night, and from Erebus and Night (or from Aether and Night) Eros is promptly born, with a primary role similar to the role he has in Hesiod's account; for this reason Plato mentions Acusilaus together with Hesiod (and Parmenides) in the passage of the *Symposium* (178a–b) where he celebrates, in the words of Phaedrus, the antiquity of that god.[44] By some means, Acusilaus's theogonic account must have found its place in the first book of a treatise on *Genealogies*, a transposition of divine and heroic myths that perhaps followed the work of Hecataeus, though still modeled rather naively after the epic tradition. Acusilaus breaks away from this tradition (as do Pherecydes and Hecataeus, in different aspects) by adopting the prose form, probably deemed better suited for a systematic and classificatory effort.[45] This explains why, among other factors, Acusilaus has normally been listed among the logographers (authors of historical writings) and was included by Felix Jacoby in his collection of fragments of Greek historians. Perhaps it would be more appropriate to call him a mythographer; in fact, the most recent edition of his fragments can be found in Robert Fowler's anthology of texts of the earliest Greek mythographers.[46] Even this arrangement poses problems, considering that

[44] Most (2007, 284) advanced the interesting hypothesis that Parmenides, by calling Eros "the first" among the gods, was trying to correct Hesiod, who grouped Eros with Chaos and Gaia in a primordial triad. The variation to the Hesiodic model implemented by Acusilaus, at any rate, seems more modest.

[45] We will deal in the next chapter with the innovation represented by prose writing.

[46] In Fowler 2000, Acusilaus occupies the first chapter, and his theogonic fragments are numbers 6 through 16.

mythography does not exhibit the traits of a proper genre before the Hellenistic period. Yet it is true that an activity of transcribing myths into prose form is established and intensified during the fifth century (with Pherecydes of Athens, for instance) and continues into the classical period in the wake of defined and widespread interest. To conclude, Acusilaus's work is relevant here because it reminds us of the fluidity of interests and overlapping of genres that characterized archaic Greek culture.

If, after these digressions, we consider the sphere of cosmological thought, it will be all the more clear how its history—along the line launched by Anaximander (if not earlier, by Thales)—unfolds under the particular influence of conscious corrections and *change*. By setting aside the idea of the gods as authors of the cosmic order, the Ionian cosmologies open an entirely new horizon; new manufacturers of a knowledge independent of ritual are reclaiming ownership of a concept of the cosmos that is quite free from mythical representation. Moreover, this critical attitude acts just as vividly within the new intellectual field itself; in fact, the theories of the Ionians develop according to a sequence that we might call antagonistic.[47]

Anaximander likely elaborated the notion of *apeiron* by reflecting on the theoretical difficulties concerning the relationship between the principle and the other substances, an issue that Thales's doctrine might have seemed to address inadequately. A substance as well defined as water lacks the qualities necessary to justify, among other things, the existence of fire (on the contrary, water and fire are mutually destructive), while the *apeiron*, precisely because it is undefined, can explain the existence of both water and fire. Nor should Anaximenes's conception, which again favors a concrete element like air, be seen as a regression to a more rudimentary understanding—as has often been the case—because of its distance from Anaximander's power of abstraction. Fragment 2[48] shows that Anaximenes may have built his argument on an analogy; if air, the substance of the soul, is the cause of life and movement for humans, then it can also be the cause of atmospheric changes and, more generally, of all becoming. Moreover, Anaximenes seems to have stressed the observation that our breath is more or less warm depending on whether it is exhaled with open or closed lips, thus inferring an important link between change in temperature and air density, and this connection could explain, on a macrocosmic level, relationships between air and the other elements and their role in physical transformations (frag. 1). The mechanism of condensation/rarefaction offers an extremely economic way of explaining elemental changes

---

[47] Schwabl (1962, col. 1519), Lloyd (1970, 20ff), and von Fritz (1971a, 23–24 and 37ff) are in agreement on this point. Tannery (1930, 92n1) argues that Thales's ideas may have been preserved not through the oral tradition but because Anaximander mentioned them in order to refute them.

[48] Mentioned above, 43.

and, unlike the *apeiron*, has the benefit of reflecting direct experience in a way that, while not especially rigorous, is certainly effective.

Another issue that is debated in a successive line of corrections is the stability of the earth. As we have already seen, Thales posited a flat earth floating on a mass of cosmic water (in this respect not straying far from the mythical model), whereas Anaximander gives the earth an approximately cylindrical shape and a position at the center of the universe measured by equidistance from the external circumference. We may surmise that Anaximander tried to overcome the implicit difficulty in Thales's theory (namely, that if we posit an element as the foundation of the earth, this element will need to be supported by something, and so on); what is remarkable is that Anaximander resorts to a form of reasoning dictated by a consideration of the symmetry of the universe. Anaximenes will later postulate that the earth is flat but floats on a cushion of air from whose condensation it was originally formed (13 A 6; A 7, 4; and A 20 DK).[49] Xenophanes will have yet another opinion; according to him, the earth stretches out below without limits (frag. 28). Aristotle, sharing a disparaging criticism by Empedocles (*De caelo*, II, 13, 294 a 21 = 21 A 47 and 31 B 39 DK), says that with this solution Xenophanes and others "saved themselves the trouble of looking for the cause (*tēn aitian*)." However, it is rather likely that Xenophanes felt the need to "stop" a search for causes of the stability of the earth that could be extended ad infinitum.

The plurality of opinions concerning the principle of becoming and the stability of the earth has been a central theme in the well-known debate, started more than half a century ago by Karl Popper, on the scientific method of the Presocratics. In the explanations and rebuttals observed in the Presocratic theories starting from the Ionian cosmologies, Popper found confirmation of his idea of a scientific knowledge that proceeds through conjectures and refutations.[50] Popper's intervention as an informed outsider elicited different reactions from the specialists in ancient thought, and among these Geoffrey Kirk responded with vociferous dissent. Contrary to Popper, Kirk

[49] Anaximenes's theoretical motivations here are not quite clear. Hankinson (1998a, 21–23) rightly stresses Anaximenes's predilection for analogic processes, whose explicatory effectiveness and logic validity he assesses correctly and case by case. However, he may go too far in arguing that the term *epipōmatizein* in Aristotle's testimony on the position of the earth (*On the Heavens*, II, 13, 294b 13 = 13 A 20 DK) is enough to attribute to Anaximenes the idea that the earth "covers as a lid" the air below it (which in this scenario would serve as a support, just as the steam produced by boiling water supports the lid of a pot). This hypothesis, while certainly tempting, does not take into account that Aristotle refers here to a doctrine shared by Anaximenes, Anaxagoras, and Democritus, without attributing to one or the other the idea represented by *epipōmatizein*. The image of the pot would in any case be hard to fit into Anaximenes's idea of a mass of air that is unlimited in every direction.

[50] See Popper 1958–59. Popper's interest in the Presocratics remained strong until the very end; see Popper 1998, a posthumous summa packed full of his ideas on the subject.

starts from the Baconian conception, according to which science proceeds from the collection of information to the elaboration of theories; in his view, some essential traits of this conception were still detectable in the Presocratic period. According to Popper, for the Presocratics the role of observation was limited to testing conjectures elaborated by reasoning; by contrast, Kirk argues that they were normally guided by *common sense* in the formulation of their hypotheses, that is, from the sense of what is possible or acceptable in the horizon of experience.[51]

There is no space here to delve deeper into the strengths and weaknesses of these positions. After all, both could be confirmed by this or that Presocratic doctrine; for example, the role of intellectual intuition in Anaximander's cosmic structure fits into Popper's framework; on the other hand, we cannot deny that Anaximenes's theory is more strongly tied to experience, in the sense that Kirk stressed. Indeed, there can be little doubt that direct observation plays an important role in the Presocratics' inquiries. What varies from case to case, however, are the ways in which observation is applied with respect to theory. In any case, the empirical references attested by our sources are not connected through a system of registration of data, though they often offer important cues for formulating new arguments. For instance, we cannot say that Anaximenes's observation of breath results in a rigorous demonstration of the fact that air is the principle, because it is not part of a systematic gathering of controlled observations in the service of an inductive process. Such an observation can produce a theory only through bold generalization; nevertheless, it surely constitutes a rectification of Anaximander's theory, and this sheds new light on the problem of the changing nature of the principle.

One additional remark on Popper's reconstruction. As noted by Giuseppe Cambiano, Popper presents the Presocratics as scientists who not only criticized the theories of their colleagues but also intentionally brought their own into the discussion in order to find the best solution to the problem at hand. This, however, is an "irenic" image modeled after the characteristics of the modern scholarly community, and it overlooks the strongly competitive environment in which the Presocratics conducted their theoretical work.[52] I might add that it is a narrow image, in the sense that it describes a discussion limited to a well-defined group of scientists who interact only among themselves, and without branching out into other fields of knowledge. What we should keep in mind instead (this point will be developed later) is that the Presocratics tend to use a dogmatic tone in enunciating their *own* truths, and to buttress their ideas by invoking personal sources of authority, while their criticisms are centered upon the truths of *others*, and their targets are natural

---

[51] See Kirk 1960 and 1961, along with the considerations of Lloyd 1967 and Algra 1999.
[52] See Cambiano 1988, 26–28.

philosophers as well as other types of savants (Homer and Hesiod preeminent among all others).

We should nevertheless give credit to Popper for this fundamental intuition; the Presocratics' inquiry adopts a critical attitude from the beginning, and this attitude fosters—from Thales to Anaximander to Anaximenes—a growing awareness of certain problems and of methods of inquiry associated with them, whether analogy, inference, generalization, or the mechanisms of polarity. The observation that such procedures were not carried out as part of a specific epistemological investigation should not lead us to overlook the significance of their having been undertaken in the first place.[53]

Throughout this chapter we have identified, among the new features distinguishing the Ionian cosmologies from the so-called mythical ones, significant theoretical questions such as limitation of the action of divine personalities in nature, formal issues such as the search for language more suitable to the description of experience, and methodological approaches (and it should be clear that this diagnosis is in agreement with Aristotle's assessment of Thales's contribution, in the first book of *Metaphysics*). Now we have added to the list the emergence of a critical attitude that characterizes the development of Presocratic thought from here on out. In the next chapter, we shall see how this critical attitude benefited from a newborn cognitive technology: writing.

[53] Cf. Stannard 1965, Hankinson 1998a, 8–25, and Hussey (2006), according to whom the conscious theoretical endeavor guiding the "new cosmology" is a clear sign of the "beginnings" of philosophy. Note that Matson 1954–55, in discussing Cornford's theses, already stressed the role of critical attitude in the thought of the first Presocratics.

CHAPTER THREE

Writing Experiments

A "Hot" Society

In the previous chapter we saw how Mesopotamian and Egyptian mythology hosted two different cosmogonic models, which seem to have coexisted for a very long period without being perceived within the collective cultural heritage as being at odds. In the Greek philosophical culture, by contrast, from the moment of its inception (with Thales), according to Aristotle, different theories follow one another at an ever-increasing pace. Each theory aims to refute the preceding one with radically different hypotheses concerning the birth and becoming of the cosmos, often by "demystifying" the preceding hypotheses. We may well say that what we have here is, in general, a substantial change in the temporal dimension of reflection.

This change is surely connected with the central role played in Greek philosophy by the interest in second-order questions, as Geoffrey Lloyd would put it—that is, an urge to explain one's theoretical choices not only by referring to previous treatments of the same problem but also by responding to the ideas of other sages in a highly competitive atmosphere. Rivalry is indeed endemic to the Greek cultural environment, which did not have, at least throughout the archaic and classical periods, institutional supports and official roles of knowledge; *phusiologoi* or physicians, geographers or astronomers must make their way not only by showcasing original and innovative contents but also by supporting those contents with quick and formally sophisticated arguments, in order to prevail over their adversaries.[1] Moreover, between the seventh and sixth centuries BCE the Greek world shows several signs of change. The center of political and social life is moving away from the

---

[1] Geoffrey Lloyd's research has constantly insisted on these themes; see for instance Lloyd 1979, 1996, and 2002a, in particular p, 151ff. I should like to stress here—even though Lloyd does not—that we can already see the signs of second-order thinking in the Ionian cosmologies, consciously constructed using modalities outside the mythic tradition.

secluded home of the aristocrat, passing through the tyrant's court, and arriving at the agora. At the same time, the intellectual prerogative once concentrated in the figure of the bard, who sang the values of a social group of which he was part (the aristocratic *oikos*) is overtaken by new intellectual roles, favored by the opening of new venues. Hesiod, in his two poems, is already breaking away from conventional values of epic poetry with his highly personal view of a world ruled by relations of justice. In a way, the lyric poets are the heirs of Hesiod's moral and religious endeavor, in variations more or less critical of the values promoted by the ruling aristocratic élite. Moreover, the sixth century sees the emergence of new forms of intellectual production, based on a new relationship with aristocratic culture that is the very essence of the rising polis. These new forms tend to delineate—following an agenda already charged with significance—areas of interest that "transcend" the boundaries of the civic community, such as the nature of the universe, through the Milesian cosmologists, and the reconstruction of Greece's past, through the historical critique of myth launched by Hecataeus, also from Miletus.[2]

Scholars such as Lloyd and Vernant have taught us that the political dimension is crucial to our understanding of some peculiar aspects of the Greek world. Vernant emphasized that the new cosmological reflection hinges upon a notion of balance, which he thinks correlates with the ideal of an equal relationship between the members of the city-state, who are equal precisely because they belong to, and share the experience of, the same polis. Lloyd too argues that this experience is crucial, but in his view it explains not the contents but the style of philosophical rationality; a fundamentally critical style, which reflects a habit of debating contrasting theses in relation to the need to take collective decisions, in court or in the assembly. Both Lloyd and Vernant, in any case, argue that Greek philosophy is a daughter of the polis, a thesis with which we can agree, while making a few obligatory remarks.

First, both scholars presuppose that equality among citizens and the habit of discussion, more or less extended to public matters, characterize the polis since its beginnings, and not just in its democratic phases. That "more or less" is problematic, for we should keep in mind that in archaic Greek society, in contexts of transition, which should be evaluated on a case-by-case basis, the decisional process must have been more limited and sporadic, as well as in the oligarchic governments of the classical period.

Another substantial objection has been raised by anthropologists, who have observed that the cosmogonic myths of traditional societies attest the same search for order and unity that, in Vernant's perspective, is a peculiarity of the origins of Greek thought.[3] In this view, the notion of cosmic order loses

---

[2] On this complex juncture, see the ever-illuminating Humphreys 1975, to which must be added Bravo 2002.

[3] Cf. Horton 1967 and Valeri 1995.

its status as a characteristic feature of Greek and Western society and, what is more, it becomes rather difficult to establish an immediate causal link between the particular structure of archaic Greek society and the birth and development of rational thought.

On the other hand, however, it is also hard to deny that such a correlation exists. For instance, we cannot overlook the fact that many times (as we shall see) the Presocratic accounts of the cosmos are connected by analogy with the notion of power, which indicates that some homogeneity between the natural and political state was seen at least at the level of conscious theorization; and this is a good point in favor of the thesis of philosophy as a "daughter" of the polis. The weaker part of this thesis, instead, is the idea that *order*, both in naturalistic thought and in the practice of governing the polis, was always thought of in terms of *democratic* equality (between the cosmic forces and the social classes, respectively). This is a great simplification that we must supplant with an in-depth analysis of the political contexts in which the various Presocratics happened to formulate their theories and their various ideological options; at the same time, we should not forget that element of "transcendence" we hinted at before, which becomes clear once we observe that when the first philosophers turn to the study of nature, they effectively cross the boundaries of the polis. Not only this; as we have amply seen in the previous chapter, the study of nature immediately follows paths that take it "outside" the city; first of all, far away from a search for principles of order and cohesion in the religious institutions of the community.

In conclusion, the position of philosophy with regard to the city is an ambivalent one; we need to seek further for the factors or "parents" that might explain its complex status. Yet it is always fruitful, from a historical perspective, to expand the scope of the search for causes; thus it is appropriate to think that a constellation of *interactive* elements may have contributed to the development of that particular critical life that characterizes the first expressions of philosophical rationality.[4] Let us now try to identify some of these elements.

---

[4] See von Staden 1992, in particular 593ff. Meier (1986) noted that an experience as complex as that of the polis requires, in turn, an explanation in intellectual terms; we can think that a certain type of "social intelligence" among the Greeks stemmed from the need to face conditions of material and political precariousness. It is worth paying special attention in this framework to a few arguments by Zaicev (1993), who ascribed the "Greek miracle" to the process of social mobilization that took place in the archaic period, both "horizontally" (consider the relocation of high numbers of citizens from the fatherland to the colonies) and "vertically" (with the aristocracy's gradual loss of power); according to Zaicev, this process instilled in large social strata the sense of an endowment of intellectual resources (the inheritance of the aristocratic "agonal spirit") that could be spent competitively in the cultural and social space. Other points have been raised more recently by Krischer (2006).

An important element is of course the particular character of Greek religion—a religion that did not require acceptance of a dogmatic corpus, since it
was not based on assumptions of faith as much as on the visibility of the cult,
which had a cohesive function for the civic community (and, of course, foundation myths and rituals varied greatly from city to city). This situation is contradicted only in appearance by what the sources tell us regarding the trials
for impiety against Anaxagoras and Protagoras, the lyric poet Diagoras, and
finally, Socrates (399 BCE). Indeed, it is not by chance that these trials took
place in Athens and in the last decades of the fifth century, that is, in a time
and space characterized by very strong internal political contrasts, during the
crisis brought about by the Peloponnesian War. We might surmise that this
was not an easy time for intellectuals, especially those who were as exposed as
Anaxagoras (who belonged to Pericles's entourage), and, at least in the case of
Socrates (which is also the only historically documented one), it is rather clear
that the prosecution used Socrates's alleged or actual inobservance of cult as
a pretext in order to silence an inconvenient critic of the Athenian political
class.[5] It is certain that Greek religion, immune (as was Roman religion) from
any opposition between orthodoxy and heresy, gives free reign to the exercise
of philosophical reasoning, which—until the time of the Neoplatonists—is
centered around nature and the role of the divine, without normally involving
institutional forms of religious practice. Philosophers do not risk clashing with
the interests of priests, because the latter do not belong to a separate caste in
charge of the preservation of dogma. Rather, they compete with the poets,
custodians of a traditional knowledge on the gods toward which the philosophers can afford to take different positions, fluctuating between partial acceptance, skepticism, and innovative revision.[6] This freedom is in place from
the earliest phase of philosophical reflection. We have already observed, in
the previous chapter, that the Presocratics do not aim so much to deny the
divine out of hand as to offer a rational explanation for the ritual aspects that
they find naive. Xenophanes represents the most famous instance of such an
attitude, such that his polemic against religious anthropomorphism can only
be understood, as we shall see, against the backdrop of a network of intercul-
tural contacts favored by commercial growth and by the foundation of the
colonies.

This last observation introduces a further factor that we need to consider:
the extraordinary opportunities for critical reception and discussion of different cultural traditions brought about by the Greek colonization in the Ionian
area (along the coast of Asia), in Sicily, and in Magna Graecia. Moreover,
the awareness of the possibility of different and alternative approaches to the

---

[5] On the debate regarding the reasons of Socrates's trial, see Sassi 2015, 177–94.

[6] On the relationship between Greek philosophy and religion in general, cf. Humpreys
1986, Most 2002, and Betegh 2006b.

same problems, besides nourishing contact with other cultures, was intensi-fied by the plurality of local situations and political structures within Greece itself. This is particularly clear from the way, or rather ways, in which the Greeks dealt with a fundamental question that we have been discussing: the problem of natural order.

A point that is not often stressed (also because it is kept relatively in the backdrop in Vernant's treatment) is that the notion of order presents at least two distinct versions in Greek thought.[7] The first, which is more frequently cited, can already be found in Anaximander's cosmology, which posits the necessity of a globally balanced relationship between the cosmic forces. Here we can glean the beginning of a reflection on that *equalitarian* relationship between the members of the polis that will be expressed in classical Greek by the term *isonomia* ("equality of rights"); a term that defines—and we need to stress this—a principle of judicial equality that is not necessarily accompa-nied by aspirations of economic equality. Yet, another important reflection on the problem of order is developed, during the fifth century, in the school of Pythagoras in Magna Graecia; and here, it is worth noting, what is elaborated is a notion of *hierarchic* order. According to Pythagoras's teachings, the cosmos is governed by a series of relationships modeled after musical chords, which represent different relationships between numbers, with the result that their combination produces a universal *harmonia*. The direct counterpart of such a vision is aristocratically oriented political activity, which the communities of Magna Graecia oppose with nothing short of violent revolts. Conversely, in the same Croton that welcomed Pythagoras, between the sixth and fifth cen-turies BCE, Alcmaeon elaborates a widely accepted definition of health as perfect equality (*isonomia*) of the forces in the body, and of disease as an im-balance due to excessive power of one of those forces over the others (in Greek, *monarchia*, or "rule of only one person"; 24 B 4 DK). Is Alcmaeon a dissent-ing Pythagorean reclaiming a democratic ideal? Without making such a bold statement, we can nonetheless argue that the notions of *harmonia* and *isono-mia* refer to two different views of the physical order corresponding to two different possible images of a changing society.

We may go beyond this list of multiple coordinates within which we are attempting to situate the emergence of archaic Greek thought. For instance, it is worth remembering that in a recent book, Richard Seaford boldly reprised an old hypothesis by George Thomson that had long fallen into disfavor, prob-ably because of its vetero-Marxist overtones. According to this hypothesis, the first manifestations of philosophical thought can be explained as the intellec-

---

[7] But see Cambiano 1982 (and Vlastos [1947] is still illuminating on many points). See Sassi 2007, in particular 191–200, for a more detailed assessment of the viability of the con-cept of *isonomia* as an explanation of the idea of physical order that begins to be formu-lated in the Ionian context.

tual outcome of social transformations triggered by the "invention" of coinage (which was actually introduced into Greece from Lydia, probably at the beginning of the sixth century, and then spread rapidly). The conventionally established value of coinage would bring about an unprecedented and powerful incentive toward conceptual abstraction. This hypothesis is attractive and there are good arguments for it, but in general it remains barely verifiable without explicit statements by the philosophers themselves (the "actors" of the process, anthropologically speaking) on the link between conceptual abstraction and the rising mechanisms of money exchange. But it is certainly worth stressing, as Seaford does, the conditions of exceptional economic prosperity (obviously related to the use of coinage in commercial transactions) in the archaic period, which benefit the Ionian cities first of all, starting with Miletus, the birthplace of philosophical cosmology.[8] Such conditions explain the social mobility that we seem to associate—through different paths that cannot always be specified—with the flourishing of archaic Greek wisdom.

However, what is even more striking, in archaic and classical Greek culture, are the expressions of the strong *awareness* of such mobility. The proud claim of the level of civilization achieved through a series of progressive reforms will become commonplace in Greek self-celebratory texts of the fifth and fourth centuries BCE; according to Herodotus (I, 58) and Thucydides (I, 6, 6), among others, the Greeks were able to go beyond a primitive, barbaric state, while the barbarians remained unchanged. The tone of these claims pushed François Hartog to recuperate a critical category that may have seemed obsolete, namely, the Lévi-Straussian opposition between "hot" and "cold" societies, that is, societies "with" and "without" a history:

> Greekness detached itself from a background of "Barbarity," as if two
> temporalities, or two different kinds of relation to time, at one point
> existed in parallel, thereby illustrating the Lévi-Straussian paradigm
> of "hot" societies and "cold" societies. The Greeks were Barbarians but
> had become Greeks, the Barbarians were Barbarians and had remained
> Barbarians. They remained a "cold" society, while the Greeks, for their
> part, became "hot," manifesting their Greek character by their ability
> to "grow."[9]

It is useful to reconsider this acute observation here, provided that we make the important observation (which we owe to Jan Assmann) that rather than counterposing *populations* with or without history, we need to counterpose

---

[8] See Thomson 1955 and Seaford 2004, 181ff.

[9] Hartog 2001 [1996], 81. One might certainly list a number of passages, especially by politically conservative authors such as Plato, which manifest a sense of hostility to change. Yet this does not prevent the same author from presenting a completely personal project (as is indeed the case in the *Laws*).

two possible *strategies* of cultural memory. According to Assmann, we can talk of a "cold" option for the societies of the ancient Near East, which, though civilized, literate, and equipped with a high level of state organization, opted to make a "cold" use of their tradition by enacting different systems for freezing the past. This does not mean that they live in oblivion; they simply remember differently. Conversely, a "hot" option characterizes Greek culture, which, from its very beginnings, tends to think about its past in terms of innovation.[10]

Egotisms

Yet, just as there is no society without history, there is no culture without innovation. And the high level achieved in fields such as mathematics, astronomy, and medicine proves that there were innovations also in the cultures of Mesopotamia and Egypt. In general, however, these cultures tend to focus on the conservation of acquired knowledge in authoritative texts that are faithfully copied. A remarkable case is represented by an illustrious writing of Egyptian medicine, the Edwin Smith papyrus, compiled around 1600 BCE, with materials dating to 3000–2500 BCE; it should be noted that the annotations of the last scribes are subordinated under the faithful interpretation of preserved knowledge. Similarly, the undeniable ability for abstraction shown in different fields of Mesopotamian culture (consider for example the level of sophistication of certain mathematical texts) is accompanied by rare and laconic expressions of self-awareness, and in general what persists is a resistance to change and a tolerance toward contradicting perspectives, which are explained in the framework of a traditional culture that revolves around the values of integration and community rather than on individual contributions.[11]

In the Greek sources, by contrast, the sense of innovation takes on a high degree of "egotism."[12] The two aspects are already connected in the works of Hesiod, who uses his name and autobiography to mark his personal territory in the context of the production and reception of poetry, which until then had been anonymous. An analogous combination is found in the lyric poets' insistence on their originality, a manifestation of that emergence of a new idea of individuality, masterfully studied by Snell and identified by Sergej Averincev as a typical trait of Greek culture, that stands out even more when we consider the absence of creative conscience characterizing the production of the wise

---

[10] See Assmann 2011 [1992], especially 51ff and 81ff.

[11] See Machinist 1986.

[12] I reprise from Lloyd (1987) the main features of the panorama that follows, as well as the notion of "egotism." Let us remember that Lloyd corroborated this diagnosis with his subsequent work, thanks to a close comparison with ancient Chinese science; see, for instance, Lloyd and Sivin 2002, 104ff.

men and prophets of the Near East (even where names are attested).[13] We should certainly consider against the same background the fact—conspicuously demonstrated by the archaeological record—that vase painters had already started to sign their works already in the eighth century, and this practice became more and more frequent.

As for the philosophers, the very fact that Thales's name was handed down from one generation to the next (even though his *ipsissima verba* are not preserved) might be interpreted as a departure from the anonymity characterizing poetic activity. At any rate, we must see that the habit of putting the name of the author at the beginning of a work represents a claim of authorship.[14] The first two figures to make claims of authorship were a historian, Hecataeus of Miletus, and a scientist, Alcmaeon of Croton, who both wrote toward the end of the sixth century BCE. Hecataeus's *Genealogies*, an exposition of mythical and historical events that can be considered the oldest historical writing in Greek, began with the following statement (I F I a FGH):

> Thus speaks (*mutheitai*) Hecataeus of Miletus. I write these things as they seem to me to be true (*hōs moi dokei alēthea einai*), since the tales (*logoi*) of the Greeks, as they appear to me, are many and ludicrous.

What is remarkable here is that the proclamation of the highly personal operation that is about to begin—a rationalistic and even derisive reassessment of the mythical tradition, and particularly of the legends attributing divine origins to certain families—is explicitly attached to the act of writing. Writing (whose cognitive effectiveness I shall explore in a moment) will indeed be used by Hecataeus to "frame," so to speak, and to denounce the multiplicity and contradictory nature of the mythical accounts that bloom in the seductive flux of the oral tradition, where historical reality is easily exaggerated and distorted (as in the stories of Geryon and Cerberus, which Hecataeus downscales in frags. 26 and 27).[15]

On the other hand, in the dedication of one of his writings, Alcmaeon, a naturalist (and possibly physician) with ties to the Pythagorean circle (with

---

[13] See Averincev 1971–73, 17ff. Recent studies have cast significant doubt on the degree of subjectivity in archaic Greek poetry; a reading that pays attention to the needs and contexts of performance shows that the lyric "I" does not voice the individuality as much as the persona the poet takes up to represent a certain ideological position (see first and foremost Kurke 2007). But this perspective too refers to a social context characterized by numerous tensions between tradition and innovation, which is what I am trying to emphasize here.

[14] The statement of authorship, on the other hand, goes hand in hand with the need to reference works in an age when the use of book titles is unknown (see below, 82n34).

[15] On the relationship between use of writing and critique of myth, see in general Brisson 1990 and 1996.

the Pythagoreans he shared, besides his homeland, an interpretation of nature based on a grid of opposing forces), places three other members of that community under his "signature" ("Alcmaeon of Croton, son of Peirithous, told Brotinus, Leon, and Bathyllus the following things"). As rightly noted by Laura Gemelli Marciano, this formulation testifies to the oral character of a teaching destined to a limited audience, which is now being written down for broader circulation.[16] The signature responds to the need, which is anything but obvious in this phase, to declare authorship of an intellectual product when this product leaves the controlled environment of its author. In Alcmaeon's case, we can even see a desire to set himself apart from the Pythagorean environment, and it is worthwhile to linger on this point for a moment.

The interpretation of Pythagorean thought is normally conditioned by a Neoplatonic tradition (through Porphyry and Iamblichus) that the Pythagoreans formed a collective identity, divided internally into two groups, *akousmatikoi* and *mathematikoi*. The *akousmatikoi* were more keen on observing the religious rules (orally) emanated by the founding teacher, whereas the *mathematikoi*, or "scholars" (of mathematical sciences), practiced secrecy (there is a famous anecdote of Hippasus of Metapontum being drowned by his fellow disciples for having divulged the discovery of the irrational, which threatened a worldview based on the conviction that all phenomena can be explained as relationships between rational numbers). This impression should certainly be put into perspective considering the great number of well-defined personalities, active in many fields, who are more or less directly related to Pythagorean contexts; indeed, we know of *phusikoi* with strong medical interests, such as Alcmaeon, and later Hippon of Metapontum and Philolaus, and also doctors such as Democedes of Croton and Iccus of Tarentum, or *mathematikoi* such as Hippasus, Theodorus, and Archytas. Thus Pythagoreanism represents only a partial exception in a panorama within which, in the wake of Popper and Lloyd, we have detected a decisive degree of individualism and critical stances. Even Pythagoreanism, in other words, must have seen an internal discussion (for example, on the number of opposites, regarding which Aristotle informs us that Alcmaeon took a personal stance, or on the organization of the cosmos), and therefore a development; and it is only against a "moving" backdrop that we can explain the emergence, at the turn of the fifth century, of a highly original product like the work of Philolaus.[17]

To conclude, the tendency to speak in the first person and/or with strongly personal tones is widespread among philosophers and scientists of the ar-

[16] See Gemelli Marciano 2007a, in particular 18–22, for the abundant points raised on the articulation and function of opening statements in the Presocratics in a context of oral communication (although this scholar devotes less attention than I would to their writing styles).

[17] Cf. Petit 1992 and Zhmud 2012.

chaic period. Consider also Heraclitus, who proclaims, "I went in search of myself" (frag. 101) to stress that he extrapolated the contents of *logos* from an isolated and highly personal reflection. And we shall see that Xenophanes, Parmenides, and Empedocles also express themselves in no less personal tones; the significant number of texts of this kind is enough to demonstrate that the combination of egotism and innovation is an integral component of Greek cultural style.

Writing technologies played a key role in this regard, allowing the individual to mark in texts (and also on vases, as we have seen), in more or less articulated forms, his particular contribution to the development of knowledge (or, in the case of vase painters and potters, the development of a skill). We have seen, for instance, that Hecataeus already exploited writing with a full awareness of its power to clarify and reassess the contents of the oral tradition, unveiling the contradictions harbored in the fluctuating world of myth, at the same time using it as a device to claim authorship of the personal contents he sets out to introduce. On the other hand, availability and use of writing are already crucial components of Eastern cultures whose scant signs of innovation we have remarked in opposition to the Greek context; the point is that those cultures did not use the technology of writing *in the same way* as the Greeks. We can infer that the relationship between literacy and writing and the development of critical thinking represents—in much the same way as the relationship between polis and philosophy—a circular problem, so that it is not possible to establish the priority of one factor over the other. Nevertheless, this is a problem that we must tackle now.

The Power of Writing

The thesis that the adoption of writing in the Greek world was the propelling factor in the birth of critical thinking was advanced years ago, in a deservedly famous study, by Jack Goody and Ian Watt.[18] The two anthropologists started from the observation that societies without writing have a "homeostatic" type of organization of their cultural tradition; oral memory works in such a way that the socially relevant elements are progressively archived, removing the rest, in a process of constant reactualization of the collective cultural heritage, which gives way to an impression (and it is indeed just an impression) of immutability. Something similar happened also in the Sumerian and Egyptian civilizations, where writing is practiced, but in a specialized form reserved for select scribal and priestly groups and finalized in the perpetuation of a specific tradition of civic and religious knowledge.

---

[18] Cf. Goody and Watt 1962–63, and the appropriate later adjustments in Goody 1977, 1987, and 2000; see also Cardona 1988.

This is also true for the beginnings of Greek civilization. Let us set aside the case of Linear A, which was used in Crete (1800–1480 BCE) to write a language different from Greek and has still not been deciphered. Now, Linear B (famously deciphered by John Chadwick in 1958), used to write Greek in Crete and other Mycenaean centers, was a syllabic writing form still far from being simplified, its use limited to restricted elites among palace administrators. Starting from the twelfth century, with the decline of Mycenaean palatial society, writing was eclipsed for a long time until a new system was introduced in Greece, toward the end of the eighth century (or in the second half of the ninth, as some scholars tend to believe today).[19] Such a system was derived from a rather simple Semitic syllabary, which was adapted with the addition of vowel signs. Thus the alphabet was born, where each symbol corresponds to a phoneme. Thanks to this "revolution," writing became available to diversified economic classes and, no longer an exclusive prerogative of specialized professional categories, it saw a speedy diffusion (among the ancient testimonies are signatures of potters already in the eighth century, but even more noteworthy from the perspective of social stratification are the graffiti drawn at Abu Simbel at the beginning of the sixth century by Greek mercenaries of Pharaoh Rhampsinith).[20]

According to Goody and Watt, this new writing technology was pivotal in determining the characteristics of Greek culture during its beginnings. Indeed, writing is an essential tool for thought construction, because it allows one to entrust one's reflections to texts that can be meditated upon later; in particular, it allows one to detect potential internal contradictions. With the visual fixation of a written text and with its reproduction, more than with the mobile forms of listening, the argument finds an objective configuration that facilitates the elaboration of abstract thinking. Moreover, recording a text facilitates recognition of reflective thinking as such, places it in a cumulative chain of results, and at the same time exposes it to criticism; in fact, it forms a base for future innovations.

These observations on the role of writing were then reprised and integrated by Ian Assmann in his reconstruction of the different forms of "cultural memory" in the great ancient civilizations. Assmann's wide framework allows us to grasp more clearly the mutual influence of the possibilities offered by the written text and the various components that model cultural tradition, such as the choice of a "cold" or "hot" option made by a specific civilization

---

[19] See Schnapp-Gourbeillon 2002, 263ff.

[20] For signatures on vases, see Schnapp-Gourbeillon 2002, 298–99. Also from the eighth century are two longer vase inscriptions in verse (one from Athens, the other from Ischia, on the so-called Nestor's cup) discussed by Henrichs (2003, 45ff) in relation to problems of Greek religion. Harris (1989) provides a broad general picture of literacy in the Greek and Roman world; for classical Athens, see Pébarthe 2006.

when it comes to preserving its memory; the elaboration, or lack thereof, of foundation myths; the relationship with political power and/or religion; the different possible images of the sources of knowledge.[21] In this view, the civilizations of the ancient Near East are the ones that opt for "freezing" the past, and therefore give writing the purpose of *conservation*. This can include the most disparate writings (mythical, cosmological, or technical; pertaining to mathematics, astronomy, medicine, or divination), yet these texts all share a social role, that is, writing endows them with canonical authority. Let us consider once again the case of the *Enuma Elish*. This text, which was religious rather than cosmogonic in character, was composed anonymously within a circle of priests and then copied for centuries without any conceptual changes, an homage to the fixed nature of ritual recitations.[22] This happened because in the ritual sphere (as well as in the oral tradition of myth) the transmission of knowledge takes place through repetition. Greek culture presents a different case, where recording the contents of knowledge in the written medium constitutes an incentive toward *variation*, the same variation that we have seen at work, coming back to the Ionian cosmogonies, in the sequence from Thales to Anaximander to Anaximenes.

Thus the link established by Goody and Watt between writing and critical thinking in Greece proves to be strong, yet it's difficult to measure its ultimate strength. It is more prudent to say that at a certain point, within that "hot" society that was archaic Greece, a complex constellation of conditions emerged in which writing (or rather, alphabetic writing) became an important factor, one that was necessary (though not sufficient) to sustain a highly competitive cultural style.[23] Moreover, the assessment of the role of writing should be

---

[21] See Assmann 2011 [1992], 59ff; the notion of images of knowledge, to which we will return in the last chapter, is reprised from Elkana 1981. Regarding knowledge and writing in the Ancient Near East, it must be noted that Cardona (1988, 15) wrote that "writing freezes experience." An analogous position has been taken more recently by Foster (2005).

[22] This text presents indeed few variants, in spite of its wide dissemination; see Maul (2015, 17–20) for more on the process of copying, memorizing, and canonizing the *Enuma Elish*. In fact, the protagonist of the earlier cosmogonic tradition was Enlil, the god of the Sumerian religious headquarters of Nippur, and Marduk, the former god of the city-state of Babylon, took his place after the rise of the city to political center of a unified Mesopotamia— actually, the composition of the *Enuma Elish* is likely to be dated to the reign of Nebuchadnezzar, 1126–1104 BCE. Moreover, after Babylon lost its political centrality, in a later version of the poem the name of Marduk was supplanted with that of Assur (cf. Frankfort, Frankfort, Wilson, Jacobsen, and Irwin 1946, 201; Rochberg 2005, 341; and Maul 2015, 29ff, 40–45). Yet these changes, dictated by contingent needs of political and social cohesion, were implemented by anonymous priests and not destined to be perceived as such, so the narrative model remained the same.

[23] With this we come rather close to considering "the introduction of a means of communication in a society as a new possibility that is offered to it [l'introduction d'un mode de communication dans une société comme une possibilité nouvelle qui lui est offerte]," as Pébarthe puts it (2006, 29). I recommend the whole introduction, for its limpid synthesis

structured by immersing it in concrete and specific contexts. First of all we should note that, regardless of the "democratic" character of Greek society pointed out by Goody and Watt, the degree of literacy is not easy to determine, nor is it reducible to a unitary definition. Obviously, literacy was rather gradual, and even at its peak in the Athenian democracy, a period of presumably significant diffusion, perhaps ten percent of the total population (this is Harris's reasonable estimate) were literate.[24] This would indicate that thirty percent of male citizens, probably the most influential and active in the political and cultural life of the period, were able to read; and in the archaic period the citizen body, a selection of the total population, must therefore have been more educated.

Surely, in certain contexts, writing may have worked—to use Marcel Detienne's words—as a powerful "publicity operator" and was "a constituent part of the political field."[25] The richest and most significant case study in this sense is probably offered by Greek law; the recording of laws in written form represents a crucial moment in the process of codification that took place around the middle of the seventh century (in Athens, with Draco, it seems) and continued at such a rate (in parallel with the development of the polis) that at the end of the sixth century the majority of Greek cities had a system of written laws.

We might surmise that the recording of laws was spurred by the ruling class's need to give public authority a visible form in order to make the community better acquainted with the city's judicial system, thereby making it more efficient. (Not by chance, an exception is represented by Sparta, which could rely on a solid educational system geared toward obedience to the laws.) It must be noted that this tendency is shared by all Greek cities regardless of oligarchic or democratic orientation. What we can better study is the case of Solon's legislation and its efficacy in setting Athens on a democratic path. Undoubtedly, Solon found in the written recording of laws a better operational tool, as demonstrated by the proud claim he puts at the beginning of the com-

---

of the last decades of studies on the problem of literacy and its interesting methodological considerations. On the appropriateness of a "multicausal" explanation for the beginnings of Greek thought, see above, 66ff.

[24] Pébarthe (2006) suggests a higher estimate (although he does not give a precise number), based on what we are able to gather from the data of scholastic and domestic education, from archaic inscriptions (many of which are private) and from the institution of ostracism, whose existence should imply (because the practice required) that every citizen participating in the assembly must have been able at least to read, and to write a name on a potsherd.

[25] Detienne 1988, xi. For an ample documentation and an in-depth discussion of the problem of legislative writing, cf. Gagarin 1986, 126ff, Camassa 1988, Thomas 1996, Gagarin 2004, Bresson (2005), who establishes an interesting comparison with the situation of written political communication in the Near East, Thomas 2005, Pébarthe 2006, 243ff, and Bertelli 2007.

plex series of reforms that he was charging with the difficult task of granting social balance among all the elements of the city: "I have written laws for the poor and the noble alike, giving to each the right justice" (frag. 36, lines 18–20). Herodotus then tells how Solon, after finalizing his reforms, traveled for a long time because he "desired to see the world" (*theōria*), from Croesus's Lydia to Egypt (I, 29–30; cf. 86ff). Even if not true, this anecdote is at least an indication of an important element in our perspective; the solution to the crisis of the polis is symbolically attributed to the impersonal stability of the law, which—thanks to writing—acts independently of its author and puts itself under the control of the collective. Here we can glimpse the beginning of a long and troubled path of practice and reflection that will lead, in Athenian culture of the second half of the fifth century, even to an identification of the *written* law as a necessary factor for a city ruled by justice. In Euripides's *Suppliants*, King Theseus closely echoes Solon's words, reminding the barbarian herald that "when the laws have been written," as they have been in his city, Athens, "the weak and the wealthy receive the same justice" (lines 430–434). Analogously, Gorgias's Palamedes lists the "written laws . . . custodians of the just" among his most beneficial discoveries (82 B 11a, 30 DK).

On the other hand, not *everyone* was expected to be able to read and understand the laws, for in that case there would have been no need for official figures such as the *mnēmones* or *hieromnēmones* ("reminders")—mentioned in a great number of inscriptions— who were in charge of preserving, through repetition, the memory of proceedings and processual norms, as well as more ancient strata of unwritten laws that often had to be taken into account as part of the integration of fundamental principles of the law (for instance, considering murder a serious crime that must always be punished). Moreover, we should not overlook the symbolic impact of a rule when written on materials such as wood, or better yet, bronze or stone, for purposes of displaying stable authority even to an illiterate public, at select locations chosen for greatest effect, such as the agora or a temple. Ultimately, in this context the transition from orality to writing must not have been as smooth as we are tempted to believe; on the contrary, we might more prudently imagine a complex dialectic between two poles, specialized knowledge and the advertisement of legislative texts.

In the context of literary communication, the trajectory from written text to reader is possibly even less linear. Here, as pointed out by Luigi Enrico Rossi, we should distinguish three moments: composition, transmission or circulation, and publication or performance. In each of these moments the use of writing is configured differently depending on the different genres, which have different modalities of fruition.

As far as poetry is concerned, writing was already used in composition in the long oral tradition of epic tales, which finds a unified form in the eighth century in the poems known to us as the *Iliad* and *Odyssey*. This is also true of Hesiod, as evidenced in both the form and content of his poems,[26] and of both monodic and choral lyric since Alcman (the extreme complexity of meter, moreover, proves that many compositions cannot be a result of improvisation). For a long time, however, the circulation and performance of poetry take place in oral form; this practice endures until at least the fourth century BCE (it obviously concerns dramatic works as well) and can be understood as the structural link between poetic performance and the occasions of festivals or symposia. For this situation of "mixed" orality, where two means of communication, oral and written, coexist in a variable relationship that influences the configuration of texts, we usually use the term *aurality*, a formulation that emphasizes that the text, though written, is not destined primarily to be read but to be heard.[27]

The case of scientific-philosophical writings is equally complex. Eric A. Havelock (who was, among scholars of the ancient world, the most determined to interpret the features of archaic Greek culture based on an opposition between oral forms and writing) tended to postdate the effects of writing and thought that the first Presocratic philosophers were actually poets working with oral composition (according to him, for instance, frag. 1 of Anaximander is spurious).[28] We might conclude instead that the high degree of elaboration shown by philosophical and scientific texts required a written medium, not only at the moment of composition but also of circulation. It is significant in this respect that Anaximander and Anaximenes chose to write in prose, which does not lend itself to being memorized as poetry does; it is clear from Aristotle that the meter of poetry served as a mnemonic device (*Rhetoric*, III, 9 1409 b 4). I shall discuss this choice shortly, and also explore the peculiar case of Xenophanes, a professional rhapsode who wrote poetry of philosophical interest (to us). As for Parmenides and Empedocles, it is true that they write in verse, but the formal configuration of their hexameters and the lack of formulaic elements invite us to think that the form in which they wrote was not dictated by memorization needs (and the reasons for adopting poetry will have to be sought elsewhere, and we shall do so later on).

More generally, talking about the circulation of philosophical writings requires a very careful differentiation of modalities and contexts. Let us begin

[26] This opinion is not unanimously accepted, but see the arguments in its favor in Most 1993.

[27] On this point, Rossi (1992) reprises a suggestion by Ong (1982). On the role of music in the oral transmission of monodic lyric, see Giordano-Zecharya 2003. The situation of philosophical and scientific writings is well illustrated by Nieddu (1984 and 1993), Thomas (2003), and Perilli (2007a).

[28] Cf. Havelock 1963, 225ff; 1983, 9, 42–43; and 1996, 25ff. A balanced consideration of Havelock's approach could benefit from the studies collected in Robb 1983, as well as the clear stance in Ferrari 1984.

with the vicissitudes of transmission for the Sentences of the Seven Sages, which offer some unique insights. Plato gives clear hints (*Charmides*, 164e–165 a, and *Protagoras*, 343a–b) that at least one original group of these maxims (certainly including the most famous, such as "know thyself" and "nothing in excess") was inscribed on the temple of Apollo at Delphi. The location was clearly suitable for a Panhellenic diffusion, which must have taken place mainly in oral form, and the conciseness of the maxims guaranteed their easy memorization and repetition. Nevertheless, there were moments of written recording. In fact, several inscriptions with lists of sayings of the Seven have been found, from Thera to Asia Minor and Afghanistan, dating from the fourth and third centuries BCE, which trace back to the Delphic original, and the more or less certain position of these inscriptions in public settings testifies to the long-lasting educational role entrusted to these expressions of early Greek wisdom.

This kind of diffusion, prodigiously various in its forms and locations, has significant Eastern precedents; we might think of the great fortune of the *Story of Ahiqar*, the autobiography of a wise counselor of the king at an Assirian court of the seventh century, almost certainly first inscribed (in Accadian and cuneiform) on a stele, and circulated between the sixth and fifth centuries in different languages and media (parchments or papyrus rolls in Aramaic, or orally in Aramaic symposia), perhaps before arriving in Attica.[29] Yet the circulation of the maxims of the Sages must also have been connected specifically with the awareness of the immediate political expendability of the norms of archaic moral wisdom; an awareness that came about rather precociously in Greece, since the list of the Seven was officially proclaimed in Athens in 582 BCE, as reported by the Peripatetic Demetrius of Phaleron in *On the Archons* (this information is preserved in Diogenes Laertius, I, 22).[30] In light of this, it is interesting to read a passage from the *Hipparchus* (a dialogue attributed to Plato but almost certainly not Platonic), where the author tells us that Hipparchus, son of Pisistratus (who ruled Athens between 527 and 514 BCE), had his own moral maxims inscribed on herms scattered along extraurban roads "so that, first and foremost, his citizens should not admire the wise Delphic writings ... but should instead regard as wise the sayings of Hipparchus; and secondly that, being able to read and appreciate his wisdom in going back and forth from there, they might abandon the fields to complete their education" within the walls of the city (228d–e). Whatever the historical value of this anecdote, these lines demonstrate an unquestionable awareness of the advertising power of writing and, at the same time, of the need to make competitive (if not manipulative) use of it, as opposed to other sources of knowledge, in order to capture its audience.

[29] See Luzzatto 1992.
[30] See Maltomini 2004.

However, this is a rather particular case. In general, we might surmise that the audience of the wise men of the Presocratic period was rather selected in terms of intellectual receptiveness. The situation may have been similar to what happened in Greek historiography with Thucydides. According to a rather late but widely accepted tradition, it seems that Herodotus gave public readings of various sections of his *Histories* (the final and complete edition was published posthumously). In this respect, he would have been following in the footsteps of his predecessors, the so-called logographers. In any case, the vivacity of Herodotean narration and its epic diction are congruent with the search for a wide audience, which might be inspired by the oral performance to revisit a moment in Greek history that was perceived as heroic (the period of the Persian Wars). Thucydides, a few decades later, overtly breaks away from this approach; his plan to write a work that is a "a possession for all time rather than a prize-essay to be heard for the moment" (I, 22) is tied to the search for an audience selected for their ability to read and also for their specific interest in the analysis of events. Thucydides requires, as will Plato, a "critical" reader who devotes his time to a careful study of the text, in the absence of its author.[31]

Yet we should remind ourselves that, until late antiquity, individual reading was normally (but not inevitably) done out loud, so even a work composed and circulated through the written medium was not necessarily destined to be read in silent isolation. One can imagine that a spoken reading of a written text (by the author, but also by interested readers who might have gotten hold of the texts in areas far away from where they were written) was an experience easily shared by a group of friends or audience.[32] This fruitful era for philosophical texts must have been various and lively, and Plato, in his acute attention to the problem of the transmission of knowledge, presents illuminating pictures of it. In the *Phaedo* (97bff), for instance, Socrates comes in contact with the philosophy of Anaxagoras when he overhears someone reading passages from his book; out of curiosity he procures a copy (on sale for little money) and reads it on his own, only to be eventually let down, as we know. Another story features a now old Parmenides, who comes to Athens from Elea in the company of his young pupil Zeno (the *Parmenides* also features a "very young" Socrates, which indicates that this dialogue is set around 450 BCE). Zeno has brought with him a copy of his writings, conceived as a defense against objections that have been leveled at the arguments of his teacher, and reads it in front of a large audience gathered in a private house; among the audience is Socrates, who starts an in-depth discussion after the

---

[31] See Yunis 2003a.

[32] The problem is known and well studied; see Knox 1968, Svenbro 1988, Schenkeveld 1992, Burnyeat 1997, Gavrilov 1997, and Busch 2002.

reading. Leaving aside the question of its historical veracity, this episode re-veals a sequence of circumstances that must have been considered normal: a written text reaches into a new environment through someone who travels with it (not necessarily the author), and even though the information is very complex and difficult, it can be shared through public reading, and a discus-sion ensues. The situation seems typical of that phase of "aural" transition where, as we saw earlier, even in the presence of the written text, reception continues to rely, albeit not exclusively, on the oral medium. Moreover, the persistence of oral channels explains why some philosophers (Thales, Pythag-oras, Socrates himself) did not feel mandated to use writing in order to circu-late their ideas. And this persistence is also explained by the particular condi-tions in which the Greek intellectual operates; given the lack of institutions designated to support his activity, the display of knowledge before a public is aimed at procuring—through direct competition with other sages—paying pupils and fame.[33]

In principle, an audience need not be literate, and oral fruition still has aesthetic appeal. It is evident, for instance, that Heraclitus puts a great deal of effort into the auditory effects of his message to make it captivating. Phil-osophical communication, on the other hand, requires understanding pro-foundly personal thoughts (and an added level of reflection, extended to a reading of the text in which those thoughts are housed), and so, tends to seek a more select audience than mythology requires, and in contexts that are not institutionalized, like religious festivals, but created ad hoc.

The panorama outlined here, though extremely concise, should give the sense of a complex situation that must be investigated by avoiding easy gener-alizations when analyzing the pairing of orality and writing against the prob-lem of the forms of rationality. Specifically, in order to examine three different approaches to philosophical writing (Anaximander, Xenophanes, Heraclitus) that are remarkably diverse to begin with, we will now also have to take into account a complex of specific coordinates, such as the cultural and social con-texts of the composition, its polemic objectives, and the presumed audience of the performance.

Anaximander: The Treatise and the Map

The ancient sources unanimously attribute to Anaximander a writing known as *On Nature*, and they emphasize its absolute originality in the Greek con-text (Diogenes Laertius, II, 1–2 = DK 12 A 1 DK; Themistius, *Orations*, XXXVI,

---

[33] This element in Lloyd's research emerged recently thanks to a comparison with the situation in ancient China; see Lloyd 1996a, 20ff, and 2002a, 151ff, and Lloyd and Sivin 2002, 104ff.

317 = 12 A 7 DK).[34] To be precise, Diogenes Laertius says that the philosopher "wrote a general exposition (*kephalaiōdē ... ekthesin*) of his opinions," a sentence that lends itself to several interpretations. Perhaps Diogenes is referring here to a summary composed later, but his words may also be describing the structure of the original writing, thus pointing to its conciseness (which would be in keeping with the pragmatic character of archaic prose)[35] or (according to a different hypothesis) to a division of the subject matter "into thematic chapters." Anaximander may have been the first author of Greek literature to write in prose. His competition was Pherecydes of Syros, who is more or less his contemporary, though each may have made independently the choice to write in prose; the point is that this choice must have represented, for both, a deliberate detachment from the literary tradition, which until then had been consistently poetic.

André Laks recently argued, with good reason, that a determining factor for the beginnings of philosophy must have been not the act of writing, per se, but prose writing in particular. Resorting to prose, in fact, implies a search for directness and unambiguousness (a search free from the restraints of prosody) and expresses a detachment from poetic discourse that is not merely formal; an emancipation from the contents of poetic discourse as well as a new relationship with the public. Whether he addresses a public of listeners or readers, the prose writer comes to the fore as an author instead of a mediator inspired by the divine voice, and aims at tones of objectivity rather than the emotional involvement of his audience. The new expressive medium, then, is instrumental to a personal claim of authority (whereas the poet's authority was guaranteed by the invocation to the Muse) coming from a new figure of intellectual looking to find his own social space.[36]

---

[34] The expression "on nature" (*peri phuseōs*) is a general indication of the contents rather than the real title of the treatise. In fact, at the time of Anaximander, the term *phusis* could designate the "specific nature" of a thing as determined by the modalities of its "generation" (it derives from the root **phu* of *phuein*, 'to generate'), but not the "nature of all things" (a meaning that is attested in philosophical texts only from the last decades of the fifth century BCE). The formulation *peri phuseōs* was acquired by the doxographers only after the (Platonic and Aristotelian) identification of the nature of the cosmos as an area of inquiry for the first philosophers, thus finding its destiny as the standard title for Presocratic writings. Generally speaking, the practice of titling a book, be it poetry or prose, is established in the fifth century, together with the affirmation of books as objects and the growth of the book market. Before that, the specificity of a work was guaranteed in the very first lines, presenting the name of the author, his birthplace, the addressee, and a brief description of the contents (the formula is variable; see, for instance, the way Alcmaeon and Hecataeus start their writings [above, 71–72, and 161ff, for Empedocles]). This situation is aptly reconstructed in Schmalzriedt 1970.

[35] Cf. Schick 1955 and Bravo 2001, 73ff, 84ff.

[36] Cf. Laks (2001b), who gives priority to Pherecydes; also Wöhrle 1992 and Humphreys 1996.

These considerations can be extended to areas other than philosophy. Consider, for instance, the work of Hecataeus of Miletus. In his *Genealogies* the written medium marks the distance from the contents of genealogical epics, acting as a rationalistic downscaling of legendary elements that it might not be an exaggeration to call "positivistic." But the adoption of prose in particular indicates that the search for a striking performance has lost a great deal of importance. Hecataeus's *Periegesis*, too, structured as a paratactic and asyndetic listing of cities followed by brief comments, probably marks a break from a tradition of hexametric *peripli*.[37]

In his writing *On the Oracles of the Pythia* (406 E–F) Plutarch will observe, concerning the abandonment of poetry in oracular responses, that among the earliest historians the adoption of prose accompanied a preference for truth over the mythical element and, analogously, that it aided the philosophers in pursuing their program of didactic clarity in a context that previously favored the astonishment of the public. It is clear that the ancients were already aware of the potential of historical and philosophical prose. Yet it should be noted that prose did not immediately become *the* writing form of philosophy, though it seems that this choice was initially shared by Anaximenes, who preferred a simple and linear style (as noted in Diogenes Laertius, II, 3 = 13 A 1 DK). But that same choice is not shared by Xenophanes, whose thought needs to be examined in light of his being a rhapsode, while Heraclitus, as we shall see, will work on an idiosyncratic rhythmic prose (and not exactly with the purpose of being clear). The poems of Empedocles and Parmenides, on the other hand, are written in the meter of epic, the hexameter (not to mention that they both refer to a divine figure as a guarantor of the truth, but this deserves a separate discussion). In conclusion, the long journey at the end of which prose establishes itself as the standard expressional form of philosophy will truly be completed only in the second half of the fifth century, in Athens, with the writings of Anaxagoras, Diogenes of Apollonia, and Democritus.[38] In its first phase, this itinerary is rather bumpy, in that it is articulated—in different social contexts—by a succession of formal choices that are always very personal, aimed at emphasizing the originality of contents (not necessarily passing through prose) for better communication and self-promotion,[39] following a coherently "egotistic" intellectual style.

However, it is worth asking ourselves what were the objectives of an Anaximander or a Pherecydes, with their personal choice of expression. It is also true that they could not be aware *ab initio* of that potential for clarity and directness of philosophical prose, which earned the praise of modern scholars;

---

[37] See Asper 2007, 79.

[38] Goldhill (2002) dates the "invention of prose" to this period and to the forms of Athenian democracy. See also the discussion here, 171ff.

[39] As aptly pointed out by Cherniss (1970).

a potential that, instead, could manifest itself in later developments. It would be just as anachronistic to try to search in this early phase for a distinction between literary genres. Yet an esteemed scholar such as Charles Kahn gave in to this temptation when he observed that, while Pherecydes's writing belongs (in implicit but clear opposition to Hesiod) to the theogonic tradition, Anaximander's treatise "does not fit into any established literary genre and hence does not aspire to represent prose 'as a division of literature.'"[40] In Kahn's view, it places itself instead in continuity with a substantial branch of technical prose with geographic, astronomical, and engineering contents (on which we have scant information), and inaugurates a new genre, that of the treatise *peri phuseōs*. On the contrary, it is clear that the prototypical nature of Anaximander's writing has been established *a posteriori* thanks to the fact that it attempted, and was successful in formulating, a new discourse on the cosmos. Pherecydes's endeavor should also be seen as an experiment aimed at rationalizing the mythical structure of the theogonies through an agenda of personal and abstract speculation; the difference is that Pherecydes's experiment does not launch any genre and remains unparalleled, presumably because its objectives still pertain to the area of traditional religious thought and because of the unresolved tension between the desire to offer a clear and orderly account of the natural events and the persistent temptation to provide allegorical representations and imaginative digressions.[41] Ultimately, then, there is no point in asking ourselves which literary genre our authors aspired to belong to or be listed under. We should instead ask: Which elements of the existing written prose might have appeared instrumental to the discourse that these authors wanted to formulate? For, even if the contents and aims of their messages were new, some model must nevertheless have inspired them.

Here we need to look at texts more complex than those written in the simple and instructive prose that was aimed at communicating or recording information and must have been in everyday use since the beginnings of literacy (and in the Ionian world it was especially favored by the frequent commercial exchanges).[42] We know that around the mid-sixth century the publication of laws had already begun, and probably some architectural writings were also being circulated. Vitruvius mentions several Greek treatises on architecture, including those of Theodotos, the architect of the temple of Hera at Samos, and Chersiphron and Metagenes, builders of the temple of Artemis at Ephesus (which in fact brings us to the sixth century BCE). These treatises are unfortunately lost, and we can only speculate about their content starting from the information provided by Vitruvius (*On Architecture*, VII, Preface, 12, and

[40] Kahn 2003, 142.
[41] See above, 51–53 and 58–60.
[42] This evidence is discussed extensively in Asper 2007.

X, 2, 11–12) and Pliny the Elder (*Natural History*, XXXVI, 95–97). It seems that this literature had an essentially illustrative and explanatory character, and thus provided, rather than a system of theoretical reflections, practical instructions to be followed for putting up the buildings, through sketches and lists of measurements and proportions, or even descriptions of special technical expedients (for instance, how to erect a column).[43] The hypothesis that Anaximander's description of a cosmos ruled by proportion and measure may have been influenced by his reading an architectural treatise is an appealing one, and an indication in this direction may be seen in the image of the earth as a column section located at the center of the universe; but given the state of our evidence, this must remain nothing more than a tempting suggestion.[44]

The hypothesis of the influence of legislative prose is more promising. The process of putting laws into writing started in the seventh century BCE. The evidence we possess for the archaic period is modest, yet certain, and it reveals a remarkable tendency for impersonal formulations of the will of the polis or this or that social institution. This impersonality is reinforced by the inscription of the laws on solid materials aimed at displaying the general and enduring validity of the law. Laks insisted on these general elements, outlining the hypothesis that in Pherecydes's attempt to naturalize theogony, the writing of the laws may have served as an important antecedent, as an expression of a human, but nonetheless permanent, institution.[45] However, as far as Pherecydes is concerned, it is not possible to go beyond a hypothesis, since both the agenda and audience for his work (which, as we have seen, is not easy to classify between theology and cosmology) are not known to us. On the contrary, we have good reasons to think that Anaximander consciously modeled his writing after the language of the laws, at least for the solemn statement in frag. 1:

> Whence is the coming-to-be of the things that are, there too their destruction happens, according to obligation: for they pay the penalty and retribution to each other for their injustice according to the ordering of time.[46]

---

[43] Cf. Wesenberg 1984 and Settis 1993, 486–87.

[44] In any case, I would not go so far as to argue that the works of the great Ionian architects were the main source of inspiration for Anaximander's cosmic model (or even for the distances he posits between the astral circles), as has been argued with great imagination in Hahn 2001 and Couprie, Hahn, and Naddaf 2003. I refer to Kahn 2002 for a balanced assessment of this hypothesis.

[45] See Laks 2001b, 147. Asper (2004) insists on the standardizing and impersonal features of Athenian legislative writing, for which see also above, 76ff.

[46] This is the extent of the fragment as reported in DK, but the original citation (in Simplicius's commentary to Aristotle's *Physics*, which draws from Theophrastus) begins with the words "according to what is due"; the preceding words (with *genesis* designating "generation" and *phthora* designating "destruction") have the flavor of an Aristotelian

The best comment on the analogy established here between the rhythms of cosmic becoming and a precise judicial situation is probably still Jaeger's:

> This is something quite different, and not at all hard to visualize. It involves the image of a scene in a courtroom. When there are two parties to a dispute, the one who has taken more than his share, whether by force or by trickery, must pay damages for his pleonexy to the party he has wronged. To the Greeks, for whom the just is the equal, this pleonexy, or taking-too-much, is the essence of injustice. We must not think of civil and constitutional rights, but simply of property rights—the daily quarrel over mine and thine. When Anaximander proposes this image as an explanation of the coming-to-be and passing-away of things in the natural world, he is obviously thinking of their very existence as dependent on a state of having-too-much, for which they must make amends by ceding to others the things they now enjoy. A very similar idea appears in Heraclitus when he says that "these live the death of those, while those die the life of these." And this atonement occurs "according to the ordering of Time," or rather, as I prefer to explain it, "according to Time's decree."[47]

Let us now consider the expressive structure of the fragment. Simplicius, who perhaps derives his opinion from Theophrastus, notes that Anaximander uses "rather poetic words." Indeed, the richness of the metaphors employed seems to respond to an emulation of poetic expression. The other fragments, though meager, confirm this impression, containing metaphors ranging from the representation of the astral openings as "pipes of a bellows" (frag. 4) to the image of the earth as a "stone column" (frag. 5) to the praiseworthy attributes of the *apeiron*, "eternal" and "ageless" (frag. 2). Thus frag. 1, while molded after a clearly judicial image (the punishment that all things must receive for their injustice), breaks away from the technical rigidity of the written laws through its stylistic sophistication. Moreover, as shown by Jaeger himself, expressions such as "according to necessity" (*kata to chreōn*), "to receive punishment and retribution for injustice" (*didonai … dikēn kai tisin … tēs adikias*), and "according to the ordering of time" (*kata tēn tou chronou taxin*) have many parallels in archaic and classical poetry and later in Attic prose. Perhaps for this reason, scholars have tended to set aside the attempt to make a close comparison between Anaximander's writing and the writing of legislative texts.[48] On the other hand, we are authorized to presume that Anaximander, in his aspiration to endow his vision of the cosmic order with the

---

translation, even though the ideas expressed may be genuine. For the general traits of Anaximander's cosmology see above, 37ff.

[47] Jaeger 1947, 35. The reference to Heraclitus draws freely from his frag. 62.

[48] The sole exception (to my knowledge) is Asper (2001, 104n156).

validating force of a judicial norm, borrowed formal patterns that had already been tested in the assertive and authoritative expression of law decrees. This presumption becomes a certainty when his writing is compared with the corpus of inscribed laws of the archaic and classical periods.[49]

First, and most obviously, this corpus contains many instances of the term *dikē* with the technical meaning of "lawsuit" and "settling" of a dispute, often concerning matters of property. Another point is that in archaic literature this term also tended to have a strictly legal connotation, rather than the more general meaning of Lawfulness or Law with a capital *L*.[50] Moreover, its antithetical term, *adikia*, also central to Anaximander's fragment, is invoked rather often to designate a crime that needs to be brought to trial. The verbs *tinein* and *tinesthai* and their cognates also frequently designate the payment due as compensation for a certain offense (the earliest instance of this being a law from Gortyn dating to the seventh and sixth centuries and concerning the right of pasture). It is true that Anaximander conveys this meaning with an expression, *tisin didonai*, that has no precedents in the legislative texts. What is more, these texts do not contain any uses of the noun *tisis* ("punishment" or "retaliation"), in keeping with a general tendency to resort to descriptions of concrete acts rather than abstract concepts. However, *tisis* is frequently used in refined literary contexts ever since Homer. This suggests that Anaximander is transposing the language of his model to a more sophisticated stylistic level. This might explain, besides the expression *tisin didonai*, the "existential" connotation of the term *chreōn*, which appears again and again in funerary inscriptions to indicate the fate awaiting the deceased.

In any case, we are brought back to a judicial context by the other expression that, in Anaximander's fragment, refers to time as the factor that articulates the rhythm of prevarication and compensation between things: *kata tēn tou chronou taxin*. Just like *tisin didonai*, this expression does not occur verbatim in the legislative texts, which nonetheless contain important references to the time factor, references that are so frequent as to seem obsessive (an impression probably due to the fact that modern law does not give the same importance to such a factor). A frequent concern, for instance (attested since the earliest surviving Greek law on stone, the Constitutional Law of Dreros, dating to 650–600 BCE), is to avoid the reiteration of public offices before a certain amount of time has elapsed. Another example of the attention paid to the element of time is represented in the recording of terms for sending someone to trial (for which we also have an archaic example in the laws of Chios, 575–500 BCE). But the most frequent situation is the one where the judicial

---

[49] In a previous discussion, some of which I am revisiting here, I provided a detailed examination of legislative writing (Sassi 2006a). On the language of archaic inscriptions in general, see Schick 1955a.

[50] As stressed by Gagarin (1974).

branch is given the prerogative to set a deadline for consolidation of a debt, payment of a fine, or compensation for damages. It is important to note that in cases such as these, or similar to these, the term *chronos* is used in combination with forms of the verb *tassein* (which indicates the act of "establishing").

In conclusion, we can argue that Anaximander elaborated his construction by drawing on borrowings from legislative texts. The interpretation according to which Anaximander wanted to outline an analogy between the physical world and the world of the polis by resorting to images of injustice and reparation is not new. However, the hypothesis that he may have carefully built the language of law itself leads us to search that analogy for signs of even stronger implications than we suspected before.

Let us consider, first, the role played in the writing of the laws by the "determination of time," with its different connotations. If we presume that the expression *kata tēn tou chronou taxin* (whose interpretation is rather uncertain) implies a reference to this particular element of regulation of the life of the polis, we can probably consider a translation like "according to the ordering of time" or, better yet, "according to the allotted time" (taking *chronou* as an objective genitive) rather than "according to the decree of Time" (taking *chronou* as a subjective genitive). The latter translation cannot be excluded altogether, since the idea of a divinized Time, supreme maker of verdicts, would certainly not be incompatible with Anaximander's view, but the former translation is now corroborated by the parallels we have seen in the judicial literature. Let us consider, moreover, that in Anaximander the *apeiron* itself is a guarantor of the cosmic "decree," a role that it exercises with the authority of a divine principle; similarly, Greek law found its legitimization by explicitly seeking approval from the local deity or by posting up the decrees on temple walls.[51] In other words, the *apeiron* is well suited to play a strong regulatory role, which can also entail giving a temporal limit to the injustice brought about by the elements (with the periodic triumph of one over the other in the seasonal cycle).

Secondly, reflecting on the nature and features of archaic Greek law will benefit our understanding of the cosmic model posited by Anaximander. Several scholars of Greek law have invited us to reevaluate the idea that there was such a thing in Greece as a general and conscious shift toward the codification of a system of laws characterized by unity and internal coherence and aimed since the beginning at a "democratic" ideal of equality of all citizens before the law. On the contrary, these scholars argue that in gradually more complex communities subjected to external pressures and internal conflict, the written record of the laws had in general (though not always) the role of settling specific problems on a case-by-case basis, not only between the ruling

---

[51] Morgan 2003, 77ff rightly stresses this interrelation of civic and religious authority in the archaic period.

class and the nonaristocratic part of the citizen body but also within the aristocratic class itself.[52] We may then ask ourselves, in light of the analogy between the material and political reality underlying Anaximander's formulation, whether he was interested in the aspect of becoming and *conflict* within the cosmos rather than in the balance that was the outcome of such a process. At any rate, we can confirm that Anaximander's reflection revolved around a notion of *dynamic* balance, a notion inspired by the "hot" context in which he lived. It is worth mentioning that, in this perspective, Anaximander's reflection is analogous to Solon's, in the sense that Solon (in Athens during those same years) was trying to intervene in the internal conflicts of his city with just measures (modeled after a notion of cosmic justice) aimed at balancing, on the political level, inequalities that were nevertheless thought to be ineradicable on a social level.[53]

Given the scarce evidence in this respect, the hypotheses we might formulate regarding the addressees and the conditions under which Anaximander's writing came into fruition are less certain. It goes without saying that in this case we cannot imagine a direct transition from the writing of a text to its wide circulation, like the one presupposed (at least ideally) by written laws (and also by the maxims of the Seven Sages, in the way that we reconstructed above).[54] In other words, it is hard to envision a sequence of inscribed reflections *peri phuseōs* in plain view in the agora of Miletus. But even here it may be useful to refer to the publication process of the laws, because precisely at the time of Anaximander this process goes through that long phase of "mixed" orality that we mentioned before,[55] during which the two channels of communication, oral and written, coexist in a variable relationship that influences the structure of the texts. In this context, Anaximander's message, though composed in a sophisticated form that imitates the force and authority of legislative writing, is destined to be transmitted orally, by its author (in its first appearances), to an audience gathered expressly for the occasion. On the other hand, it is clear that we are dealing with a particular message that aims to draw the attention to *original* contents. This message, then, is addressed most likely to an audience more restricted than one composed of citizens committed to complying with the laws of the community or attracted by poetic performances. A new message called for new occasions. But what were these?

---

[52] See Hölkeskamp 1992 and 1999, as well as Gehrke 1995.

[53] See above, 39ff for a first argument in favor of this reading of frag. 1, to which must be added Engmann 1991 and Gagarin 2002. On Solon, see Vlastos 1946 and above, 42ff. Martin also reads Anaximander's fragment (and Solon's reforms) in direct correlation with the problem of the unity of the polis, which is dynamic rather than static (2003, 32–33).

[54] See above, 78ff.

[55] See above, 77–78ff.

To answer this question, it may be useful to remember that Anaximander's interests were not restricted to the nature of the cosmos. This is falsely suggested by Aristotle's focus on this aspect in his physical treatises and the evidence contained in a doxographic tradition markedly influenced by the Aristotelian perspective. For instance, Anaximander was also interested in geography, probably drawing most of his information from the stories of merchants and sailors passing through Miletus, but perhaps also from personal experience (the sources mention his participation in the foundation of a colony on the Black Sea, as well as a trip to Sparta; 12 A 3 and A 5 a DK). His role in this context is far from negligible, if it is true that "he was the first who dared to draw the inhabited earth on a tablet," as reported by an ancient author who quotes Eratosthenes, the great geographer and astronomer of the third century BCE (Agathemerus, I, 1 = 12 A 6 DK). This testimony, aimed at marking the birth of cartography, is well in agreement with the tradition attributing to Anaximander the first writings on nature.

Christian Jacob rightly observed that the idea of putting a graphic medium at the service of a representation of the earth (more precisely: of the entirety of the inhabited earth, unperceivable in everyday experience) presupposes a significant ability of abstraction, not just in the author but also in the recipients of his message.[56] Even in this case, then, as in the case of the writing on nature, Anaximander must have addressed a selected and, so to speak, intellectualized audience and presented them with the cartographic drawing accompanied by an oral illustration aimed at onlookers-listeners.

On the other hand, Jacob denies that the map was of any use to travelers, soldiers, or politicians, arguing that its existence is already justified by Anaximander's project of a general study of nature. This opinion is influenced by a Platonic-Aristotelian prejudice, according to which the philosophical interest originated as pure contemplation. As far as geography is concerned, we come to different conclusions if we consider Herodotus's account of Aristagoras of Miletus, even though it refers to a slightly later circumstance. Aristagoras, sent on a diplomatic mission to Sparta to seek the help of King Cleomenes against the Persians (499 BCE), brings a bronze tablet on which was drawn the perimeter of the Earth, including the oceans and all rivers, which he uses both to inform the king of the political situation of the Ionian cities and to show him how the military campaign would be carried out (V, 49, 1). We should note that Ionia and Miletus were facing pressure from the Persian empire after the overthrow of the Lydian monarchy, precisely in the period of Anaximander's maturity; it will be easy to deduce that his map also may have been seen as a means of geopolitical information by the citizens most closely involved with the revolt taking place.

[56] See Jacob 1988.

Let us now consider whether our remarks on the possible origin and influence of Anaximander's map can prove helpful in understanding the context in which the first treatise on nature was written and began to circulate. Admittedly, we know almost nothing about the framework within which the first natural philosophers worked, but precisely because of this we cannot exclude that they expected some practical outcome from the transmission of their knowledge. Thus we cannot rule out the possibility that Anaximander presented his cosmology, modeled on an ideal symmetry, as a view "from above" aimed at instilling balance in the choices of the city elites whom he was addressing. In this mileu, judicial terms and notions must have worked as an entry point for a public Anaximander was calling on to share a common vision of the "things" of the city. At the time, Miletus was an economically prosperous and culturally flourishing city, threatened in its independence and burdened by repeated power struggles between tyrants and oligarchs as well as social tensions. Some litigations needed to be assigned to competent but external figures; we know of an intervention by the Parians—of uncertain date, but it is not impossible that it dates to the mid-sixth century.[57] The polis-cosmos analogy would then work in two directions; not only, as has long been established, is the relationship between opposites in the cosmos represented in terms borrowed from conflicts (mainly about property) that pervade the polis, but this picture of the cosmos can in turn serve as a model of that dynamic balance, guaranteed by adequate laws, that Anaximander thinks the city needs.

Finally, we might surmise that Anaximander's message was addressed to a select public of high-ranking citizens who shared social and political interests, were familiar with legislative texts, and could therefore discuss them together with other aspects of the polis, on occasions created ad hoc. I would not exclude the possibility that this kind of conversation may have taken place during convivial gatherings. Beyond the primarily ludic character of its manifestations, the institute of the symposium found its deeper motivation in the display of solidarity among aristocratics and in social harmony. With its special emphasis on the orderly demeanor of the symposiasts and on the formal arrangement of the songs, the symposium represented a sort of aesthetic projection of an ideal political order.[58] Therefore it could host, besides the poetic performances that were mandatory for every participant, speeches on love in both poetry and prose (along the lines of the ones idealized in Plato's

[57] Precious observations on the sociopolitical picture of Miletus can be found in García Quintela 1996 and Seaford 2004, 198ff, who both considered the hypothesis of a "close encounter" between Anaximander and the laws. See also Gorman 2001, 87ff.

[58] Ford (2002; especially 25–45) brilliantly develops this point. For what follows, see also Pellizer 1990.

Symposium) as well as conversations on various themes of moral or political wisdom (the Sentences of the Seven Sages, for instance, were also read at symposia). I do not wish to further develop this hypothesis in relation to Anaximander. Yet it is certain that a message such as his, which presupposed a high degree of reflection, called for a prearranged time and space, and it seems natural that such an environment was provided by a private home, be it the author's or a fellow citizen's.

In conclusion, we might surmise that the first writing on nature was read publicly, for the first time, in a rich home at Miletus. We might also hypothesize that reading was followed by a discussion aimed at commenting on the analogy between conflicts in the cosmos and those taking place in the ever-changing local society. We can see another indication concerning this last aspect (the possibility of a *discussion*) by comparing the birth of cartographic representation and the beginnings of natural inquiry, noting that, upon exhibiting its data, the map lends itself to discussion and criticism. We know that Anaximander's map was reprised and rectified by Hecataeus a few decades later, in the same Miletus where it must have remained visible to anyone who was interested. Anaximander, probably inspired by that same preoccupation with symmetry that emerges from his description of the cosmos, had indicated a bipartite division of the surface of the earth (imagined as being circular in shape) into a northern continent (Europe) and a southern one (Asia). Hecataeus complicates the picture, perhaps basing his account on additional geographical data that he may have gathered during his travels to Persia and Egypt, which are reported by the doxographical tradition. However, he still has a geometrical outlook, for he represents Scythia in the shape of a square, Asia Minor and Arabia as trapezoids, and Africa as divided into three zones that are in turn divided vertically in half. Significantly, this leads Herodotus to mock Hecataeus (IV, 36, 2):

> And I laugh when I see how many people have now drawn maps of the earth, and yet none of them gave a reasonable explanation of it. For they draw Okeanos as encircling the earth, which they think is round as if drawn with a compass, and they make Asia as big as Europe. For myself, I will show in a few words the extent of each of these parts, and how they should be drawn.

Note how Hecataeus is struck with the same weapon—corrosive writing in the first person—that he himself had used against the mythical genealogies. Herodotus vividly expresses the intention to substitute the geometric and abstract space of the first cartographers with a more flexible and concrete representation (probably inspired, we assume, by further exploratory journeys). In fact, later he will present a description of the earth that proceeds like a periplos, from one population to the next. But there would never have been a sequence of different points of view nor a tangible progression of knowledge, if a first, and then a second, geographical representation had not been drawn on a tablet.

The sequence from Anaximander to Hecataeus to Herodotus may, then, be considered an exemplary instance of the connection of writing and cultural variants in the sense described by Assmann.[59] The map worked at once as a text for preserving specific contents, but it also invited its users—in specifically motivated social contexts—to elaborate and criticize. Nevertheless, the rectifications that followed did not hide the traces of the previous phases; a snickering Herodotus who proclaims his intention to go beyond the sketchiness of the early maps still contributes to preserving the memory of those first attempts. In the case of Anaximander, the material form of the book provided a stable support for his views on the cosmos, thanks to which they were preserved in cultural memory and at the same time launched a long line of discussion exceeding even the author's intentions.

Xenophanes, Satirist and Polemicist

Xenophanes was born in the Ionian city of Colophon around 570 BCE. Following a series of political upheavals (the restoration of a tyranny in Colophon and the Persian conquest of Asia Minor between 546 and 544 BCE), he left his fatherland at the age of twenty-five, and from that moment onward "sixty-seven years tossed about *his* reflection (*phrontis*) throughout Greece," as he recounts in a work that he must have written at the age of ninety-two (frag. 8 DK). His career is that of an itinerant poet, so, in the Panhellenic context, his publication method requires continuous traveling from one audience to the next. However, as noted by Havelock, Homer or Hesiod would never have called their poetic activity *phrontis*; with this term, Xenophanes declares his detachment from the traditional themes of epic poetry, as well as the desire to explore new intellectual frontiers.[60]

His long journeys take Xenophanes to many Sicilian cities (Syracuse, for instance, at the court of Hieron) and to Magna Graecia. A popular biographical tradition, moreover, links him to Elea, and at its colonization he is reported to have dedicated a poem. This tradition also indicates Xenophanes as the teacher of Parmenides, which is doubtful. The thirty-four fragments we possess, which amount to one hundred twenty-one lines in various meters (dactylic hexameter, elegiac couplets, iambic trimeter) include two sizable elegiac poems, a number of passages (almost all of which are hexametric) on cosmological, theological, and gnoseological themes, as well as a group of verses

---

[59] On Assmann's categories, see above, 74–76. For a more in-depth study of the relationship between the models of Anaximander, Hecataeus, and Herodotus, cf. von Fritz 1971, 32ff, and Gehrke 1988, in particular 177ff.

[60] Havelock 1966 (reprint 1982), 235.

whose contents we might classify under the label of cultural criticism. It is natural to think that the latter were part of the so-called *Silloi*, a satirical writing that the ancients attributed to Xenophanes. The other, speculative fragments are harder to place within Xenophanes's opus. In keeping with a common cliché, the ancient sources also attribute to Xenophanes a poetic work *On Nature*, but he does not seem to have focused his ideas on the physical world in a single work.

An analysis of the communication strategies at work in Xenophanes's verses is extremely helpful in understanding his role in the history of philosophy, without sacrificing either the variety or the originality of his work. Some information provided by Diogenes Laertius sheds some light: "He wrote in epic verse, as well as elegy and iambic poetry, against Hesiod and Homer, attacking them for the things they said regarding the gods. Yet he himself recited (*errhapsōdei*) his own writings" (IX, 18 = 21 A 1 DK). Xenophanes is presented here as a rhapsode, that is, a performer of poetry, and we might well speculate that he earned his living by performing at festivals, public contests, symposia, and tyrants' courts. This professional identity is evidenced in one of his elegiac lines, echoing the normal ending of many Homeric Hymns (for example, the *Homeric Hymn to Aphrodite*, line 293), where the poet announces the end of the current song and the beginning of the next: "I now proceed to another tale, and I shall show a path" (21 B 7 DK, line 1).[61]

Yet, while the rhapsode's prerogative was normally to perform (by heart) a traditional repertoire (mostly of Homer, but other poets as well), Xenophanes presented original material in his performances. What is more, he was harshly polemical against poetic tradition, and his particular target was the representation of the Olympian gods in the poems of Homer and Hesiod.[62] The information provided by Diogenes is famously confirmed by some of the preserved fragments, which attest to a lucid and aggressive critical stance against the anthropomorphic representation of the divine (frags. 11 and 12):

> Homer and Hesiod have attributed to the gods everything that
> is a cause for reproach and blame among men:
> theft, adultery and mutual deceit.

> They spoke of a number of illicit divine deeds:
> theft, adultery, and mutual deceit.

In Xenophanes's view, this portrayal of the gods, which Homer and Hesiod modeled on the world of men, is morally inappropriate; what is worse, thanks

---

[61] See Collins 2004, 147–48.

[62] Ragone (2005) offers a rich reconstruction of the historical context of Colophon between the sixth and fifth centuries BCE, permeated by a "Homeric" culture aimed at perpetuating traditional educational models, and makes the attractive hypothesis that Xenophanes may have already elaborated his polemical ideas in his homeland.

to those poets' influence on the fabric of Greek culture, it has become part of the mainstream (frags. 10 and 14):

> ... since from the beginning all have learned according to Homer.

> But mortals believe that the gods are born
> and have clothing, voice and body like their own.

What emerges from these lines is an opposition between the common opinion of "mortals" and that of the wise man speaking (which is obviously the right one). This idea appears frequently in Presocratic literature as a powerful promotional motif. The wise man, in this case Xenophanes, candidly exposes the notion that gods are similar to men, and his irony turns into sarcasm as he outlines the possible versions of anthropomorphism among other populations and even—paradoxically, but why not?—in the animal kingdom (frags. 16 and 15):

> The Ethiopians say that their gods are snub-nosed and black,
> the Thracians that they have light blue eyes and a rosy complexion.[63]

> But if oxen, horses or lions had hands,
> or were able to draw with their hands and do the work that men can
> do,
> horses would draw the forms of their gods similar to horses,
> and the oxen similar to oxen, and they would fashion their bodies
> in the same shape as they each had themselves.

These texts also reveal how the development of modes of critical thinking may have been benefited, in archaic Greece, through contact with other belief systems during an era characterized not only by politically motivated migrations but also by thriving exchanges and colony foundations, such as the era of Xenophanes. Indeed, the mechanisms of his criticism of anthropomorphism emanate directly from the discovery of a cultural diversity whose main corollary is the awareness that Greek culture is itself a *construction*, one due mainly to the works of Homer and Hesiod, whose hegemony as poets and educators is the main target of Xenophanes's polemic.

Yet Xenophanes does not only rebel against the poets' inappropriate representation of the Olympian gods; he also refuses to be passive and reinforce the set of values underlying the entire poetic tradition. A strong critical stance also emerges in the two longest elegies preserved, even though they send us back to the aristocratic context of the symposium. The first elegy stages a

---

[63] Note that the text of this fragment is the result of Diels's reconstruction after a paraphrase by Celsus. It nonetheless has a place in the history of ethnography. Elsewhere I have argued that the adjective *purrhos* more likely designates the overall complexion rather than the hair (Sassi 1982b); see also Sassi 2001, 20ff.

"moralized" banquet scene characterized by a sense of religious decorum. After the appropriate ceremonial instructions and the necessary invitation to honor the gods and avoid hubris, the author invites celebrants to drink, though not to excess, and praises the man who, having taken drink and being incited by memory and the practice of virtue, speaks of noble deeds and not "of the battles of Titans and Giants and Centaurs, fictions of the ancients, nor of "furious conflicts, for there is no use in these" (frag. 1, lines 21ff). This is a clear break from the mythical tradition—as well as from the partisan political poetry of authors such as Theognis and Alcaeus—in the direction of an ideal of virtue that anticipates classical notions of moderation. In the other elegy, fighting on a different but neighboring front, Xenophanes makes a highly personal statement about the superiority of his intellectual attitude, compared to the cult of physical strength and athletic prowess glorified by aristocratic society. We should note that here, at line 12, Xenophanes does not hesitate to emphasize "our wisdom" (*hēmeterē sophiē*). But we should also note that this self-promotion takes place inside the symposium; in these compositions, as we have seen, Xenophanes is working within the same framework as other contemporary monodic poets, who eschew epic tales in favor of themes they deem more appropriate for the atmosphere of the banquet (first and foremost the theme of *erōs*, as in the case of Anacreon and Ibycus), as well as an opportune moment to proclaim their professional distinction.[64]

In conclusion, Xenophanes employs traditional poetic forms such as elegy or epic hexameter to promote an original and personal agenda. It is clear that his aim is to reach the same vast public whose cultural identity has been formed by attending rhapsodic performances. In fact, even his meter reveals (besides an obvious search for expressive efficacy, which in itself may also be the goal of a text destined to be read) a significant concern for the memorization of contents in a context of aural fruition. A good indication of this is the repetition of the same line in frags. 11 and 12 (cited above); more generally, other elements that can be explained in this way are the parodic variations of Homeric formulae and frequent use of repetitive patterns.[65] These elements are not found only in polemical texts. Consider, for instance, the cosmological framework of frag. 30, where many terms are repeated, and also the last line reprises the contents of the first, in a ring composition typical of oral formulations:

> The sea is the source of water, and source of wind;
> For neither would in the clouds the force of wind come about
> blowing from within without the great sea

[64] For the interpretation of the two elegies, on which much has been written, see at least Di Donato 2005. See also Vetta 1983, xlviiiff; Ford 2002, 46–66; and Gostoli 2005.

[65] See the analyses of Hershbell 1983, Classen 1989, and Wöhrle 1993b.

nor streams of rivers nor rainwater from the sky,
but the great sea is the begetter of clouds and winds
and rivers.

It is reasonable to think that even those texts that we call cosmological, theological, or gnoseological were addressed to an audience not made up specifically of "philosophers," and that they fulfilled the same expressive needs as the more openly polemical ones. The critical stance and the personal, sometimes even aggressive style of Xenophanes are some of the main features of his discourse.[66] We shall explore his gnoseological stance later.[67] For now, it will be worthwhile to pause and consider his "theology," which gives particularly good insight into the complementary destructive and constructive purposes of his thought.

I want to stress here that Xenophanes is far from wanting to deny the existence of the gods per se. Rather, his intention is (as it will later be Plato's) to "reform" the traditional belief, purging it of its philosophically unacceptable traits. Xenophanes's own image of the divine, then, is constructed precisely through a *negation* of the human attributes, that is to say, of those characteristics that poets such as Homer and Hesiod naively extrapolated from the human world to represent the workings of the gods. In fact, Xenophanes's only god is "not at all similar to mortals in body or thought" (frag. 23); "it is unfitting for him to move here and there, but he shakes all things without toil by the faculties of his mind" (frags. 25–26); having *no* sense organs, he sees, hears and thinks "in his entirety" (frag. 24; this image may allude to a spherical shape).

About this representation—in itself a remarkable result of a sophisticated intellectual process and of a certain ability of abstraction—the ancient tradition constructed the view, largely accepted in the modern period, that Parmenides learned the central principle of the unity of being from Xenophanes.[68] Admittedly, we cannot exclude that Parmenides may have been able to hear Xenophanes perform at Elea, and may even have been interested in his idiosyncratic idea of the divine. However, it is completely anachronistic to make Xenophanes the founder of the Eleatic "school" or the creator of ontological monism. Having said this, it should be clear that Xenophanes's thought, unlike that of Parmenides, fights the battle on the side against the cultural monopoly of the Homeric-Hesiodic tradition. If further proof is needed, one could point out that his "theological" fragments contain a series of precise references

[66] This is an old intuition by Rudberg 1948, who inspired the title of this section.

[67] See below, 146ff.

[68] In a famous passage in Plato's *Sophist* (242c–d), Xenophanes is mentioned as the forefather of the "Eleatic ancestry," a position that will be consolidated by Aristotle in the first book of *Metaphysics* (986b 18–27). I have dealt with this problem elsewhere (Sassi 2006c).

to the language and imagery of epic poetry, such as the image of Zeus, who shakes Olympus with a nod (*Iliad*, 1, lines 528–530).[69] These references are certainly parodic in nature, and they aim to emphasize Homer's distance from contemporary religious culture. At the same time, the reprisal of familiar expressive forms was used to ease the reception of new contents for an audience gathered in the traditional setting of the symposium.

The Obscure Heraclitus

Reading Heraclitus brings us, again, to a highly specialized expressive environment. His style, already regarded by ancient rhetoricians as a prototype of obscure writing,[70] seems to represent a remarkable exception to that search for a language capable of a "direct grip" on reality that we have seen as a significant feature of many of the philosophers' writing choices. But this exception is more apparent than real, in the sense that Heraclitus, too, in his own way, is intimately adherent to the reality he describes; a reality whose deeper sense reveals itself only to those who are able to decipher it under the contradictory surface of the sensible world. For, according to Heraclitus, the field of things that are before everyone's eyes (but most people are not even aware of this) is pervaded by an incessant tension (or better yet, a "war") between opposing forces. This tension is revealed by phenomena such as the mutual transformation of the elements and the alternation of day and night, and also, on the existential level, by the cycles of sleep and wakefulness, which represent, on one hand, the transition from ignorance to knowledge and, on the other, the contiguity of death and life. This tension is also reflected in the insurmountable conflict of different points of view, so that, for instance, water that is good for fish is undrinkable and lethal to men, or "the road up and the road down are the same thing" (because the road is the same, only entered from different sides; cf. frags. 8, 10, 51, 53, 54, 60 and 88).

Heraclitus's universe is in a state of perpetual conflict, both as a whole and as the sum of its parts. It is broadly believed that Heraclitus intended to cor-

---

[69] For further remarks on this point, I refer to Gemelli Marciano 2005. This richly documented study advances the interesting hypothesis that Xenophanes's criticism of religious anthropomorphism may have been inspired by the characterization of the supreme god Ahura Mazda in ancient Persia (which was resistant to iconographic representations). However, I do not think that this lessens the speculative character of Xenophanes's thought, as argued by Gemelli; in light of my objection to Burkert's argument (see above, 38–39), I believe that a conceptual element imported from another cultural context still requires a theoretical adjustment to the new context. Moreover, I think that Xenophanes's verses should not be dismissed as nonphilosophical just because he was a rhapsode. I elaborated on these issues (and more) concerning Xenophanes's religion in Sassi 2013b.

[70] See Fuhrmann 1966, 70 for a list of relevant passages.

rect the notion of balance in Anaximander's cosmos. But this opinion does not hold true if we see also in Anaximander's fragment (as we tried to do above) a focus on the conflict between cosmic forces rather than on the need for mutual compensation. In either case, moreover, the view of cosmic conflict is presented as an image-projection of a marked instability of the social fabric, in which the internal disputes between citizens constitute a "physiological" factor. A good indication of this is offered by the terms used in frag. 80 of Heraclitus:

> It is necessary to know that war is common (*xunon*) and strife is justice (*dikēn*), and everything happens according to strife and necessity.

The traditional image of Heraclitus as the philosopher for whom "everything flows" must be corrected with the important remark that, in his view, stability is inseparable from mobility, just as unity is inseparable from conflict, that is to say, "the invisible accordance (*harmoniē*) is stronger than the one that is visible" (frag. 54). Beneath the proliferating dissonances of reality the wise man has discovered that the opposites are connected by a force that, even when pushed to an extreme, never goes beyond the breaking point (as in the curvilinear structure of the bow and lyre, whose ends are drawn near each other in a "conjunction (*harmoniē*) turning back on itself"; frag. 51).

Heraclitus posits the existence of a *logos* intended as "reason" and "rule" of becoming, identifying it with the ever-mobile and impalpable substance of fire (a natural element that seems to take up the role played by water, *apeiron*, and air for the Ionians, but which also becomes—in an entirely new way—an existential marker of change). *Logos* in Greek means also "speech," and Heraclitus uses the term and its double meaning to refer to his personal message and, *at the same time*, to its notional core—the *logos*-principle of all things. Thus Heraclitus stresses that his message should not be acquired passively; its contents must be *understood*. This motif emerges clearly in two fragments that probably belonged to his earliest writings.[71] Here, in assertive and protreptic tones, humankind is urged to undertake nothing short of a conversion from the sleep of reason in which it normally lives; only when men emerge from their solipsistic isolation will they gain an awareness of the meaning of the wise man's words and, simultaneously, of the profound meaning of the reality in which they are immersed (frags. 1 and 2):

> This *logos*, which always (*aiei*) is, men are incapable (*axunetoi*) of understanding, both before having heard it and after having heard it once. For, although everything happens in accordance to this *logos*, men

---

[71] As Glenn Most pointed out to me, we might surmise that the very beginning, now lost, featured an emphatic announcement of the name of the author, something like this: "Thus speaks Heraclitus [from Ephesus, and/or son of . . .]."

resemble inexperienced people, when they experience the words and actions I describe, by dividing each thing according to its nature and saying how it is. But the other men forget the things they do when awake, just as they forget what they do when asleep.

Although *logos* is shared (*xunou*, like war in frag. 8), most people live as though they have their own intelligence.

The will to free most men from their condition of ignorance is accompanied by criticism of some clearly well-known wise men against whom Heraclitus is competing. It might seem odd that, according to the textual evidence, Heraclitus's attacks affect neither Thales nor the duo of Anaximander and Anaximenes. Admittedly, the Ionians are never explicitly mentioned in the pre-Aristotelian tradition, exception made for Thales and his emblematic role (Heraclitus refers to him in frag. 38 as "the first to study astronomy"). And we need not necessarily try to "aristotelically" link together the different *phusiologoi* in a chain of consecutive scientific acquisitions. Yet the general lines of Heraclitus's thought may be read as a response to Ionian naturalism revisited through an existential lens.[72] One might think, then, that Heraclitus chooses an approach that holds an implicit message for the Milesians; for instance, by electing to give a prominent role to a substance such as fire, whose novelty is self-explanatory, he implies the acknowledgment of a shared set of references. Heraclitus's criticism is more explicit, if not violent, not only against Homer and Hesiod, the most renowned representatives of epic tradition, but also against others who, like Xenophanes, Hecataeus, and Pythagoras, had firmly distanced themselves from that tradition (frag. 40):

Knowing many things (*polumathiē*) does not teach understanding, or it would have taught Hesiod and Pythagoras, as well as Xenophanes and Hecataeus.

That this polemic addresses such disparate personalities is an obvious sign that Heraclitus is not reflecting within an already established philosophical tradition. The victims of his sarcasm are all those wise men who downscaled knowledge to a heap of exterior notions, being incapable of relating the plurality of reality to the fundamental intuition of its unity. Let us read further (frags. 42, 57, and 129):

Homer deserves to be cast out of poetic competitions and struck with a stick, and so does Archilochus.

Hesiod is the teacher of most; people are certain that he knew very many things, he who did not recognize day and darkness. For they are one.

---

[72] This persuasive thesis comes from Kahn (1979).

Pythagoras son of Mnesarchus carried out his inquiry (*historian*) further than all other men and, choosing from these writings, built up his own wisdom: a knowledge of many things (*polumathiē*), an evil craft (*kakotechniēn*).[73]

The treatment of Pythagoras is remarkably harsh, as he is presented as a quack who put together other people's ideas and passed them off as his own. This is also an indication that Heraclitus regards *polumathiē*, a fault shared by his adversaries, as an even more dispersive model of wisdom, in that it stems not from personal meditation but from putting together the knowledge of others. It is clear that according to Heraclitus, "knowing many things," which is a shallow showing-off of ideas, tends by its very nature to become popular, and the process is made even easier (and we may well surmise that this was seen as an aggravating factor) when these authors resort to using enticing expressive techniques.

This polemic, then, has the clear purpose of bringing the contents of Heraclitus's message to the fore in a competitive way. Consistent with this approach, on the formal level Heraclitus does not seek immediate and improvised success among an audience willing to be allured by a flow of poetic lines; rather, he aims to trigger instances of individual reflection. This is why he breaks up his discourse into a series of poignant sentences, each of which constitutes a (very dense) unit of meaning. And within each sentence, an expressive choice tends to play on two intertwined levels.[74] On one hand, this choice aims to reproduce, through frequent and complacent use of antitheses, the contrastive structure of the sensible world, even emphasizing it for those who are not yet aware of it. On the other hand, the exaltation of contrast triggers, through antiphrasis, recognition of a generally organized framework governed by a (divine) principle of unity. A good instance of this irreducible duplicity, which is the recipe for the notorious Heraclitean "ambiguity," may be seen in frag. 67:

The god: day night, winter summer, war peace, repletion hunger. It is altered just as [fire], when commingled with spices, and gets its name from the fragrance of each of them.[75]

---

[73] Mansfeld (1989) rightly pointed out that the formulation of frag. 129 does not imply a reference to written works of Pythagoras (who did not write anything, *pace* Riedweg 1997), but nonetheless presupposes a context in which the book is a relatively common object.

[74] This does not rule out that these various thoughts (which are sometimes provided in the compact form of the aphorism, sometimes in longer and more complex sentences) may still have been organized in a meaningful sequence. On the problem of the unity of Heraclitus's book, see Granger (2004), who reprises the reading of Kahn 1979 (see below, n.76).

[75] This fragment presupposes the analogy between the cosmic divine principle and the fire on the sacrificial altar, where different kinds of incense are burned.

Heraclitus must have aimed at an audience capable of confronting a written text and going back to it time and again in order to understand its many implications. Remarkably, Aristotle mentions in his *Rhetoric* (III, 5, 1407b 11 = 22 A 4 DK) the difficulty of establishing the punctuation of Heraclitus's text, to the extent that it is often unclear whether a certain word should be read with what precedes it or with what comes after it. This observation is better understood if one remembers that Greek writing was continuous, that is, it lacked both word spacing (which will be standardized only during the time of Charlemagne) and punctuation marks (which will be applied regularly only after the invention of printing). Aristotle mentions the very text of frag. 1 ("this *logos*, which *always* is, men are incapable of understanding") to remark that it is not clear whether that "always" qualifies the (external) validity of *logos* or men's (generalized) deficit of knowledge. We are probably closer to Heraclitus's intentions if we give up trying to resolve this ambiguity and admit that the adverb can refer to both what precedes it and what comes after it, according to a construction *apo koinou* (and one could cite many such instances).[76] However, when reading the text aloud, it is useful to pause on one point or another of the phrase, which naturally leads to favoring one of the two possibilities. Therefore Aristotle's perplexity, together with the general sense of ambiguity of Heraclitus's sentences, is better understood in relation to the reading of a *written* text.

In light of these observations we have no reason to doubt that Heraclitus was also addressing an audience of readers. This is confirmed by the baffling juxtaposition in frag. 48 of *biós*, the Greek noun for bow, and *bíos*, the noun for life. There is an antithetic wordplay between the two terms, which share the same phonemic sequence but are stressed differently (though accents were not marked in writing at that time). This wordplay must have been aimed at an aural/oral audience, but at the same time it might also have served as an invitation to stop and reflect inquiringly on the text.[77]

The name of the bow (*biós*) is life (*bíos*), but its work is death.

Let us remember that frag. 1 is a clear invitation to "listen to" the *logos*.[78] Heraclitus, then, was relying on the impression brought about by his personal reading (presumably declaimed in tones of an inspired prophet rivaling those of bards and rhapsodes) to snatch his listeners away from the easy attraction of poetry. Which is to say, he does not ignore the efficacy of reading out loud;

---

[76] It is enough to scan the translation in Kahn 1979, who felicitously played on the category of ambiguity (and of the subsequent multiplication of textual references) in his reading of Heraclitus. See also Kahn 1983.

[77] According to a process carefully reconstructed by Dilcher 1995, 129ff.

[78] See above, 99–100.

on the contrary, he pays a great deal of attention to sound effects. A close philological reading has shown that his rhythmic prose is structured according to
a series of metrical correspondences between antithetical elements aimed at
effectively mirroring a reality conceived as an identity of opposites.[79] At the
same time, by substituting the hexametric flow with a broken-up sequence
of aphorisms, Heraclitus sets himself apart from the rhapsodic tradition to
which Xenophanes was still tied. His independence from this tradition is also
indicated by the fact that during his lifetime he seems to have communicated
his message solely to the citizens of Ephesus; coming from an aristocratic
family (even a royal one, if we accept what Diogenes Laertius tells us; IX, 6),
he did not need to travel and make a living as an itinerant poet.

Heraclitus does not limit himself to the double play of orality and writing.
He also draws from a variety of preexisting expressive models, whose potential he develops in relation to a constant objective: to wake up his audience.[80]
First, several elements suggest that the context of the mysteries was an important source of inspiration for Heraclitus, with regard to both contents and
style. It is true that he does not seem to claim to be immortal, which is the
main aspiration of the followers of the mysteries; instead he thinks that every
soul is dissolved into a cosmic vital force.[81] Nevertheless, the awareness of the
precariousness of the individual's existence and the urge to transcend mortality through a superior unity of life and death—two central elements in Heraclitean thought—are also at the very foundation of the mystic experience, and
in both cases they are expressed in a series of antitheses symbolically related
to the basic opposition of life and death, such as light and darkness, day and
night, waking and sleeping. This consistency with tradition is remarkably confirmed by the verbal sequences inscribed, together with a few symbolic draw-
ings, on three bone tablets dating to the fifth century BCE and found inside
a sacred area at Olbia Pontica (a colony of Miletus on the Black Sea). Among
other significant things, these tablets contain the earliest mention of "Orphics" (*orphikoi*) as members of a specific group, yet more interesting to us
here are three brief phrases that are structured around such remarkable oppositions as "life death life" (*bios thanatos bios*), "peace war" (*eirenē polemos*),
and "truth falsehood" (*alētheia pseudos*).[82] In fact, the first two pairs of opposites recur in significant aphorisms by Heraclitus (in particular see frags. 48,

---

[79] As meticulously shown by Deichgräber 1962. Robb 1983 provides a catalog of stylistic elements that are related to an agenda of auditory efficacy and memorization.

[80] Cf. Snell 1926 and Hussey 1999, 91–93.

[81] On this point, see below, 117ff.

[82] For a substantial treatment of the Orphic character of these writings (which were
published in 1978), see Zhmud 1992. The reading *orphikoi* has now been carefully confirmed by Bravo (2007, 75–76).

62, 67 and 88), and the opposition between truth and falsehood is the inspiration for Heraclitus's self-presentation as a truthful wise man in contrast to those who only pretend to be such. However, these oppositions have a different meaning in the Orphic context, where peace and truth denote the condition achieved by the initiated, in contrast to the turmoil and deceptiveness characteristic of the mortal condition. In Heraclitus, instead, the same oppositions stem from the awareness that, in reality, the cosmic conflict adumbrates a fundamental balance.[83] Yet the question we should be asking is not whether Heraclitus's thought might have influenced these texts from Olbia, or whether specific elements of the Orphic doctrines might have attracted his attention, perhaps with the result of soliciting from him a work of appropriation and transformation. What is important is to point to an affinity; a perception of reality in contrasting terms, one that uses antithesis as the stylistic method most suitable to express it. Heraclitus's predilection for antithesis is indeed a common trait between his discourse and the liturgy of the mysteries, both Eleusinian and Orphic; and the same can be said of asyndeton (also present in the Olbia tablets) and of paronomastic juxtaposition (e.g., *bíos* and *biós*).

It is also interesting that Heraclitus, when he solemnly declares his own *logos* in frags. 1 and 2, uses the tones of a hierophant (the priest who announces the mysteries). Here he is referring to his audience of listeners as uninitiated (*axunetoi*, found in frag. 1, may have been a "technical" term in this sense) and addresses them with a *prorrhēsis*, that is, a preliminary speech similar in tone to the one uttered by the first priest in the antechamber of the holy circle at Eleusis and promising access to the mysteries only to those who might subject themselves to initiation. The final revelation, both in Heraclitus and in the mystery cult, takes place through seeing and at the same time hearing a truth reserved to very few people.[84]

Communication by way of enigmas also belongs to the practice of the mysteries, which can be understood only by the initiated. And the use of enigmas, wordplay, paradoxes and surprising and moralizing tales is characteristic of archaic wisdom, where the ability to propose or decipher verbal puzzles brings about, or increases, the fame of the *sophos*.[85] Not only does Heraclitus love enigmatic formulations, as we know, but he also programmatically refers to enigmas as the paradigmatic form in which reality presents itself;[86] knowl-

---

[83] As rightly noted in ibid., 77–78.

[84] On the relationship between Heraclitus and the mystery, see the excellent work by Schefer (2000; on frag. 1 in particular, see pp. 56–60), but see also Thomson 1953, 83, and Roussel 1990. We may interpret Strabo's mention that the royal *genos* of Ephesus, among other privileges, oversaw the priesthood of Eleusinian Demeter (22 A 2 DK) as a sign that Heraclitus was acquainted with the mystic environment.

[85] See Rossetti 1992.

[86] See Hölscher 1974.

edge must advance through riddles such as the one that not even poor Homer was able to solve, in an apologue minted ad hoc (frag. 56):

> (They say) that, when it comes to recognizing what is manifest, men are deceived like Homer, who was the wisest. For boys who were killing lice fooled him by saying: "What we see and grasp, we leave behind, while what we did not see nor grasp we are taking away."

Another strong model of wisdom communication, also mentioned in programmatic terms in a famous fragment, is the oracular response, be it of Apollonian or Sibylline inspiration (frags. 93 and 92):[87]

> The lord whose oracle is at Delphi does not tell nor hide, but gives signs (*sēmainei*).
>
> ... the Sibyl by her frenzied mouth ...

The second quotation, which represents the earliest source regarding the tradition of the Sibylline Oracles, is also the more problematic. While Heraclitus's emphasis on the aspect of the Sibyl's divine possession—one that he was unlikely to have identified with—seems indeed to indicate that he prefers the "style" of Delphi, his communicative strategy shares some significant traits with the prophecies of the Sibyl. It is not only a matter of obscurity, which is currently the best-known feature of these prophecies and also one that Heraclitus may have borrowed from other expressive models, as we have seen. More similarities can be seen in the predilection for the use of the first person (both Heraclitus and the Sibyl tend to speak for themselves rather than as the mouthpiece for the divinity); in their addressing the harangue—using mostly melodramatic, but occasionally apocalyptic, tones—to the whole of humanity rather than to a specific addressee; in the frequent references to an auditory process that simulates a direct and oral communication, even in the case of a written text (divination in Greece took place most often in oral form, but the prophecies of the Sibyl had circulated in book form since the archaic period).[88]

At any rate, Heraclitus borrows from oracular practice the fundamental idea of the intentional construction of a polysemic text. A good example of this is again the articulation of frag. 1, which lends itself to two different interpretations depending on whether we read the temporal adverb *aiei* with what comes before or after it. This is the same mechanism at work, for instance, in the paradigmatic phrase of oracular style: *ibis redibis non morieris in bello.*

---

[87] Warren rightly underscores this feature in the title of his chapter "The Oracles of Heraclitus" (2007, 57–76).

[88] On the characteristic obscurity of oracular style, seen as the beginning of "the history of the semantic problem, of the reflection on the signifying power of words," see Fuhrmann 1966, 51ff. On the peculiarities of Sibylline prophecy, see Manetti 1997 and 1998; Baumgarten 1998, 52–60; Crippa 2004; and Lightfoot 2007, 14ff.

This sentence, too, prefigures two different fates, namely, to survive or to die at war, depending on the position given to the negative particle, whose interpretation is entirely open, due to the absence of punctuation. However, there is a clear and substantial difference; Heraclitus's ambiguity, unlike that of the oracles, is never aimed at confusing the individual, who is helpless in the face of looming disaster. Instead it aims to shake one's conscience and invite one to a lucid understanding of reality.

Finally, to this plurality of expressive models we must add the influence of moral maxims, which are brief and sententious, precisely like many of Heraclitus's aphorisms.[89] Here, too, the stylistic similarity corresponds to an intellectual affinity; Heraclitus's ideal of wisdom—the result of moderation and introspection—is the same as the one that emerges from the Sentences of the Seven Sages, and in both cases the assertive invitation to a moral regeneration is expressed in the form of a pithy and categorical statement (see, for example, B 112 and B 116 DK).

To conclude, exploring Heraclitus's writing workshop has led us to discover a melting pot of almost too many ingredients, and it would be superfluous to comment on the unique quality of the final product. Besides, that excess of signifiers, which we can approach only through philological and historical effort, must have been immediately captivating—both emotionally and intellectually—for contemporary audiences.

Heraclitus's message, then, is virtually accessible to anyone who would undertake an endeavor of insight, but it addresses a select audience capable of understanding an ever-complex web of references to forms and contents. This same elite must have been variously involved, or able to be involved, in governing the polis, and this leads us to hypothesize circumstances of diffusion not unlike the ones we postulated for Anaximander. Not by chance, Heraclitus resorts—in order to emphasize the normative and sovereign character of *logos*—to an analogy with the human law, presented as a factor of inner stability of the polis not less important than the necessity of defending it from external enemies (frag. 44: "The people need to fight for the law as they do for the walls [of the city]"). Adding an explanation that is absent in Anaximander, Heraclitus claims that the power of the law is guaranteed, in turn, by the reference to a divine principle common to all things, most likely identifiable with *logos* itself (frag. 114):

Those who wish to speak sensibly (*xun noōi*) must rely on what is common (*xunōi*)[90] to all [also, to all things], just as a city does on the

---

[89] See the argument in Granger 2004.

[90] Note here the play of assonance, which is obviously not merely formal; the emphasis is on the recurring Heraclitean notion of what is "common."

law, and even more strongly. For all human laws are nourished by the one, divine law; for it dominates as much as it wants and suffices for everything, and is even in excess.

On one hand, the political sphere provides the two complementary images (conflict and the mediating power of the law) that are most suitable for representing the problem of balance in the cosmic change. On the other hand, and coming full circle, the divine principle of balance is pointed to as the ultimate principle to which human actions need to conform. Between the political and metaphysical planes there sometimes seems to be a complete osmosis rather than mere mutual exchange; a text like frag. 33, for instance ("It is law also to obey the will of one and one only") lends itself well to this multilayered interpretation.

It does not seem impossible, then, that Heraclitus expressed his ideas on "all things" in contexts of discussion about important decisions for the city (though not necessarily limited to these). This hypothesis can be corroborated by the biographical tradition, which refers to Heraclitus's eminent position (as an aristocratic) in Ephesus, an element that would be congruent with the promotion of a unique and sovereign principle. Moreover, this perspective gives credit to Diogenes Laertius's reference (IX, 5) to a division of Heraclitus's book into three sections dealing with three different subjects: "all things," the things of the city, and the divine. This information probably presupposes the existence of a Stoic reworking of Heraclitus's text, but we have reason to believe that Heraclitus differentiated these three areas of his doctrine and also correlated them through a series of analogies and references to illuminate them—Charles Kahn, in his masterful reconstruction of Heraclitus's book, has drawn many fruitful conclusions from these observations.

In his aspiration to gain authority within the city, Heraclitus (as Anaximander had done before him) modulates his tone on at least one occasion to emulate that of a legislator. This instance occurs in a cosmological text where Heraclitus contemplates the possibility of the Sun altering its regular course (by moving too close to the Earth, for instance, or by pausing longer than usual during the day or during a solstice), remarking that this infringement would be followed by necessary reparation through the agency of a sovereign principle of order. This statement is guaranteed to have an effect because of Heraclitus's metaphorical reference to vivid figures of Greek religion, such as the Erinyes or Justice itself, that embody the inevitability of divine sanction. As we know, Anaximander had already mobilized figures of the civic order as guarantors of the natural order, and Parmenides will do the same by positing an "avenging Justice" as the guardian of the cosmic gate where the paths of day and night take turns (frag. 1, line 14). But here we should note first of all that Heraclitus's fragment also recalls, on a structural level, the textual style of a law, where the description of the crime (often in the future indicative) was typically followed by the mention of the judicial figures designated to deal with it (frag. 94):[91]

> The Sun shall not overstep his measures, otherwise the Erinyes, ministers of Justice, will find him out.

These considerations offer a new element for the interpretation of the ancient tradition according to which Heraclitus deposited his book, as a votive offering, in the temple of Artemis at Ephesus (Diogenes Laertius IX, 6). Some see this as an act of "religious preservation typical of an age without libraries"[92] that went hand in hand with the authorial agenda of self-presentation as exceptional and superior, which we saw at work in Heraclitus's expressive strategy.[93] We can agree with this, as long as we see that depositing the book in a sanctuary is an indication of an attempt to gain greater accessibility for the writing rather than of a jealous preservational instinct. In a very interesting contribution, Lorenzo Perilli has provided ample confirmation of the role played by temples, in all phases of the Greek world, as places for preservation and consultation of heterogeneous library materials (not only books proper, but also any scientific, judicial, and documentary texts).[94] We may add that archaic temples were where the vast majority of laws were *shown*, in addition to being preserved, in order to instill a religious respect for them and at the same time to parade how objective, stable, and permanent they were.[95] Nor should we forget that even the diffusion of the Sentences of the Seven Sages had followed this path.[96] A "monumentalization" of his writing before the citizens of Ephesus—as if it were a series of regulations—may well have been one of the objectives Heraclitus set for himself when he decided to deposit his book in a temple; but the other, more important objective must have been to make it *available*.

The philosopher's ambitions are not limited to a local context; even though he is interested in the social fabric of his fatherland, Heraclitus has broader

---

[91] Similarly judicial tones are also found in frag. 28 (quoted in its entirety below, 149): "Justice will surely prove guilty the forgers and witnesses of falsehoods."

[92] Cavallo 1988, 30.

[93] On this point, see Cambiano 1988b, 70–71, and Cambiano 1996, 837. On self-presentation in terms of novelty as a way for accruing the status of the ancient philosopher, see also Cambiano 2013, 55ff.

[94] See Perilli 2007a. It is natural to think that the writings of architects (including the one regarding the temple of Artemis at Ephesus; see above, 84) were stored in the very temples they put up.

[95] Precisely in the area of the Artemision at Ephesus, a legal inscription (certainly a part of a broader legislative program) from 500 BCE is preserved, relating to the requirement of validating a testimony by means of a sacrifice to Zeus (Körner 1993, 314–15).

[96] See above, 78–79.

horizons in mind. The breadth of his vision is enabled by the means of com-munication he has chosen; unlike the laws, the book is meant to be copied and distributed beyond the boundaries of the polis. It is possible that Hera-clitus's writing may have traveled on one of the ships that carried different goods, including books in wooden chests, from one side of the Aegean to the other (as reported by Xenophon, *Anabasis* VII, 5), and reached some region of the Greek world and then fell into the hands of the author of the famous Derveni papyrus (420–400 BCE). Here Heraclitus is alluded to as a "classic" to refer to in order to find doctrinal elements comparable to the concepts of the Orphic hymn that is being commented on. One of the two direct quota-tions found in the text is from frag. 94, which mentions the "measures" of the Sun and the supervising action of the Erinyes (the other quotation is from frag. 3, which ascribes to the Sun the "width of a human foot"). In the vicissi-tudes of transmission, any link to that specific Heraclitean text and the con-text in which it was elaborated, and thus any sense of its possible pragmatic implications, was lost. At any rate, the Derveni author is interested in the possibility of making a free comparison between Orphic themes and the Her-aclitean motif of the harmony and stability of opposites in the cosmic frame-work.[97] Writing does not only guarantee that thought is fixed; it also allows it to step outside the city spaces in which it was developed, and enables it to fly off to new places and find other readers, other readings.

[97] Of course, the mystical traits of Heraclitus's thought must have favored the recep-tion of this book in Orphic contexts. After Burkert (1983), who was the first to focus on the two Heraclitean quotations, see Sider 1997 and Rangos 2007, in particular 48–50. On the notion of cosmic justice in the Derveni papyrus, see Kouloumentas 2007.

CHAPTER FOUR

Adventures of the Soul

The Soul, the Cosmos, and an Orange

About sixty years ago, during a lively opening lecture at the Meeting of the Aristotelian Society (which was published shortly thereafter and soon marked a pivotal point in the study of the Presocratics), Karl Popper emerged as an adamant proponent of a "return" to that golden age of "rationality."[1] At the beginning of his address, the philosopher indicated the reasons for his enthusiasm; on one hand, the "critical attitude" inaugurated by the Ionians, and on the other, the "simplicity" and "boldness" of the questions they asked, from the very beginning, concerning the basic problem of the *cosmos* and of *knowledge*, which are inseparable:

> For it is of considerable interest to see how their practice as well as their theory of knowledge is connected with the cosmological and theological questions which they posed to themselves. Theirs was not a theory of knowledge that began with the question 'How do I know that this is an orange?' or 'How do I know that the object I am now perceiving is an orange?' Rather, their theory of knowledge started from problems such as 'How do we know that the world is made of water?' or 'How do we know that the world is full of gods?' or 'How can we know anything about the gods?'[2]

Popper was convinced that understanding the world around us, our place in it, and our knowledge of it are all part of the same problem, and that this problem is *the* philosophical problem par excellence. Against the widespread Baconian notion according to which the gnoseological problem pertains to our knowledge of an orange rather than to our knowledge of the cosmos, Popper remarked that with the Presocratics "our Western science ... did not

---

[1] See Popper 1958–59.
[2] Ibid., 2

start with collecting observations of oranges, but with bold theories about the world."[3]

Popper then developed an analysis of the different solutions that were gradually developed by the Presocratics, applied to the problem of cosmic becoming, and then put into use in their methodologies. As we saw in a previous chapter, this analysis sparked a lively debate on the relationship between observation and theory in the formulation of the Presocratic doctrines, as well as on the particular "critical" attitude that informed their development.[4] This debate, however, ended up overshadowing Popper's strong claim of an *implicit* (because fundamental) interconnectedness between cosmology and theory of knowledge, which had nevertheless provided the starting point of his argument. It is now worth focusing on that claim; though without attempting to evaluate here its theoretical legitimacy in terms of philosophy of science, I believe it will be useful to reflect on it from a historical perspective.

I will begin by observing that the first Ionians do not seem to have *expressed* an interest in gnoseology. As far as we know, Thales, Anaximander, and Anaximenes did not accompany their inquiry on nature with a conscious reflection on the procedures and validity of that inquiry. Each of them, as we have seen, resorted to some type of empirical observation or analogical reasoning, but the impression is that these processes emerged spontaneously, so to speak, during the elaboration of their theories, while their innovative character within a certain methodological program was not emphasized. However, just a few decades later, authors such as Xenophanes and Heraclitus, who are well aware of the implications of the new cosmological inquiries, elaborate claims on the validity of human knowledge in relationship to divine knowledge, and/or on the relationship between data gathered by the senses and the action of reason, with respect to gaining knowledge.[5] We may say that Popper's suggestion is confirmed; it nevertheless needs an important integration. Assuming that there is a link, original or nearly so, between cosmology and theory of knowledge, should we not ask ourselves whether cosmology involves, a fortiori, a notion of the *subject* of that knowledge?

It is time to recalculate our route of exploration. Up to now, following the outline provided by the first book of Aristotle's *Metaphysics*, we concentrated on the cosmological models, which are after all the most visible, or at any rate the best documented, product of the Presocratics' reflection. Yet we cannot ignore that the study of physical nature was soon accompanied by, and interwoven with, an interest in the nature and workings of something that we now

---

[3] Ibid., 3.

[4] See above, 61–63.

[5] In connection with the problem of the authority of wisdom, in the next chapter I focus on a variety of Presocratic texts touching on the relative values of reason and the senses.

call "soul" and the Greeks called *psuchē*. We'll remember that Aristotle himself devotes the entire first book of his treatise *On the Soul* (*Peri psuchēs*, in three books) to a careful review of earlier opinions on this theme, whose theoretical importance he acknowledges—with the consequence that the reconstruction of Presocratic psychology, like that of Presocratic physics, is strongly dependent on the information provided by Aristotle and by a doxographical tradition largely mediated by Aristotelian patterns (an important case in point is Theophrastus's *On the Senses*).

It is remarkable that in the work of a Presocratic, Heraclitus, *psuchē* occurs for the first time with the meaning that will characterize it throughout the development of Greek culture, namely, as a principle that unites vital and cognitive processes (perceptions, emotions, thought); one that does not only cover the field of biological life but also the field that we (after Descartes) call "mind." Yet the formation of a unitary notion of *psuchē* is not linear, either before or after Heraclitus. In the following pages, we shall focus on some of its phases by trying to follow the outline suggested by Popper's observations; we will ask if, and how, the Presocratic discourse on the soul emerges and develops at the same time as the discourse on the cosmos.[6]

From Breath to the Self

The Greek term *psuchē* is etymologically linked to the verb *psuchein*, which means "to blow" and "to cool down" (not necessarily by blowing on something), and with the adjective *psuchros*, "cold." In the language of Homeric epics, it denotes the vital "breath" that shows itself upon leaving the individual, either with his or her last breath or by coming out of a mortal wound, before continuing on to the underworld as a "weak and almost incorporeal doppelgänger of the living person,"[7] a shadowy existence far from glorious deeds and full use of the senses (and, it should be noted, also exempt from rewards or punishments for one's actions in life). But even in the sphere of worldly existence, the entity called *psuchē* takes up a merely vegetative role, while other elements in Homer are involved in the cognitive sphere; *thumos*, for example, which denotes the impetus of passion; or *kēr*, the heart, with which the hero converses as if he were talking to a part of his "divided" self, in moments of hesitation; and finally, *phrenes*, the diaphragm, the seat of thinking. The latter is sometimes represented—when its mechanisms are clearer and better identified—as a function of *nous*, since the prerogatives of the different "organs" are far from being rigorously defined. A rather sophisticated

---

[6] A firm stance regarding this question is taken in an essay that is not recent, yet still noteworthy: "a concern for this inner dimension emerged gradually in the Presocratic period by differentiation from the outer dimension, i.e. from the cosmos." (Seligman 1978, 5)

[7] Vegetti 1992, 202.

analysis of this linguistic framework enabled Bruno Snell to formulate a fortunate diagnosis; according to him, the preference for concrete and exteriorized descriptions of the mental processes and the absence of precise definitions of the psychic elements that characterize the Homeric representation reflect a "primitive" phase of Greek culture, where a unitary notion of soul has not yet been developed. Nor does Snell think it possible to extract a unitary notion of the body from the Homeric text; indeed, the scholar observed just as acutely that the term *sōma* is used only when referring to a corpse, while a living body is described with terms that represent it as a plurality of elements, such as *rethē* or *melē*, "limbs."[8]

We may object to Snell's framework—which is based on the assumption of a one-to-one correspondence between elements of thought and semantic units—by remarking that the lack of a linguistic term does not necessarily imply the absence of the corresponding concept. Moreover, notions such as "self," "soul," and "subject" do not constitute objectively defined territories that come into focus as the "spirit" gradually construes itself (à la Hegel). On the contrary, these notions are forms of experiential organization, and we should study their variations and tensions within determined contexts, in order to avoid evaluating them according to a teleological criterion of presence/absence derived (more or less implicitly) through comparison with later theoretical frameworks.[9] With the due precautionary remarks out of the way, however, we may describe the initial phase of the Presocratic discourse on the soul as a path that starts with a traditional concept of *psuchē* as vital breath (and thus intended as a *vital principle*) and is later complicated with the introduction of a notion of the soul as a *cognitive principle*).

In this sense, the very fact that the Presocratics tend to place the soul within a cosmic framework shows that from the very beginning, their path diverges from the Homeric one. According to Aristotle, Thales believed that the universe was penetrated in many, if not all, of its parts by a *psuchē* acting as a moving principle, and he saw a sign of this in the magnet, a seemingly inanimate object, and its ability to attract iron (Aristotle, *On the Soul*, I, 5, 411a 7 and I, 2, 405a 19–21 = 11 A 22 DK; Diogenes Laertius, I, 24, mentions Hippias as one of his sources and adds that Thales "formed his conjecture" by observing magnets and amber). Thales's reasoning develops a hylozoistic premise according to which the entire universe is animated to some extent, and this premise does not appear to have been linked to any clear distinction between the living and the nonliving.[10] Some sort of differentiation, however,

---

[8] See Snell 1953 [1947], 1–22.

[9] Vegetti is very clear on this point (1996b, 431–33).

[10] For an analysis of Thales's argument seen as a "paradigm of empiricism," see Hankinson 1998a, 12–13. See also above, 43, for Thales's statement that "everything is full of gods."

seems to have taken place with Anaximenes, who formulates the first direct reflection on the human soul (frag. 2):

> Just as (*hoion*) our *psuchē*, ... being air, controls and holds us together, so breath and air surround (*pneuma kai aēr periechei*) the entire cosmos.[11]

We have already mentioned this short text—in connection with methodological questions—as an early instance of analogical mode,[12] and we must cite it again here to note that this analogy is established between the role that the air-soul has for "us," living (i.e., breathing) beings, and the role that the air-element plays in the cosmos. Anaximenes, then, reprises the Homeric notion of a soul-breath and gives it a role that is at least as active as that of cosmic air, and even stands out in comparison, since it supports our vital functions.

The claim of a functional analogy (and more, of a material identity) between the two entities would not be possible if these were not perceived as separate. Through the surface of a definition of *psuchē* seemingly dependent on the illustration of the cosmos, then, we can glean the elements of a focus on the psychic principle as that which defines human beings in opposition to the surrounding world.

Yet, as we previously suggested, it is in Heraclitus that we can see the first, unmistakable signs of a conception that identifies the same entity as the center of cognitive processes that is also posited as a principle of life. The claim that knowledge is the product of the activity of the *psuchē* and not of the senses is not, for once, too enigmatic:

> Bad witnesses are eyes and ears for men, if they have barbarian souls (*barbarous psuchas*).

The Greeks famously call "barbarians" all those who do not understand or speak Greek, the language compared to which all others amount only to meaningless stammers (*barbar-* is an onomatopoeic sound indicating a stutter). This sentence should then be taken to mean that the information provided by the sense organs is useless, even misleading, for individuals who lack

---

[11] The text of this "fragment" (introduced by Aëtius I, 3, 4 to illustrate Anaximenes's choice of air as *archē*) probably underwent the replacement of some Ionian morphological features with forms of the so-called *koinē*. The term *sunkratei* is not attested before the second century CE, and the use of the term *kosmos* before Heraclitus is unlikely. But the particular use of *hoion* in this text is not attested in the *koinē*, and Aëtius's subsequent clarification ("*aēr* and *pneuma* are used synonimically") may indicate that the preceding words were taken as a literal quotation. Moreover, *periechei* is an appropriate description of the relationship between *archē* and cosmos as posited by Anaximenes (see above, 43), and there is no reason to doubt the overall image represented here.

[12] See above, 60.

the ability (characteristic of an "apt" *psuchē*) to coordinate and structure empirical data into a nonsuperficial understanding of reality.[13]

Another maxim, "I went in search of myself" (*edizēsamēn emeōuton*, frag. 101) echoes the Delphic invitation "know thyself" (*gnōthi sauton*). In fact, Heraclitus declares that he himself has *already* carried out an internal examination, and in order to define this process he uses a term that emphasizes the dynamic sense of a completed investigation. However, the most significant difference lies elsewhere. While the Delphic maxim invited men to recognize their own limits, Heraclitus comes to a rather different conclusion at the end of his inquiry; as he succinctly drives it home in another aphorism, he recognizes that the internal dimension has an unfathomable depth to it (frag. 45):

> As far as you may go, you will not find the limits of the soul, even if you travel every road; so deep (*bathus*) a *logos* it has.

It is not easy to unravel every nuance of this dense fragment. In particular, it is unclear what meaning we should give to *logos*, a term whose polysemy (meanings ranging from "speech" to "thought") is only intensified by Heraclitus's sophisticated ambiguity. Here *logos* denotes something like the "intimate reason" and the essence of the soul, which lies "deep" for those who embarked themselves in search of it, with the futile intention of finding its boundaries as if it were a circumscribable, *definable* territory. We know that for Heraclitus the real nature of all things "loves to hide" beneath the manifestations of the sensible world (frag. 123). Yet, at the same time, the *logos* of frag. 45 can be the soul's self-consciousness, which may expand—given the subjective and objective nature of thought—ad infinitum.[14] This reading is corroborated by another fragment (115) presenting the *psuchē* as an entity that does not need external nourishment for its potentially boundless development:

> The soul has a *logos* that augments itself.

The play on images of opposition between the finite and the in(de)finite underscores the psychic reality's resistance to explanation in spatial terms, that is, in terms of location in the body and the interaction between its organs, as conceived by Homer. Indeed, archaic Greek poetry presents traces of a notion of soul comparable to Heraclitus's; in this regard, Bruno Snell pointed out the capacity of attributes such as *bathuphrōn* and *bathymētēs* ("of deep counseling," "of deep mind," in Solon and Pindar) to "voice this new idea, that intellectual and spiritual matters have 'depth.'"[15] It is more than likely that Heraclitus had great interest in the development of the sphere of subjectivity in

---

[13] Nussbaum (1972a) rightly observed that, for Heraclitus, the cognitive ability of the soul amounts to its *linguistic* competence.

[14] This is pointed out very well by Hussey (1999, 104–5).

[15] Snell 1953 [1947], 16.

archaic lyric poetry, one of the most celebrated elements of the genre. How-ever, he not only emphasizes the "depth" of the soul but also aims at integrat-ing this peculiar entity into a cosmological model. The fact that this endeavor proves to be difficult, as we shall see momentarily, does not diminish Hera-clitus's role in the process of formation of what we may well call a *theory* of the soul.[16]

At least until Plato, who discusses the essential affinity of the soul for the domain of the intelligible, the material characterization of the soul is not op-tional; Presocratic psychology consistently rests on a "physicalist" assumption shared with the representation of the soul in Homer and archaic Greek lyric, which will be adopted in turn by the tragic poets.[17] Similar to Anaximenes's soul-air, Heraclitus's soul is akin to the principle identified in the cosmos, i.e., fire, with the implication that the properties of mobility and lightness of fire are reflected in corresponding qualities of intelligence. Given the contradic-tory picture provided by the ancient sources, it is unclear whether the Hera-clitean *psuchē* is more precisely a form of vapor or breath (though neverthe-less fiery) or a mixture of water and fire, or a commingling of fire and air. The latter is the most recent suggestion, and the most attractive, as a mixture of fire and air provides a good explanation of how the soul can get through several phases of dryness/wetness, corresponding to different levels of intelligence.[18] In any case, Heraclitus traces an ideal hierarchy where the highest position is occupied by the dryest soul (in such a way that its *logos*, we might surmise, adheres more closely to the *logos* of cosmic fire), while the lowest positions are taken by souls that, having given in to physical pleasures and passions, have variously "dampened," like the clouded soul of a drunkard who does not know where he is going (frags. 118 and 117):

A gleam of light; a dry soul, the wisest and the best.

A man, when he has gotten drunk, is led by a youth, staggering, not understanding where he is going, because he has a wet soul.

[16] This is a central point in Schofield 1991. For the following observation, see the still valuable treatment by Verdenius (1966).

[17] In general, see Gill 2001,170–71 and (especially, but not solely, for tragedy) Padel 1992. Anaxagoras seems to have been the first to introduce a dualism between mind and matter; as described at the beginning of frag. 12, the *nous* must be "unmixed" with any of the other things in order to have total domain over them (on the issues encountered by Anaxagoras on this point in explaining the modalities of knowledge, see Sedley 2007, 11–30. Heraclitus, too, declares that "what is wise (*sophon*)" is "separated" (*kechōrismenon*) from all things (frag. 108), but this separation should not be taken literally, perhaps. For Hera-clitus, the god tends to coincide with the *logos* and to share its quality of immanence (frag. 67); thus divine knowledge can attain that "synthetic" vision of the opposites that is nor-mally impossible for humans to achieve (compare frags. 102 and 78 with the commentary of Kirk, Raven, and Schofield 1983, 190–91).

[18] See the excellent arguments in Betegh 2007.

Intellectual tension does not fail only those who indulge in physical pleasures. Heraclitus, to whom we are indebted for a strong statement about the independence of the individual's destiny from the intervention of gods or protecting demons (frag. 119: "a man's character is his *daimōn*"), also reflects on the interplay of reason and passion and its role in molding one's nature (frag. 85):

> It is hard to fight against anger (*thumōi*); for whatever it wants, it purchases at the expense of the soul.

Giving in to strong emotions such as anger also slackens intellectual tension, and there is a physical explanation for this process, too; the fire of passion thrives at the expense of the soul in the sense that the latter, once dampened, becomes dull. (It should be noted that the term *thumos* is linked to the verb *thuein*, which has the rather tangible meaning of "to ferment" and "to seethe,"[19] as well as to the Latin word *fumus*). The wet condition can be enjoyed by souls who are not aware that this brings them closer to death; but in fact, the waning of consciousness, like the one that occurs during sleep, brings about a state similar to complete annihilation (frags. 77 and 26):

> Getting wet is pleasure, not death, for souls.

> A man, when dying, kindles a light in the night when his sight is extinguished; living, he touches the dead man during sleep; when awake, he touches the sleeper.[20]

For Heraclitus, then, souls die of a death by water; and from water they are reborn, in a cycle of transformations within which they play a role similar to that of fire in the cosmic cycle (frags. 36 and 31):

> For souls it is death to become water, for water it is death to become earth, from earth water is generated, from water soul.

> Transformations of fire: first sea, of sea half is earth, the other half burning lightning.

With Heraclitus, the view of the physical world inherited from Ionian naturalism takes on existential connotations, and the view of the soul is "naturalized." The soul has the prerogatives of a principle of movement and, at the same time, of knowledge, as it is made of the same matter as the cosmos and there is full integration between the psychic states (lucidity and inebriation, sleep and wakefulness, life and death) and the framework of universal change. In this framework, however, the possibility of expansion of the self finds insurmountable boundaries marked by the limits of the ever-precarious individual

---

[19] As already observed by Plato in *Cratylus* (419e).

[20] This "contact," which implies a continuous transition in both senses, justifies the identification of living and dead, awake and asleep, young and old delineated in frag. 88.

existence. Personal immortality is excluded from Heraclitus's horizon, as he regards the desire to procreate (thereby acutely anticipating a theme that will be developed by Plato in *Symposium*, 208e) as men's pathetic attempt to overcome their mortal condition (frag. 20):

> Having been born, they want to live and have allotted deaths, and they leave behind children to have the same destiny.

But frag. 36, quoted above, is the one that reveals best of all the mortality of the soul as an inevitable consequence of the role assigned to it, a part of the cosmos, in the cycle of transformations. For, once the individual souls have dissolved into water, what takes place is not a rebirth of the "old" souls but the generation of new ones from water that has gone through a process of transformation into earth. In this respect it is particularly remarkable that at the very end of the fragment the plural *psuchēisin* switches to the singular *psuchēi*, as though representing the soul as a vital global force of all living beings.[21]

It is useful at this point to mention a distinction, proposed by Gábor Betegh, between two models of the relationship between soul and cosmos that are of paramount importance in Presocratic thought.[22] One is a "portion model," where the soul is identified as a portion of the material (or materials) that has the role of cosmic principle. This model underlies both Anaximenes's and Heraclitus's constructions, and Heraclitus's is the one that shows both its advantages and limits. The fiery composition of the soul enables Heraclitus to give it a cognitive function, explaining it in terms of a material interaction with the cosmic environment; on the other hand, however, it hinders the full development of a sense of personal identity. Yes, Heraclitus invites men to look within themselves individually, but the goal of this introspective process is to reintegrate the information that cannot be relayed by the senses into a deep understanding of the rhythm of becoming, which corresponds to the revelation that the soul is a particle of the same *logos* that governs the cosmos;

---

[21] This is an important intuition of Mansfeld 1967, 18–19; on the mortality of the soul in Heraclitus, see Centrone 2007, in particular 145–48. This framework should also be used to decipher the meaning of the difficult frag. 62 ("Immortal mortals, mortal immortals; the ones [both the immortals and the mortals can be the subject] living the others' death, yet dying their life."). This text has mostly been interpreted as an opposition between divine and mortal conditions, or (by Nussbaum 1972b, 163ff) as a reference to courage as a virtue enabling men to gain a particular state of immortality. I tend to connect this fragment with the sequence of destruction and rebirth of the souls, in which men, individually mortal, find an immortality of their own—a "collective" one, so to speak; they are thus both "mortal" and "immortal," in that they feed on the life of prior individuals, which, envisioned as a global vital energy, is always present; yet they are unmistakably "dead," *other* than the prior and future living.

[22] From here on, though I autonomously develop a few specific points, I refer to Betegh 2006a.

moreover, upon the death of the individual, this particle will return to the whole that it came from.

Another notion of personal identity is developed in the context of what Betegh defines the "journey model." Like the other paradigm, which is connected with the Homeric notion of soul-breath, this model is also based on a set of traditional beliefs, with one substantial difference; the moving core in this case is a mystical faith in the immortal and divine nature of the individual soul, whose essence stands out even more in that it is unscathed after the vicissitudes of its journey in the cosmos.

Restless Souls

We are going to select two of the many legendary tales on prodigious, at times shamanic personalities that populate the archaic Greek world. The protagonists are Aristeas of Proconnesus (an island on the Propontis, modern-day Sea of Marmara) and the Thracian Salmoxis. According to Herodotus's account in the fourth book of his *Histories* (devoted to the Scythians), the corpse of Aristeas, after his sudden death in a fuller's shop, disappeared mysteriously as the fuller was hastening to warn his relatives; meanwhile, a passerby claimed to have met and talked to him outside the city. Aristeas reappeared six years later, and after composing an epic poem about the faraway Arimaspians (among whom he arrived "possessed" by Apollo), he died a second time, only to reappear two hundred and fifty years later, at Metapontum.[23] Here he exhorted the citizens to put up a statue for Apollo, who had come to Metapontum with him and honored them with his presence; "and he, who was now Aristeas, had followed him; and when he followed the god, he was a crow" (IV, 15).

In the same book Herodotus says that the Getae, a Thracian people, believe that they are immortal in the sense that their dead go to their god Salmoxis. He adds that he also heard from the Greeks that in reality Salmoxis was a man, one of Pythagoras of Samos's slaves who, having been freed, returned to his fatherland. Here, according to Herodotus, he began to spread ideas regarding the immortality of the soul (it is implied that he learned these from Pythagoras) while having a subterranean chamber built for himself, where he lived for three years while the Thracians mourned his death and

[23] The Arimaspians were said to be one-eyed (see Herodotus, III, 116 and IV, 13, 27; ancient ethnographic sources often attribute physical anomalies to the peoples living at the boundaries of their known world), who inhabited the northern coast of Pontus (the modern-day Black Sea). In the narrative of book IV, the reference to the Arimaspians is an occasion to mention Aristeas. See Bolton (1962) for an attempt to reconstruct the poem on the Arimaspians but also for a careful analysis (119–41) of the biographical tradition on Aristeas (even though the scholar tends to rationalize its more unusual elements as the result of later additions).

then reemerged, living proof, we might say, of the veracity of his statements on the soul (IV, 94–95).

A flight around the world for Aristeas, in animal form and accompanying Apollo, and a stay in the underworld for Salmoxis; these are both journeys of learning, in territories thought to be off-limits, carried out by personalities who, passing through a state of apparent death, defy the boundaries that the body normally imposes on the expansion of the soul. The undeclared yet necessary baggage taken on these journeys is the gift of memory, thanks to which the soul holds a recollection of its peregrinations and is thus able to communicate the knowledge acquired abroad to those who have stayed "on earth," in the form of an erudite message.

These tales must have represented a prototype of journeys in search of an ultramundane truth, such as the one evoked by Parmenides in the proem of his writing (on which we will focus in the next chapter), or the journey of Er in Plato's narration. Yet if what we are looking for is a conscious thematization of memory as a prerequisite for psychic identity—an indisputable tenet of cognitive science—we will more easily recognize it in that complex of eschatological beliefs that intertwine Orphic, Pythagorean, and Dionysian elements that developed in Greece between the sixth and fifth centuries BCE. As we shall soon see, this framework is dominated by the belief in metempsychosis, mostly in connection with the notion that the human soul, divine and immortal in essence, is condemned to a series of reincarnations into different bodies (sometimes of different species) on account of an original fault (not always specified or specifiable), which must be atoned for with an ascetical lifestyle and/or a process of purifying rituals that also serve to restore the memory of the previous lives. This theme is the basis for an embryonic notion of moral responsibility that is, together with memory, the other essential element for the definition of personal identity. We will now consider a few details of the various paths along which a religious need for individual salvation and uniting with the divine brings forth a *reflection* on the soul.[24]

Let us begin with Pythagoras. Born in Samos around 570 BCE, at about the age of forty he settled in Croton, where he founded a philosophical and religious community destined to have a long-lived influence on the intellectual and political life of the cities of Magna Graecia. Around his figure soon flourished a legendary tradition depicting him as an extraordinary wise man; he once stood in the theater at Olympia flaunting a golden thigh, a sign of divine origin; he was spotted at multiple places at the same time (at Croton and at Metapontum); he had (like Aristeas) a strong tie with the cult of Apollo, so much so that the Crotonians called him Hyperborean Apollo (Aristotle, frag.

[24] Dorothea Frede 2004 provides a positive assessment of the contribution of Pythagoreans and Orphics to a reflection on the soul, paying special attention to its importance for Plato.

191 Rose and Aelian, *Varia Historia*, II, 26 = 14 A 7 DK); finally, he presented himself as living proof of the transmigration of the soul, claiming that he remembered several of his reincarnations, including the Homeric hero Euphorbus (Diogenes Laertius, VIII, 4–5 = 14 A 8 DK).

Pythagoras's belief in metempsychosis is confirmed by ancient sources such as Xenophanes and Ion of Chios.[25] But we cannot ascertain whether he learned about metempsychosis by contact with other civilizations (as usual, he is said to have traveled East). According to a passage in book II of Herodotus, devoted to Egypt, the Egyptians were the first to claim that the soul is immortal and transmigrates into different beings—of air, sea, and land—and returns to a human body after wandering for three thousand years; this *logos* was adopted by some Greeks, ancient and recent, whom Herodotus enigmatically avoids mentioning by name (Herodotus, II, 123, in 14 A 1 DK = frag. 423 Bernabé). However, Herodotus's account is curiously inaccurate, since metempsychosis is not otherwise attested in Egyptian religion (unlike the immortality of the soul, of course, and metamorphosis into animal form, which the historian may have mistaken for metempsychosis). Supposing that this notion reached Greece through other cultures, for its origin we must look in India (where it is attested since the beginning of the sixth century BCE), or more probably in the central strip of Eurasia, where, not by chance, some of the deeds of Aristeas and Salmoxis take place; the dissociation of soul and body during ecstatic trance might be seen as an important antecedent of the idea of transmigration.[26]

Whether imported or not, among the Greeks the theme of metempsychosis finds a particular configuration closely tied to a development of the spiritual dimension of the soul. As will be shown by the reading of some Orphic texts that will follow shortly, this is certainly visible in the Pythagorean context as well. Pythagoras constructs his self-image as a wise man by presenting himself as one who, thanks to the experience of many lives, has accumulated an extraordinary wealth of knowledge. Not only does this image become a strong factor for bringing the community together around its leader (combined with the performance of a series of purification rituals including, in connection with the premise of transmigration, a strictly vegetarian diet); it also guarantees the validity of a new wisdom that hinges on the idea of the numerical harmony governing the cosmos discovered by Pythagoras himself.

In the next chapter I return to the features of Pythagoras's self-presentation, but it must be noted here that it is based on the assumption that the soul has kept a *memory* of its prior lives. Empedocles also celebrates this prerogative

---

[25] I will come back to frag. 4 of Ion of Chios and to frag. 7 of Xenophanes in the next chapter.

[26] On this point, see Bremmer 1983, who emphasizes the shamanic elements in Greek culture, along a line inaugurated by Meuli and Dodds (but see below, 167n73).

in his portrayal of a wise man who has lived many lives, which probably refers to Pythagoras.[27] Thus it is rather likely that in connection with the belief in metempsychosis, Pythagorean thought developed an appreciation for the value of memory as an elemental constituent of the individual self. We are not sure whether this framework included a notion of punishments or rewards awaiting the soul in the afterworld commensurate with one's moral conduct while living. Indeed, Ion of Chios, who writes around the middle of the fifth century BCE, praises Pythagoras's remarkable wisdom and ascribes to him the statement that some human souls (he is referring to Pherecydes's) may be granted bliss in the next world on account of their intellectual and moral merits (36 B 4 DK). A Pythagorean interest in this notion is attested only here, and scantily; but, as we shall see now, the theme left stronger traces in the Orphic context.

In another passage of book 2 of the *Histories* (II, 81), Herodotus refers to the prohibition of entering sacred spaces or burying the dead in woolen garments, as specified in Egyptian and Pythagorean customs, which are "in agreement with the so-called Orphic and Bacchic" rituals. The taboo of wool may be connected to the fear of compromising the integrity of the animal, which according to the belief of metempsychosis might be a transit point for a human *psuchē*. In any case, such close affinity regarding a burial custom indicates that Pythagoreans and Orphics must have shared a general background of beliefs on the immortality of the soul. This is not surprising, if we consider the well-documented presence of mystery cults, both Orphic and Dionysiac, in Magna Graecia, that is, in an environment particularly inclined, between the sixth and fifth centuries BCE, to be open to questions of spiritual needs and the demands of salvation.

The search for a solution to the precariousness of human existence in a promise of personal immortality and through close contact with the god—which was not guaranteed by the strongly civic structure of traditional religion—is a trait shared by all the so-called ancient mystery religions, regardless of their diverse rites and mythical references (another common trait was the secret character of initiation rituals). For classical Greece, think of the cult of Dionysus, the cult of Demeter whose main center was at Eleusis, or even the Samothracian and Andanian mysteries.[28] Orphism, however, shows a penchant for theogonic and cosmogonic reflection that has no parallel in other mystery cults—not even in Dionysism, with which it nevertheless shares significant elements of mythical etiology as well as of cult.[29] Furthermore, al-

---

[27] See below, 150.

[28] A large corpus of texts pertaining to the mysteries through the Hellenistic period, as well as a rich commentary, can be found in Scarpi 2002.

[29] The cosmo-theogonic texts are found ibid. I, 356–75, as well as in the first section of the edition of Orphic texts by Bernabé 2004; for a guide to the contents, see Bernabé 2002,

ready at the end of the sixth century BCE, this reflection was entrusted to a literary corpus (the "heap of books" in Plato's *Republic*, 364e) traditionally attributed to the mythical singer Orpheus. The importance given to writing is another characteristic trait of Orphism, not only in relation to other mystery cults but also more generally in the world of Greek religion, where the oral dimension prevails.[30]

However, the role of writing did not make Orphism a "book religion," nor has there ever been an Orphic orthodoxy. On the contrary, the central themes of Orphism, which were not particularly systematic from its very first formulations, underwent several contaminations over time, mainly with Pythagoreanism. From then until late antiquity, the earliest phase of Orphism was overlapped with a series of theoretical accumulations that were especially heavy during the religious revival of Orphic and Pythagorean beliefs in the neo- and middle Platonic periods. Nevertheless, it is not impossible to reconstruct a constellation of themes that appear to be already well defined at the end of the classical period, also thanks to the discovery of a few, exceptionally important documents. Let us consider the bone tablets from Olbia, which we mentioned earlier,[31] or the papyrus famously discovered in 1962 among the remains of a funeral pyre at Derveni (near Thessaloniki). The Derveni papyrus contains a commentary, on an Orphic theogony, that is centered around the relationships of the elements in the cosmos and formulated through numerous references to naturalistic Presocratic doctrines (the papyrus dates to the fourth century BCE, but the commentary seems to belong to the fifth).[32] Let us consider, in particular, the group of gold lamellae found from 1876 to

---

211–16. The structure of the cosmos, dominated by the intervention of divine figures (ruled by Zeus) on situations of disorder, is in line with the features of mythical representation. The multiplicity of models that coexist in the long tradition of Orphism, the result of variations implemented by anonymous itinerant seers of the kind described by West (see above, 57), also pertains to the sphere of "calculated imaginings" (see above, 58). Burkert 1992, 124–27 saw this as a combination of "cathartic practice and speculative mythology"; according to him, the recitation of the Orphic cosmogony has a function analogous to that of the various cosmogonic texts of the ancient Near East, whose reading (magically) enacts the restoration of an original order (of society or, in medical practice, of the body). However, we should not miss the special case of Orphism, insofar as it does not aspire to restore an exterior and mundane status quo but the original purity of the soul, thereby making way for an existential dimension, which is an important innovation in the history of Greek thought.

[30] See Henrichs 2003. If I am not mistaken, the first to bring the attention to "Orpheus's writing" was Detienne 2003 [1989], 132ff, followed by Baumgarten 1998, 70–121, and Calame 2002. For the difference between Orphism and Dionysism on this point, see Di Benedetto 2004, 30ff.

[31] See above, 104.

[32] For the Derveni papyrus, which I do not examine in depth due to the chronological limits of my inquiry here, see at least Laks and Most 1997, Betegh 2004 and Piano 2016, as well as the critical edition of Kouremenos, Parássoglou, and Tsantsanoglou 2006.

recent years in Magna Graecia, and also on Crete, in Thessaly (at Pherae, for example), and in Rome (a crucial date was 1969, the year when an important lamella was found at Hipponion, modern-day Vibo Valentia in Calabria). The chronology of these artifacts spans a period from the end of the fifth century BCE to the third century CE, but scholars agree that the religious model behind these texts (a sort of memorandum for the afterlife, addressed to the initiated deceased) may date to the beginning of the fifth century.[33] This dating hypothesis seems to have been recently confirmed by the discovery of more artifacts from Olbia; two inscribed lead lamellae found at two different locations within the polis, which Benedetto Bravo thinks are connected to a religious context of initiation. The scholar interprets one of the texts (dating to the second half of the sixth century) as a similar memorandum for a dead woman associated with an Orphic group. The other text (dating between the end of the sixth and the beginning of the fifth century) contains, according to Bravo, moral directions regarding the behavior necessary in order to avoid the reincarnation of the soul.[34]

In light of this evidence, it has become more difficult to deny the existence of something like an Orphic "movement," one that required of its followers, scattered all over the Greek world, neither the observance of a dogmatic creed nor the exclusive acceptance of one cult (hence the overlaps with Pythagorean, Dionysian, and Demetriac elements) but rather acknowledgment of some fo-

[33] After Pugliese Carratelli 2001, a milestone in the scholarship on the Gold Tablets, further important assessments are Edmonds 2004, Tortorelli Ghidini 2006 (with an edition and Italian translation), Graf and Iles Johnston 2007 (with an edition and English translation). See Tortorelli Ghidini 2006, 36–53, for its in-depth exploration of the Orphic character of the Gold Tablets, which has often been denied for part or all of them; for instance, by Calame 2002, 389–92 and Calame 2006, 229–89, which nevertheless offers several excellent readings; and by Graf and Iles Johnston 2007, who argue that the tablets belonged to the Dionysian context, into which Orpheus was "drawn" for some reason. Tortorelli Ghidini argues for the existence of a common "religious model," beyond the differences in context (geographical and chronological) and the discrepancies between the formulas used and the divinities being summoned (Persephone or Dionysus). For a more careful analysis of these discrepancies (which I cannot explore here), see Ferrari 2007, 115–165. In 2007 a new lamella was published, datable to the end of the fourth and the beginning of the third century BCE, found during the illegal excavation (1904) of a tomb in the vicinity of the Neolithic site of Magoula Mati, near Pherae in Thessaly (it made it into Graf and Iles Johnston 2007, 38–39). The fact that both Demeter Chthonia and the Mother of the Mountain are mentioned in the text has led scholars to note that, in the "fluid fabric" of Greek polytheism, Orphism was soon able to encompass both Dionysian and Demetriac elements (Persephone, daughter of Demeter, is mother to "Orphic" Dionysus), as well as other cults, in various and nonhierarchical combinations; see Ferrari and Prauscello 2008, especially 207.

[34] See Bravo 2007. Of the two readings, I think the former is more solidly corroborated by the extant text.

cused points of inspiration.[35] Among these points was the awareness of humanity's debt to the gods, creators of the cosmos and of humankind itself. In fact, one of the foundation myths of Orphism is the story of generating the human race from the ashes of the Titans, who were struck with thunder by Zeus for killing and dismembering Dionysus (his son by Persephone). This story, which was already circulating by the middle of the sixth century BCE (Pindar frag. 133 Maehler clearly refers to the "ancient pain" that Persephone demands be redeemed), represents the notion that human beings carry within themselves a seed of pernicious rebellion, as well as traces of divine birth. In any case, the most characteristic trait of Orphic eschatology (which fascinated Plato, as is especially clear in the *Phaedo*) is the duality of an immortal, divine soul trapped in a body as if it were a tomb or prison, whereas death is seen as liberation.[36] The soul is condemned to transmigrate from one body into the next, probably because of the Titans' crime, and only through a special way of life (ascetical exercises, vegetarianism) will it be worthy, after death, of reuniting with its principle. The initiation rite probably included a reading of theogonic texts aimed at commemorating the vicissitudes of the primordial divinites that culminated in the death of Dionysus and revealing the roots of the present suffering. A reminder of cosmic history, then, was the first step toward purification.[37]

Orphic eschatology thus seems to have encouraged both a focus on moral responsibility[38] and an appreciation of memory as a tool of (redemptive) knowledge. Both notions come to the fore in a remarkable representation of the soul's journey in the Gold Tablets. Such documents have normally been found in burials, folded or rolled up and tied to the neck of the deceased. The texts inscribed on them (in formulations of different lengths) contain instructions to the deceased—sometimes a sort of vade mecum—for obtaining salvation in the afterlife. The instructions are to be followed during a journey—

[35] Orphic eschatological texts are collected in the accurate edition by Bernabé 2004, 349–54. I generally agree with the trend of optimistic reconstruction started by Guthrie 1952 and continued, among others, by Bernabé and Tortorelli Ghidini, against the skeptical stance of Edmonds 2004 (see also Edmonds 1999, who denies the Orphic character of the myth of Dionysus's dismemberment).

[36] On the modalities and effects of the "transposition" of Orphic discourse on the soul in Plato's philosophy (to borrow Auguste Dies's very effective formulation), see the clear discussion in Bernabé 2007.

[37] According to Obbink 1997, the cosmological exegesis carried out by the Derveni author was also conceived as a form of initiation.

[38] According to the foundational mythology of Orphism, the individual is not directly responsible for the original fault, but the need for purification paves the way—it is not clear to what extent—for moral discourse. One might be tempted to think of the role of the "sins of our ancestors" in Christian theology, but it would be risky to make much of this parallel.

with stops along the way sometimes described—that ends with the infernal gods' request for recognition by the initiated. Before being put in the grave to accompany the deceased in his journey, these texts were probably recited during the funeral ritual. In any case, they anticipate a sort of postmortem continuation and completion of the initiation received during life, for a soul that is detached from its body but not yet redeemed. Below is the text of the Hipponion lamella, which features a particularly rich topography of the netherworld:

> This is the work of Memory, when you are about to die
> down to the well-built house of Hades. There is a spring at the right side,
> and standing by it a white cypress.
> Descending to it, the souls of the dead refresh themselves.
> Do not even go near this spring!
> Ahead you will find from the Lake of Memory
> cold water pouring forth; there are guards before it.
> They will ask you, with astute wisdom,
> what you are seeking in the darkness of murky Hades.
> Say, "I am a son of Earth and starry Sky,
> I (masculine) am parched with thirst and am dying; but quickly grant me
> cold water from the Lake of Memory to drink."
> And they will announce you to the Chthonian King,
> and they will grant you to drink from the Lake of Memory.
> And you, too, having drunk, will go along the sacred road on which other
> glorious initiates and *bacchoi* travel.

(TRANSLATED BY GRAF AND ILES JOHNSTON 2007)

Mnemosyne, a mythical figure of Memory, is present only in one group of tablets, perhaps because it had more exposure to Pythagorean influences. In this particular text, Mnemosyne appears already in the *incipit*, as if it were the *author*; what follows is a series of injunctions addressed, in the future tense, to the soul of the initiated (in another group of tablets from Thurii the instructions are followed directly by the deceased, who addresses the guards of the underworld in the first person). Once in the house of Hades, he or she will have to proceed toward the fresh water coming from the lake of Mnemosyne, avoiding the spring where the other souls gather; this is clearly the spring of Forgetfulness, used by those souls which have not been purified by initiation and are destined to reincarnate after the deletion of each and every memory of the life they just abandoned. This element is reprised and amplified in the myth in Plato's *Republic*, 621a, where the souls that are destined to return to Earth stop by the plain of *Lēthē*, or "Oblivion," to drink water from the *Amelēs*, the River of Unmindfulness. In order to gain access to the spring of Memory, the initiated will have to present the guards proof—as a sort of safe-conduct— that he or she is aware of his origin, both corporeal ("earthly") and celestial/ divine. Once granted permission to drink from the spring, the soul will be able to "fly away from the heavy and painful cycle" of births (using the expression found in tablet III from Thurii) and finally set upon the path of blessedness. As effectively pointed out by Calame, the soul's declaration of its genealogy serves not only as a "passport" but also as a "password."[39] Having proven its identity as "pure (coming from) the pure,"[40] the soul of the deceased is admitted into the circle of those who have gained an immortality comparable to that of the gods.

Two passages from the first book of Aristotle's treatise *On the Soul* attest that both Orphic and Pythagorean thought hosted a material notion of the soul. In both cases, moreover, this notion can be connected to the Homeric breath-soul. According to Aristotle, "some" Pythagoreans identified the *psuchē* with the moving motes visible in sunbeams, while others identified it with what moves the motes, thereby subscribing to a treatment of the soul as a cause of movement and getting especially close to the atomists, for whom psychic atoms are spherical in shape—and therefore the most mobile—and regularly enter animal bodies through respiration (*On the Soul*, I, 2, 404a 16 = 58 B 40 DK). Later in the book, Aristotle criticizes the theories that emphasize the motive and cognitive function of the soul that is typical of animals and overlook the vegetative and nutritive function, which is common to all *empsucha* (including plants). In this context Aristotle mentions a *logos* contained in the "so-called Orphic" poems according to which "the soul enters from the universe into breathing beings, carried by the winds" (I, 5, 410b 27 = frag. 421 Bernabé). We can see that both options presuppose a "portion model" in which the soul is identified with the element (air) that is found in largest quantity in the cosmos. Yet there is no evidence, in Aristotle or elsewhere, that such a model was used, either within Orphism nor Pythagoreanism, to give a deeper understanding of the material interaction between soul and body or of the modalities of cognitive processes. This is not surprising at all, since in these contexts corporeality tends to be seen as an obstacle to the intellectual and moral progress of the soul. Moreover, the notion of a breath-soul

---

[39] Calame 2006, 243.

[40] This is the initial formula used by the deceased to introduce himself or herself to the infernal gods in tablets III, IV and V from Thurii (frags. 488–490 Bernabé), a formula that emphasizes the significance of "an ascesis pursued not only by him, but also by his biological or ritual parents" (Ferrari 2007, 144).

is not incompatible per se with a pattern of metempsychosis.[41] It is worth noting that the word *metempsuchosis* is not derived directly from *psuchē* but instead is formed by the preposition *meta* (which denotes succession and change) with the verb *empsuchoō*, "to animate"; even though the term is relatively late (occurring for the first time in Diodorus Siculus),[42] it is not impossible that it preserves the memory of an image of "reinsufflation" of the soul. The winds in the Orphic *logos* mentioned by Aristotle, then, are not exactly assigned the task of providing movement and other functions of the body on account of their airy consistency; rather, it is possible that they originally served as the "tools of a cosmic law" of atonement, one that forces those souls that are not yet perfectly pure to enter new bodies.[43] Similarly, "some" Pythagoreans may also have reflected on the airy nature of the soul in relation to an appreciation of the *first* act of respiration with which it enters the body.[44]

In conclusion, the belief in metempsychosis, in both Orphic and Pythagorean versions, provides fertile ground for the articulation of a notion of personal identity relating to the aspects of intellectual memory (of one's prior lives) and of moral responsibility (with respect to original fault). On the other hand, it does not seem to have sparked any interest in the interaction of the soul with the body (and, through it, with the cosmos) during cognitive processes. The "journey model" stresses the places visited by the soul, not the elements that constitute it, and consequently it cannot be applied in the very instances where, as we have seen, the "portion model" is most effective (at least in Heraclitus's use of it). We may ask, at this point, whether a unitary

[41] The same cannot be said of the theory of the soul as *harmonia* (a balance of the elements of the body) that can be ascribed to the Pythagorean Philolaus of Croton; on the difficulties of Philolaus's theory on this point, see Barnes 1979, 186–93.

[42] The earliest authors who refer to a transmigration of souls (Pindar, Empedocles, Herodotus, Plato) provide concrete descriptions of the process, with several periphrases; for example, the soul is said to "wear" the new body, or "penetrate" it; alternatively, the individual "is reborn" (*palin gignesthai* is Plato's favorite expression). On this point, and in general for a valid reconstruction of the issue of metempsychosis between Orphism and Pythagoreanism, see Casadio 1991.

[43] Ibid., 126. See also frag. 422 Bernabé.

[44] Regarding Pythagoreanism, it is perhaps significant that the birth of the cosmos is explained through a "first respiration" that ensures that the surrounding *pneuma* is inhaled into the heavens (Aristotle, *Physics*, V, 6, 213b 22 = 58 B 30 DK). According to Philolaus, a Pythagorean, the embryo is warm, and therefore its first act upon being born, necessary to moderate its temperature, is respiration. Yet Philolaus's doctrine does not show traces of the "primitive" model; he evidently bases his theory on empirical considerations (the warmth of the newborn, the observation of his first reaction to the outside world), and he also builds his cosmological system on an analogy with the embryo, so that the cosmos originates from (and rotates around) a central fire; see Huffman 2007.

discourse on the soul might find more favorable conditions in a joint adoption of both models, and, in fact, such an endeavor seems to emerge from the fragments of Empedocles, to which we now turn our attention.[45]

Empedocles and His Daimōn

The biography of Empedocles of Akragas (ca. 495–435 BCE) contains a wealth of information regarding both the prominent role he played in the (democratic) politics of his native city and the more or less spectacular way in which he died—according to the most popular version (Diogenes Laertius, VIII, 67–72 = 31 A 1 DK), by throwing himself into the crater of Mount Aetna to obtain immortal fame. The biographical tradition attributes to him two writings in hexameters, one dealing with physics and cosmology and traditionally titled *On Nature*; the other devoted to the theme of purification and the salvation of the soul, and significantly titled *Purifications (Katharmoi)*. Though it is often difficult to assign passages to one poem or the other, the fragments that have come down to us present Empedocles as a cosmologist and magician, physician and thaumaturge, which inspired Werner Jaeger to call Empedocles a "philosophical centaur" and a "prodigious union" of natural science and mysticism.[46]

Whether one wants to call it a union or, perhaps more appropriately, an interweaving, this is the interpretive knot that, to this day, snares anyone who approaches Empedocles's work. Scholars of the past (including Diels and Wilamowitz) hypothesized that Empedocles converted from philosophy to religion in his old age, and ascribed *Purifications* to a second phase, where the "theological" thoughts of the philosopher are concentrated. This hypothesis clearly overlooked the religious inspiration that breathes from the physical poem.[47] Catherine Osborne delved deeper into the problem and argued that Empedocles authored a single poem on nature, which some scholars call the *Katharmoi*, containing all the extant citations and treating religion and philosophy as equal in importance.[48] However, this conclusion is contradicted by textual data with which we will have to deal in the next chapter, and especially by the fact that the two fragments have two separate proems.

The cards were reshuffled with the publication, in 1999, of the Strasbourg papyrus, discovered in 1990, which contains a few fragments from Empedocles's

---

[45] I refer to Betegh 2006a, 43–48 for a reading of the Derveni papyrus as an attempt to integrate the two models that ends, by analogy, in a juxtaposition.

[46] Jaeger 1986 [1936], 292. See Vegetti 1996 on the figure of the physician-and-seer (*iatromantis*) whose features can be recognised in Empedocles.

[47] See the criticism already addressed by Kahn (1960) to the 'biographical' hypothesis.

[48] See Osborne 1987 and Inwood 2001, 8ff.

work and has extraordinary significance for the reconstruction of his thought (besides the fact that they are the first, and only, fragments of a Presocratic to come down to us via direct tradition).[49] The longest fragment is a continuation of a known text transmitted as part of the writing *On Nature* (frag. 17 DK); a scholion confirms this title for the contents of the papyrus. And it is noteworthy that the new portion of text includes a line already known and ascribed to *Purifications* on account of its contents (frag. 139, which we will mention again). Even more significant is that the new text features elements of a demonological conception that had previously been thought to be confined to the cathartic poem. All in all, the new text definitively proves that in Empedocles the physical and religious dimensions are neither separate nor complementary, but rather, one penetrates the other, all bound together by a mystical perspective in which the physical world is the setting for the soul's toil and potential salvation.

The more acute interpreters of Empedocles did not need the Strasbourg papyrus to understand that the fate of the cosmos and of the soul are parts of the same story.[50] And we should become accustomed to regarding the interconnectedness of philosophy and religion as anything but anomalous; on the contrary, it is fundamental to a significant part of Presocratic thought (as I showed in this chapter through analyses of Heraclitus and the Pythagoreans). The fact remains that in Empedocles this interconnectedness seems to create more problems than it solves, specifically when it comes to formulating a unitary discourse on the soul; his eschatological conception, in other words, still presents some difficulties.

The general lines of Empedocles's cosmology may be read as an answer to the problem posited by Parmenides concerning the explanation of becoming; according to the rigid logic of the Eleatics, if Being must meet the requirements of immutability and eternity, nothing can come into being (in that it would come from a state of nonbeing); therefore the change that we perceive in nature is nothing but the product of a deceitful opinion dictated by the senses. Empedocles bypasses this difficulty by ascribing self-identity, eternity, and equal powers to four fundamental elements (fire, air, water, and earth; called "roots" in frag. 6.1) and to the two forces that move them, Love and Strife.[51] Thus the things perceived by the senses are not mere appearances

[49] See Martin and Primavesi 1999. The papyrus dates to the end of the first century CE.

[50] See Osborne 1987a and, in particular, Kingsley 1995, as well as the good intuitions of Seligman 1978, 12–17). At any rate, the fact that the Strasbourg papyrus provided the ultimate proof for this reading is confirmed by both Curd 2001 and Kingsley 2002; see also the acute observations of Wildberg on the role played by natural philosophy in Empedocles's "religious project" (2001, in particular 55–56).

[51] The relationship between Parmenides's ontology and the models of Empedocles and Anaxagoras for explaining nature has been emphasized by Curd (1998).

but derive from the elements commingling in different proportions through the action of Love and Strife (frag. 8):

> ... there is no birth (*phusis*) of any of the mortal things,
> nor end of destructive death,
> but only mingling and separation of mixed things,
> and this is called birth by humans.

Empedocles builds within this framework a demonological[52] doctrine by combining Hesiodic elements and elements of the mystery religions.[53] In the Hesiodic myth of the "races," the men of the oldest generation, the golden one, after benefiting from the most prosperous life conditions, thanks to the friendly protection of the gods, are made to disappear under the earth but, as Zeus commanded, continue to linger on earth as *daimones*, hidden from view by a cloak of air, who watch over and protect humankind (Hesiod, *Works and Days*, lines 109–126). In the *Theogony* (lines 782–806) Zeus decrees that, should there be a "discord and feud" (*eris kai neikos*) among the Olympians and should one of them commit perjury, he will have to atone by spending a year lying in bed "without breath and without voice," and an additional nine years away from banquets with other gods, returning to Olympus only in the tenth year. Empedocles reworks these elements into the image of a *daimōn* that is exiled from his blessed existence, until then shared with others "who have received as lot a long life," because of perjury and blood crimes perpetrated under the dark force of Strife. This hint (in the final line of the fragment

---

[52] What follows is based on texts whose interpretation may generally be agreed on. In particular I shall avoid insisting on points involving controversial matters, such as the articulation of cosmic cycles or the number of cosmogonies and zoogonies. Some scholars argue that the cosmos is (being) formed through the separation of the elements from the perfect original unity of the Sphere (frags. 27 and 28), and once the main cosmic masses have been separated by Strife, Love intervenes to aggregate their parts into men and animals (see, for instance, Bollack 1965–69). According to another interpretation, the cosmic cycle is articulated into two symmetrical moments and is constantly repeated, starting from the Sphere, where the separating power of Strife acts gradually (in the first of two cosmo-zoogonies admitted under this interpretation) until they are completely separated and a new cosmo-zoogony starts under the influence of Love (see O'Brien 1969, followed by Martin and Primavesi 1999, among others). Considering the variety of opinions emerging on this and other points in Primavesi et al. 2001, the Strasbourg papyrus does not seem to have shed particular light on documentation that remains generally obscure. However, I think that some of the points mentioned above fall into place if we accept the suggestion by Sedley 2007, 31–74, who hypothesizes a first phase governed by Love and a second ruled by Strife. Sedley situates the Sphere at the beginning and at the end of a cosmos that includes several periods of alternate power of the two cosmic forces, in such a way that the byproducts of Love have not been deleted in the present world, governed by Strife, and what the student Pausanias is being invited to "see" (Strasb. pap., a, ii, 30) is the natural world *as a whole*.

[53] See Seaford 1986, in particular 6–9.

cited below) indicates that the fall of the *daimōn* is parallel (or simultaneous) with the interruption of the primordial state governed by Love at the hands of the cosmic force of Strife. At any rate, the *daimōn* is sentenced by a law of necessity to an expiatory journey through the cosmic masses, by which he is incessantly rejected (frag. 115):

> There is an oracle of Necessity, a decree of the gods, an ancient one, eternal, sealed by broad oaths:
> whenever one taints his limbs with a crime of bloodshed,
> and also by his error swears a false oath,
> the *daimones*, who have received as lot a long life,
> must wander thrice ten-thousand seasons away from the blessed,
> being born in this time in all different forms of mortal beings
> who encounter during their life one painful path after another.
> For the force of the ether chases them away into the sea,
> the sea spits them out toward the earth's surface, the earth toward the rays
> of the gleaming sun, and he [i.e., the Sun] into the whirlwinds of the ether:
> Each one receives them from another, all hate them,
> and among them is myself, too, exiled by the god, wandering,
> because I relied on raging Strife.

Laura Gemelli Marciano argues that this representation refers to the figure of the god "exiled from the Sky par excellence," that is, Apollo; according to the founding myth of Delphic ritual, after killing the serpent Pytho, he is condemned to a *sequence* of wanderings that ends with a ritual purification.[54] Thus Empedocles would be putting himself under the auspices of Apollo and might be linked, through this connection, to Pythagoras. Moreover, the disparagement of bloodshed pertains to two themes of Empedocles's teaching, both connected to a belief in metempsychosis: repudiation of blood sacrifice and abstention from eating meat.[55] As we have just seen, Empedocles declares that he himself is an exiled *daimōn*. Other texts reveal that when he was rejected by the cosmic elements and fell into the arduous world, he transmigrated through different kinds of living beings before acquiring a human form. At this point, our hero is well into his cathartic journey, close to freedom from reincarnation, and he presents himself as an immortal, a god who delivers

---

[54] See Gemelli Marciano 2001, in particular 224–26.

[55] The consumption of meat is deplored, in highly expressive tones, in frag. 139 (see Strasb. pap., d 5–6). See also frags. 128 and 130, which depict a sort of golden age in which men and animals have friendly relations and Aphrodite is sovereign instead of Ares, god of war, or any of the other gods. Since she is honored with painted animals and herbs, the altars are not soiled with blood from sacrificial victims.

truths, acquired during his long cosmic journey, about the birth and death of natural beings, and who has tools for understanding nature (frags. 118, 117, 146 and 112):

> I wailed and shrieked upon seeing the unfamiliar place.

> For once I was already a boy and a girl
> and a bush and a bird and a mute fish leaping out of the sea.

> And in the end they are seers, hymn singers and doctors
> and come as princes among humans on earth,
> and from there they blossom up as gods, highest in honors.

> Friends, you who dwell in the great city beside the yellow Akragas,
> atop ...
> I salute you! An immortal god, no longer mortal,
> I come to you honored among all ...[56]

The formula "an immortal god, no longer mortal" shows an extraordinary affinity with the words used in the Gold Tablets to refer to the initiated as someone who has become, or is about to become, "a god from a man" or "a god instead of a mortal."[57] This and other comparisons raise the question of the relationship between Empedocles and Orphism on one hand, and Empedocles and Pythagoreanism on the other. The arguments of those who maintain there is a close and direct relationship between Empedocles and Orphism (such as Christoph Riedweg) have been the object of a lively and articulate debate;[58] yet, besides the undeniable differences, there are also undeniable shared elements, including a belief in reincarnation. Let us remember that in 476 BCE, during Empedocles's youth, Pindar wrote an ode to celebrate the victory at the Olympian games of Theron, tyrant of Akragas, in which he expressed a view of punishment, purification, and rebirth of the soul inspired by Orphism or, more generally, mysticism (second *Olympian*, especially lines 56ff; see also frags. 131 a–b and 133 Maehler). Similarly, it is difficult to ignore that there was contact with Pythagoreanism, considering the connection between philosophy and religion that we have been stressing, which characterizes the intellectual climate of southern Italy at this time.

---

[56] The text of frag. 112 is quoted in its entirety on p. 166 and reconsidered from the perspective of Empedocles's authorial self-presentation. Akragas is the Greek name of both the ancient city and the nearby river.

[57] The observation is in Kingsley 1995, 258ff. The texts in question are the tablets from Thurii II and III (frags. 487, 4 and 488, 9 Bernabé). In both texts the famous formula "a kid you/I fell into the milk" follows, where the kid is Dionysus's sacred animal, the sacrificial victim with which both the god and the initiated tend to identify. Milk is a symbol of regeneration.

[58] See Riedweg 1995. Betegh 2001 has shown that a significant relationship with Orphism is also visible in Empedocles's cosmology.

However, in Empedocles's view, the transmigrating entity—the *daimōn*—is not the same as a soul (as we will see shortly). Moreover, the fault that he is trying to expiate is not a collective inheritance of humankind (as in the Orphic myth of the Titans); the author of this fault is he himself, the divine being who, with Empedocles's birth at Akragas, finally gained access to a human body. It is likely that with this representation Empedocles meant to make a highly *personal* contribution to the notion of moral consciousness. It is more difficult to see whether he was attempting to join his moral theme with the theme of cognition in a coherent framework; we turn now to this question.

As Charles Kahn wrote, in a study that, though not recent, is chock-full of insights that remain valid, Empedocles seems unable to bridge the gap between the problem of the immortality of the soul (which implies acquiring or reacquiring a divine essence and is normally reserved for a specific psychic entity) and an explanation of cognitive processes (perception, feeling, thought), inasmuch these are operated by the physical (and mortal) compound.[59] We can agree with Kahn's assessment, especially if we add that the immortal *daimōn* is not a soul, as assumed by the ancient commentators and a few modern interpreters still. On closer inspection, in frag. 115 this term does not denote a feature that is shared by various individuals; it is a quality of *special* individuals endowed with a divine nature; both Love and Strife are *daimones* in this sense (frag. 59, line 1).

It is also remarkable that, in the only passage where *psuchē* is attested in Empedocles, the term defines the soul as a material biological principle.[60] As Jean Bollack aptly noted, for Empedocles the soul is "life and blood, and all the psychic, sensorial, emotional and even cognitive processes are part of the body."[61] Moreover, Empedocles himself lays the foundations for a physiological explanation of sense perception that will find great favor in the Presocratic period. The main idea is that material effluences continually flow out from all things, and when they pass through different channels in the body (the perceptual organs), they encounter its inner components; the encounter of similar elements brings about the various perceptions. On this basis Empedocles, who does not make an explicit distinction between perception and higher intellectual processes, thinks that all things somehow partake in "thought" (hence the term *panpsychism*). However, he seems to assume that humans can attain a higher level of knowledge thanks to a particular organic material, blood, which consists of perfectly equal parts of earth, air, water, and fire (frag. 98);

---

[59] See Kahn 1960 (1974), in particular 436–37.

[60] This is the case of frag. 138, quoted by Aristotle in his treatment of metaphor in *Poetics*: "drawing [that is to say, consuming, extinguishing] life with bronze." The Homeric language seems to suggest that we are dealing with the notion of soul-breath.

[61] Bollack 2003, 65.

this gives humans the ability to discern all things, which are in turn made of the same four elements, but in different proportions (frags. 109, 107 and 105):

> With earth we see earth, with water water,
> with ether divine ether, and with fire invisible fire,
> Love with Love, Strife with baneful Strife.

> from these [the four elements] all things are joined and condensed
> and by these they think and feel pleasure and pain.

> nourished [i.e., the heart?] in the waves of throbbing blood,
> where above all is located what humans call thought;
> for the blood around the heart is thought for humans.

As we can see, Empedocles's account of the soul joins the "portion model"; here blood is a substance of the body endowed with cognitive abilities thanks to its material affinity with the main components of the macrocosmos. According to Empedocles, however, "before they were formed as mortals and after having dissolved," men "are nothing" (frag. 15 line 4). This means that the psychic principle located in the blood is destined to dissolve with the death of the body. Moreover, it is unclear how the *daimōn*, a decidedly immortal entity, interacts with the elements of the body, given that the body is described (in frag. 126) as an "unfamiliar cloak of flesh." It is even less clear how it can interact with the elements of the cosmos. David Sedley has observed that the *daimones* must be flesh-and-blood organisms (otherwise we would not be able to explain how they could have committed the sin of eating meat) and hypothesized that when they "become" other creatures (thereby undergoing a *transformation* rather than a proper transmigration), what remains to guarantee continuity is nothing more than a principle of "subjective consciousness."[62] This hypothesis is worthy of attention, but if we accept it we are forced to admit that Empedocles's view of the *daimōn* is essentially geared toward a moral discourse and, as it happens in other contexts where the "journey model" of the soul is at work, does not deal with knowledge *of the world*.[63]

---

[62] See Sedley 2007, 32 and 50–51 (in particular n62). However, I should also like to mention the hypothesis that the *daimōn* may have an ethereal consistency such as the one attributed to the soul in the archaic period; see Gemelli Marciano 2006, 667–68.

[63] This hypothesis also does not allow us to clarify how former lives can be known. David Sedley noted in a personal correspondence (2/20/2008) that "Empedocles only declares that he has been these other organisms, not explicitly that he remembers having been," although this ability "may be explained by his extraordinary clairvoyant powers which have enabled him to break the usual barriers presented by metamorphosis." For an interesting attempt to reconstruct the peculiar "mnemotechnique" of Empedocles' *daimōn*, cf. Rappe 2001, 64–67. In any case, as also shown by the acute interpretation of Osborne 2005, there are plenty of reasons to regard the *daimones* as agents responsible for their

Therefore, the entity that for Empedocles is the protagonist of a cosmic journey of salvation appears to lack the material requirements that he himself deems necessary for standard cognitive functions. This should also mean that not all humans are fallen *daimones*, and that only the latter are destined to reacquire their original divine nature, thanks to extraordinary intellectual faculties (whose nature, however, is not specified). But then, what is the point of Empedocles's teachings to his student Pausanias? Perhaps to offer him the greatest possible amount of knowledge of nature that can be attained with the scant cognitive tools that all humans who are not *daimones* have at their disposal? And would this not indicate (paradoxically) a divide between the ideal of spiritual salvation—reserved to very few in its entirety—and that of the knowledge of nature, downgraded to second best in this scenario? In my view, the extant fragments of Empedocles's work do not allow us to answer this question. The only certainty is that, in the interweaving of mysticism and philosophy that characterizes this phase of Presocratic thought in general and Empedocles's thought in particular, the eschatological concern and the search for moral regeneration that goes with it pose serious obstacles for the construction of a theory of soul that satisfies the unity of the individual as a living *and* thinking (and moral) being. Lest this assessment seem too simplistic, we shall look for further proof in a (rather concise and apropos) framework of the later developments of ancient psychology.

To Each His Own (Compound)

The history of Presocratic psychology before Empedocles contains several instances of theories motivated by the need to clearly distinguish the functions of the soul and, at the same time, to give a unitary explanation of it. In the last few decades of the fifth century, for example, Democritus regards the soul as an aggregate of atoms. In his doctrine, the atoms are the fundamental constituents of the cosmos, indivisible elements of Being (which is eternal and unchanging) that are different from each other only in terms of their geometrical features (size and shape), their position, and their arrangement; their aggregation and disaggregation in the void brings about the various sensible objects. At the core of this theory lies the same need that we saw in Empedocles of bypassing the problems posited by Parmenides concerning the study of Being.

More or less contemporaneously, Diogenes of Apollonia constructs a complex account of perception and intelligence, in which air is the *archē* of the cosmos. This notion would appear to have been borrowed from Anaximenes and to be rather unsophisticated, were it not for the fact that Diogenes equips

---

own actions, for which they are punished according to a moral code to which they had subscribed.

it with the attribute of *intelligence* following the model of Anaximander's *nous*. Thus the same air acts both as a principle of order within the cosmos and as a principle of life and knowledge in the field of living beings; moreover, the notion that this principle is present, in different degrees of "thinness," in different animal species enables Diogenes to arrange the latter into a scale of cognitive abilities, as well as to distinguish animals from humans and humans from one another.

Making excellent use of the model outlined by Empedocles for explaining sense perception, both Democritus and Diogenes trace the sensory processes to contact between elements outside and within the body. This leads them to underscore the material affinity between soul and cosmos and thus to apply a "portion model," which does not prevent them from outlining a distinction between sensible and rational knowledge; the latter is explained by Diogenes, and probably by Democritus as well, through the notion of a concentration of the matter of the soul in the brain, seen as the coordination center of sensation.[64]

There is no doubt that with Democritus and Diogenes the theory of soul and intelligence reaches a high level of elaboration. Yet one cannot help but note that these thinkers, as far as we know, do not take into consideration the problem of personal identity, thereby avoiding the wall hit by thinkers such as Empedocles and Heraclitus. This may confirm the difficulty (which we already observed) of integrating this problem into a general theory of the soul. It must be said that such an integration seems to have been attained by Plato, not by coincidence in the *Timaeus*, where the legacy of Presocratic naturalism is more evident. It is here that Plato combines the model of transmigration, with all its moral implications, and the notion of a complex composition of the single soul, part of which is immortal and divine in nature (made of the same constituents of the cosmic soul), while another part (responsible for sensations and emotions) is engendered upon its encounter with the body during incarnation.[65]

Yet this theory, too, is lacking in the eyes of Aristotle, who aims to bring together the two trends that characterized the preceding theories, including Plato's—for until the time of Plato the biological and cognitive functions of the soul had been regarded as two different issues, or at any rate they had not been unified in a consistent theory. Aristotle embarks upon an entirely new

[64] For a detailed assessment of Democritus's and Diogenes of Apollonia's (but also Empedocles's and Anaxagoras's) theories on sense perception, see Sassi 1978. The bibliography on specific problems and moments of Presocratic psychology is endless; for a general orientation see at least the titles listed in Everson 1991, 220–24 and Long 1999b, 394–95. See also the general framework outlined with great acumen by Laks (1999).

[65] For a different explanation of Plato's "success" in the psychology of the *Timaeus*, see Betegh 2006a, 46–48. I find that Fronterotta 2007 gives the best assessment of the constitution of the soul in the *Timaeus*.

path when, in the second and third books of his treatise *On the Soul*, he classi-fies living beings according to a scale of increasing degrees of complexity, cor-responding to a sequence of psychic faculties. The nutritive/reproductive principle of the soul (shared by all living beings, including plants) is accom-panied in animals by the sensitive one (which distinguishes them as such), and is closely associated with the locomotive one (animals move toward what they perceive and desire); yet only the human animal is endowed with reason.

Aristotle's achievement cannot be underestimated; the notion of *psuchē* now works as a unitary explanatory principle for *all* living beings, character-ized by the variable combination of *all* vital functions. This twofold move is made possible by assuming a necessary and mutual relationship between (each) soul and (each) body; on the contrary, in Aristotle's view, all his prede-cessors (especially, but not only, those interested in the immortality of the soul) had made the mistake of regarding soul and body as two entities in a casual relationship with each other, without searching for "something in com-mon" that is the only thing that allows one to explain their interaction (I, 3, 407b 13–26):

> The mistake of this [i.e., the one in the *Timaeus*] and most other theo-ries on the soul is that they attach the soul to, and put it in, the body without determining why this happens and which are the conditions of the body. And yet this would seem necessary, for it is by having something in common that the one acts and the other is acted upon, that the one is moved and the other moves; there is no interaction be-tween things taken at random. But these thinkers only attempt to de-fine the nature of the soul, without adding any details about the body which is to receive it; as though it were possible—as in the Pythago-rean stories (*kata tous Puthagorikous muthous*)—that any soul en-tered any body. This is just like saying (as each body appears to have its own form and shape) that carpentry can find its way into flutes; on the contrary, each craft must employ its own tools, and each soul its own body.

In conclusion, let us note that Aristotle's construction of a systematic and uni-tary psychological theory required doing away with two aspects that had heavily influenced the discourse on the soul in prior formulations and were intimately interdependent. Aristotle leaves out of the horizon of *On the Soul* both the religious concern for the immortality of the soul (an aspect that in-terests him, if at all, only in relation to the problem of the knowledge of the first principles) and the problem of moral conduct (whose study is reserved for specific treatises on ethics, in accordance with the rigorous compartmental-ization of knowledge in Aristotle's work). At last, eschatology does not live here anymore.

CHAPTER FIVE

Voices of Authority

The Odd Couple

In a well-known passage of the tenth book of *Republic* (606e–608b), Plato returns to the negative effects of poetic mimesis, already denounced in previous sections of the dialogue, to stress that the only poems that may be admitted into the city are those honoring the gods or praising noble actions, while Homeric poetry should be rejected in its entirety. To those who sing Homer's praises because he "educated Hellas" and even base "their whole life" on the ethic code of the *Iliad* and the *Odyssey*, Plato responds that the only merit of Homeric poetry is its formal excellence, which, however, carries with it pernicious repercussions on the moral level; for to grant the Homeric Muse access to the city means to pave the way for the domain of emotionality; pleasure and pain will become the guiding criteria for human actions instead of the ordering power "of the law and of what is each time commonly agreed to be the best reason." Thus the coexistence of irrational beguilement and rational argumentation is impossible for the sake of the polis; according to Plato, this is an "ancient quarrel" (*palaia ... diaphora*) that crucially divides poetry and philosophy.

This formulation clearly bespeaks a strong "teleological narrative."[1] Plato is projecting into the past—as if into a primal and constitutive situation—a contrast between poetry and philosophy that became a reality only in his younger years. Moreover, as far as we know, archaic Greek culture lacked a unitary notion of poetry or literature; in this period, the various "genres" of song were distinguished according to the different performance occasions rather than following the formal and abstract criteria that would later inspire their classification in a context of literary theory, starting in the fifth century BCE. And it is only toward the end of this century that the nouns for "poetry"

---

[1] Ford 2002, 46 (see also 10–13 and 46ff).

(*poiēsis*) and "philosophy" (*philosophia*) are applied to specific genres that differ in objectives, contents, and form, and that prose is established as the main means for communicating philosophical contents. Furthermore, Plato exacerbates that division when, in constructing his political utopia, he characterizes poetry as the place of irrational persuasion par excellence, all the while indicating rational argumentation as the exclusive prerogative of philosophy. Yet, as we know, Plato himself is anything but indifferent to the communicative power of poetry; in contexts that require stronger persuasion,[2] he eschews neither mythical narrations nor a writing style that aims at high emotional involvement, which he achieves via the dramatic structure of the dialogue. With this he shows he has inherited an ancient attitude of the philosopher to emulate, rather than deny, the poets' qualities and prerogatives. And this attitude, contrary to what Plato is trying to emphasize, is an integral part of the beginnings of philosophy.

In the first chapter, in an attempt to identify the outlines of a philosophical thought in that melting pot of competing forms of wisdom, traditional and otherwise, that is the archaic Greek world, we set out to emphasize, among other elements, the interest in "all things," that is, the intention to explore the nature of men and of the world. This indication was brought to fruition in the second chapter, dedicated to the first cosmologies, and in the fourth, which dealt with the discourses on the soul. As we have already noted, since Homer and Hesiod the archaic poets present themselves as authors of a *global* discourse on the cosmos that will soon play a central role in Greek education.[3] For this reason the places and the occasions of poetry, in continuity with its initial mold, appear naturally predisposed to host moral reflections, whether in sympotic gatherings or during festival celebrations. On the other hand, in the first half of the sixth century, while the long-lasting monopoly of the poets on *paideia* is being established, a favorable combination of factors brings about new speculations about the nature of the cosmos in the Ionian world. At this point, the inquiry bifurcates in two directions that are documented, *in statu nascendi*, in a writing by that poet-political thinker and contemporary of Anaximander, Solon. In these powerful verses, Solon compares the origin of a snow- and hailstorm from a cloud to the enslavement of a people at the hands of a tyrant, and ascribes the cause of it to the "ignorance" of the *dēmos* itself. What needs to be done instead (by applying, we are led to believe, a forecasting ability like that of a meteorologist) is to stop the leaders before they prevail, which in turn requires an "all-encompassing knowledge" (frag. 9, line 6 West). Here the "knowledge of all things" is the awareness of the complex political tapestry showcased by Solon as a thinker and man of action, while

---

[2] See above, 19–21. On Plato's search for a synthesis between poetry and philosophy and on its realization in the mimesis of the dialogues, see Giuliano 2000.

[3] See above, 30–31.

the natural world is evoked only as an analogy to emphasize the potential violence of the upheavals within the polis.

Let us now try to interpret this situation by adapting rather freely some of the valuable explanatory categories formulated by Yehuda Elkana.[4] We might say that the construction of the Ionian cosmologies brings about the delineation of a certain "body of knowledge." The fact that this phase apparently lacks deliberate descriptions of a methodological problem does not diminish its importance for the beginnings of the science of nature. What is important is that a program of inquiry is established *de facto*, thanks to the identification of new concerns, accompanied by new procedures, for correlating them to the data of knowledge. Moreover, the growth of knowledge depends on the production of apt "images," that is, a set of conceptions around the nature of truth, the sources of wisdom, and the addressee. While the body of knowledge consists of thoughts about the world, these images (which, as Elkana argues, are socially determined) express thoughts about knowledge itself, and thus constitute "second-order thinking." It is true, *systematic* thinking of this kind does not emerge from the conceptions of the Ionians, even though these conceptions show a critical stance toward the mythical framework that must be anything but conscious. At any rate, the Presocratics that immediately followed show ample evidence of a process of constructing and self-justifying the images lined up in the game of appropriation and/or denial of the communicative modalities of poetry.

The stakes are highest when it comes to the ways of granting *authority* to the body of knowledge. We shall see, in fact, that a certain number of authors stress their detachment from the poetic tradition (while laying the foundations for a new tradition of knowledge) in combining the choice of new contents with new and more appropriate *guarantees of truth*. (Let me note incidentally—I have already touched on this point and shall do so again—that this development also implies a particular audience and focused occasions of performance).[5] For instance, while the mythical bard summons the Muses, the patron goddesses of the art of poetry, to support the veracity of his message, Alcmaeon and Xenophanes prefer to focus on explicating a personal methodological agenda. Both Parmenides and Empedocles follow a different, yet somewhat parallel, path. It is true that these authors remain within a mythical framework when they turn to their religious revelations (conveyed by the solemnity of epic meter); however, turning to their religious revelations does not exclude their employing rational processes. We might say that with Parmenides and Empedocles, philosophy cohabitates with poetry in the context of the hexameter; but the products of this coexistence, as I will try to show, are closer to philosophy than to poetry.

---

[4] See Elkana 1981, 13–21 and Elkana 1986, 40–48.
[5] See above, 70ff and 82ff.

Farewell to the Muse

The Muses are evanescent figures of the Greek imagination. In Ancient Greek, *mousa* is both a common noun used to refer to poetic "song" accompanied by music and also the name of the divine daughters of Zeus and Mnemosyne (Memory), who like to approach humans and give them the task of celebrating a world of gods and heroes with verses to be ingrained in collective memory. The Muses have features of autonomous personalities in Greek mythology, yet they are represented in most literary and iconographical sources as graceful maidens who love to dance in choruses (often led by Apollo), and they are barely distinguishable from one another; although all nine of them are mentioned by name since Hesiod, only in the Hellenistic period are their respective prerogatives specified. We might be entitled to see in them the personification of an abstract notion (of artistic inspiration, to be concise), as long as we note their special status—an "incorporeal" one, so to speak—so that they reveal themselves to their chosen ones essentially through voice. In observing this, Penelope Murray reprises a suggestive definition of the ancient muse as a "voice of language"—which we owe to Joseph Brodsky[6]—and draws a conclusion that is important for our purposes here. The evanescence of the Muse (whose collective identity is mostly expressed by use of the singular form) makes her a figure that we may call *ad usum poetae*, in the sense that each author enjoys a personal, and personalized, relationship with her; thus a figure that owes its immense fortune in the Western poetic tradition to its extreme flexibility, which made possible unlimited appropriations.

It is significant that a literature characterized by the most absolute anonymity, such as that of Mesopotamia, does not contain anything of the sort; here the texts are presented as the direct result of the revelation of a preestablished traditional "treasure" that is immune from authorial intervention.[7] This comparison invites us to see in the Muse a useful *topos* for the poet's self-presentation as an author independent from the traditional repertoire. This is also true in a seemingly anonymous context such as that of the Homeric poems, where the Muse is summoned more than once as a guarantor of the veracity of the bard's story (as well as of the ordered structure of the account, so that it will be both pleasant and trustworthy). We will remember in particular the opening of the catalog of ships, where the Muses are called upon to sanction the veracity of the knowledge that the poet will exhibit of things that are distant in time and space and cannot be acquired through the modalities of ordinary knowledge (*Iliad* 2, lines 484–487):

---

[6] See Murray 2005, 150. The following exposition on the status and prerogatives of the Muse in Homer, Hesiod, and beyond presupposes the readings of Roochnik 1985, 40–45, Finkelberg 1998, 68–99, Most 1999b, 342–43, Scodel 2002, 65–89, and Brillante 2006.

[7] See Xella 2006.

> Tell me now, o Muses who dwell on Olympus,
> for you, o goddesses, are everywhere and know everything,
> while we only hear the fame, and see nothing,
> (tell me) who were the leaders and commanders of the Danaans.

Thanks to their divine nature, the Muses are ubiquitous and therefore—given that direct and visual knowledge is superior to the simple oral recounting of an event—omniscient. The task of the Homeric bard is to act as a mediator of this knowledge for the mortals, partially filling the abyss of ignorance that separates them from the world of the gods; his *sophia*, which grants him a central role in society, lies in the skillful use of formal means to this end.

Hesiod's relationship with the Muses is slightly more complicated. As we have seen,[8] in the proem of the *Theogony* (lines 26–28) he recounts how his "conversion" to poetry came about (it is not easy to determine whether the episode is perceived as real or whether it is the artificial construction of a poetic persona). The Muses approach him on the slopes of Helicon where he—a humble shepherd —is grazing his flock, and rebuke him with words that insist on the privilege granted to him, among the many shepherds who are incapable of rising above the small-mindedness of everyday life:

> Shepherds who dwell in the fields, bad disgrace, nothing but belly!
> We know how to say many lies (*pseudea*) that resemble truths
>   (*etumoisin homoia*),
> But when we want, we also know how to proclaim true things.

The emphasis on the trustworthiness of the contents that will be consigned to the budding poet should not be doubted; Hesiod will start his song "from the Muses" (as they themselves bid him to), and not only can they sing delightful hymns to their father, Zeus, but they can also speak of "the things that are and the things that shall be and the things that once were" (line 38). What is less clear, however, is the reference to the songs that are similar to truths yet false, which the Muses are also capable of inspiring. Scholars have hypothesized that Hesiod may be distancing himself from mere fiction, yet it needs to be noted that he himself does not disdain the fiction of animal tales in *Works and Days* (lines 202–12). Problematizing further, scholars have asked whether Hesiod may be trying to break away from the elements of falsehood he perceives in the Homeric poems and other theogonic accounts by asserting the veracity of his own story. The difficulty of identifying the potential target of this criticism has led even a scholar as attentive as Jenny Strauss Clay to argue that the poet is referring to the uncertainty of the truth of his own message; but it is simply unimaginable that a didactic poet like Hesiod, who in the *Theogony* (lines 226–232) lists Lies (*Pseudea*) among the pernicious progeny

[8] See above, 33.

of Strife (*Eris*), is authorizing a deceptive message.[9] Rather, it is plausible that Hesiod, having assessed the variety of existing versions of the same myth brought about by the desire of poets to distinguish themselves during their performances, perceives this tradition—hypostatized in the Muse—as a repertoire that effectively includes both true and false stories; and this is why he must convince his audience of the superiority of his own version.[10]

Whereas the Homeric bard placed himself easily (or so it seems) within the existing tradition, Hesiod invites us to consider its complexity. This move, however, is not based on any explicit criteria of argumentation. Rather, the truth of the contents that the Muses pass down to Hesiod is consolidated through poetic efficacy, memorability, and the author's own *ēthos*. In this sense, the poet does not cross the line, albeit thin, that separates him from a philosophical conception of knowledge—let us remember that earlier, in considering the cosmogonic model of the *Theogony*, we similarly assessed Hesiod's position in relation to the history of philosophical thought.[11]

Throughout archaic poetry, the Muse continues to play her role as the poet's ally, but the emphasis gradually shifts to her contribution to the trustworthiness of the poetic account rather than to its formal beauty. At the same time, expressions of "professional" awareness become more frequent as the poets become more and more able to command, through innovation, the means and potential of their *technē*.[12] In short, after Hesiod the quality and extent of the Muse's assistance become negotiable. At the same time the sense of the unbridgeable gap between human and divine knowledge comes to the fore and takes on highly pessimistic overtones. A good example of this can be seen in an iambic writing by Semonides of Samos (also known as Semonides of Amorgos), active during the second half of the seventh century BCE (frag. 1):

> Boy, loud-thundering Zeus has control over the outcome
> of all existing things, and arranges them in whichever way he wants,

---

[9] See Strauss Clay 2003, 58–59. According to Detienne (1996 [1967], 72–73), these lines are declarations of a fundamental ambiguity of poetic utterances, while Arrighetti 2006 rightly defends against this kind of argument with the coherence of Hesiod's didascalic program. However, in a recent essay, Strauss Clay succeeds as sharply as ever in reconciling the "ambiguity" and "enigmatic character" of Hesiod's Muses with the poet's trust that he will be instructed by them not only about the gods, but also about natural phenomena (2015, 108–17).

[10] Scodel 2001, 112–23 is convincing on this point.

[11] See above, 32–37.

[12] The process that I am describing here is, of course, rather simplified. I must at least mention Pindar's original stance in calling himself an "interpreter" (*hermeneus*) and "prophet" (*prophētēs*) of the Muse's oracular message; cf. Ledbetter 2003, 64–68. This trait, together with the intentionally obscure style, puts Pindar near his elder contemporary, Heraclitus; but Heraclitus, as we know, speaks only for himself.

while there is no intelligence (*nous*) among men, but day by day they
    live (*epameroi*)
like beasts, knowing nothing (*ouden eidotes*)
of how the god will bring everything to its end.

It is worth pausing a moment to reflect on the characterization of humanity as living "day by day." The expression recurs, in different versions of equal
meaning (*epameros, epēmeros, ephēmeros, ephēmerios*), in various contexts
of archaic lyric that exhibit a high degree of existential pessimism (the most
famous of these passages is probably the one in Pindar's eighth *Pythian*, line
95: "Creatures of a day (*epameroi*): what is one? And what is one not? Man is
the dream of a shadow"). This expression is not meant to emphasize, as one
might initially think, the brevity of human existence, "ephemeral" like that of
an insect living "a day only" on earth. Rather, as Hermann Fränkel demonstrated with his usual acumen, the formation of the term implies that humans are "exposed to the day" (from the preposition *epi* and the noun *hēmera*)
as to a limit that prevents them from knowing what will happen to them the
next day; in other words, men are *ephēmeroi*, not because they are short-lived
but because their existence is marked by an instability that they are incapable
of determining beforehand, let alone overcoming.[13] In archaic literature this
theme is often interwoven (especially in iambic, elegiac, and sympotic contexts) with that of the helplessness (*amēchania* is the key term here) of a
human being who is sadly aware that his or her destiny depends on the will of
the gods. Yet this awareness does not necessarily translate into passively let-
ting go. On the contrary, it is often exhortatory; the thematization of not-
knowing, while marking the space for human actions, also invites this space
to be filled with rational ones (we saw an instance of this earlier, when Solon
counters the ignorance of his fellow citizens with an exhortation to *panta
noein*).[14]

In any case, the not-knowing on which the poets pause to reflect concerns
human existence and what the future holds for it, whereas the philosophers
bring into question the possibility of knowing the events that are taking place
presently in the real world. Moreover, the philosophers' attitude tends to an
epistemological optimism that is quite the opposite of the poets' pessimism.
Let us consider the unequivocal declarations of authors who, while they do
not deny the superiority of divine knowledge and even observe its characteristic immediacy, precision, and universality, prefer to emphasize the capability

---

[13] See Fränkel 1946. Cf. Romeyer-Dherbey 1999 for a valorization of the theme of
"man's random time" in Pindar.

[14] See above, 140–41. For other passages, see Föllinger (2007), who brilliantly outlines
this situation. See also Lesher 1999, 225–28.

humans possess to broaden their view of nature through their own cognitive tools. Among these is the *incipit* of Alcmaeon's writing (frag. 1):[15]

> Alcmaeon of Croton, son of Peirithous, told Brotinus, Leon and Bathyllus the following things. About invisible things, about mortal things the gods possess certainty (*saphēneian*), while humans judge by conjecture (*tekmairesthai*).

The use of the verb *tekmairesthai* to indicate human cognitive ability is remarkable. If we consider that *tekmērion* in Greek denotes a strong "sign," which tends to be distinguished from *sēmeion* (which also means "sign" or "clue") in terms of its greater probative strength, we can note that Alcmaeon is claiming the validity of a knowledge (the only one achievable by humankind) that proceeds through inference from signs, that is, from the data observable in nature. In other words, he is calling on the collaboration between reason and the senses as the source of his own medical and naturalistic learning.

Xenophanes proclaims an analogous independence from the traditional sources of knowledge in various passages. In a well-known fragment, he very clearly distances himself from those mythical accounts that present civilization as a by-product of the gifts offered to humankind by divine or semidivine figures (for instance, fire from Prometheus, or agriculture from Demeter and Triptolemus). On the contrary (frag. 18):

> The gods did not reveal everything to mortals from the very
>   beginning,
> but in time, by searching, they [mortals] find something better.

Another equally famous and significant text shows that Xenophanes's stance on knowledge develops coherently along these lines (frag. 34):

> No man knows (*iden*), or ever will know, the truth (*to...saphes*) about the gods and what I say about all things; for even if one succeeded in saying the complete truth, yet he himself would not know (*oide*). In fact, opinion (*dokos*) is given about all things [or ... for all men].

The interpretation of frag. 34 has a long and tormented history. Antiquity, as well as some modern scholars, favored a skeptical reading, according to which Xenophanes is denying completely the possibility of humans' knowing anything about the gods or about the cosmos as a whole (and the *dokos* in the last line should be read as pure "illusion"). The prevailing opinion nowadays, however, is that Xenophanes's skepticism is well mitigated by the clear defini-

---

[15] Already partially quoted above, p. 72, in relation to its position at the beginning of a written text.

tion of a specifically human sphere of cognitive abilities.[16] Here, as in frag. 1 of Alcmaeon, a prominent role is given to having clear and precise knowledge (*saphēneian* in Alcmaeon, *to saphes* in Xenophanes), presented as an exclusive possession of the gods. The instances of the verb *oida* (whose root **vid* is the same as in the Latin *videre* and the English noun "vision") to indicate true knowledge as a direct and completely absorbing experience, which humans by nature are unable to achieve, is remarkable in this sense. Yet, as in Alcmaeon, this observation is immediately tied to the proclamation of a specifically human cognitive ability; Alcmaeon's *tekmairesthai* corresponds in Xenophanes to the possibility of formulating an "opinion" on the gods and on all things. This meaning of the term *dokos*—and a neutral one; an opinion can be either true or false—is confirmed by another text of Xenophanes, where we find another instance of the verb *doxazō* (another term connected to the root **dok*), again in the context of an evaluation of an opinion's cognitive potential (frag. 35):

> Let these things be opined (*dedoxasthō*) as resembling true ones (*eoikota tois etumoisi*).

It is interesting to note the term *etumos*, which stresses the level of "authentic" truth and at the same time echoes the words with which the Muses announce to Hesiod that they can say "many lies that resemble truths (*pseudea polla ... etumoisin homoia*; *Theogony*, line 27).[17] But Xenophanes has transformed the topos of the opposition between divine and human knowledge, abandoning the notion that the gods facilitate the achievement of the truth and focusing instead on the possibility that humans are able to advance, solely with their capacities, insights that, if not absolutely certain, at least "resemble" and are "appropriate to" the reality they are meant to describe. This is the sense of *eoikota* in frag. 35, which we may also translate as "possible" or even "likely," referring to the positive connotation of cognate words such as *eikōn* ("image," "reproduction," "portrait") and *eikazein* ("to compare," but also "to make conjectures").[18]

For the sense of Xenophanes's *dokos* it is still interesting to recall the words with which Hecataeus of Miletus opens his *Genealogies*: "I write these things as they seem to me to be true (*hos moi dokei alēthea einai*)."[19] Here the verb *dokein* introduces a rearrangement of Greek mythology that will be carried out through personal perspectives and critical opinions regarding the tradition. We know that, just like Hecataeus and Alcmaeon, Xenophanes did

---

[16] See Fränkel 1925, Rivier 1956, Heitsch 1966, Lesher 1992, 149–86; Ioli 2003 (selected from the endless bibliography on Xenophanes's gnoseology).

[17] See above, 143.

[18] See Turrini 1977, Bryan 2012, Sassi 2013a.

[19] The fragment is quoted in its entirety above, 71.

not simply state his agenda but fulfilled his desire for knowledge with a positive inquiry into the natural world and even constructed an image of the divine inspired by criteria of "plausibility."[20]

Finally, we may note an affinity with Heraclitus's gnoseological stance. It is interesting that Heraclitus directs his sarcasm toward Hecataeus and Xenophanes, of all people, because he accuses them of *polumathiē*, that is, of having a broad knowledge not subject to critical examination. The goal of Heraclitus's polemic, of course, is to emphasize his own superiority in elaborating a personal conception of the reality of all things through a careful reading of the information provided by the senses. The statement "I went in search of myself" of frag. 101 must not be interpreted at the expense of the cognitive contribution of sense perception, which Heraclitus all but underestimates (frags. 55 and 107):

All things of which there is sight, hearing, learning; these I prefer.

Bad witnesses are eyes and ears for men, if they have barbarian souls (*barbarous psuchas*).

As noted earlier, the Greeks call foreign people "barbarians," meaning that they speak an incomprehensible language and also do not understand Greek, so Heraclitus calls "barbarian" the souls of those who cannot go beyond the seemingly unrelated indications of the sensible world to grasp the deeper structure of reality; the philosopher, however, manages to do so because he is able to cultivate internally the sense of the unifying *logos* of all things.[21] Even Heraclitus, then, relies on a cooperation between reason and the senses as the source of his knowledge, and therefore (joining, in spite of himself, the line inaugurated by Hecataeus, Alcmaeon, and Xenophanes) can do without revelations sent by gods or Muses; everything he needs he carries within himself, in his critical thinking.

Power Games

Joannes Stobaeus recounts that Pindar, in referring to some unspecified/ unidentified *phusiologountes*, said that these "naturalists" limit themselves to "picking an unripe fruit of wisdom" (*atelē karpon sophias*) (frag. 209 Maehler). This criticism is probably not aimed against natural inquiry per se, but against those authors, such as Alcmaeon or Xenophanes, who carried it out without appealing to divine sources. Elsewhere Pindar warns that "blind are the minds of men if one without the dwellers on Helicon seeks ... the path

[20] Curd 2002, 126–29 takes a firm position on this point. See also Sassi 2013b and above, 97.

[21] For complementary considerations on frags. 101 and 107, see 117–18. For an evaluation of Heraclitus's "rationalism," to which I subscribe, see Curd 2002, 120–24.

of deep wisdom (*batheias sophias hodon*)" (*Paean* 7 b, lines 18–20); here the assistance of the Muses marks a clear distinction between the pious work of the poet and the activities of those who pretend to be *sophoi* without actually being such.[22]

But not all those who had something interesting to say regarding the soul and the cosmos distanced themselves from supernatural guarantees of truth. In the case of Pythagoras, for instance, we have good reason to think that his belief in metempsychosis was instrumental to his self-presentation as a wise man whose extraordinary knowledge was accumulated in the course of his many previous lives, which he recalled clearly.[23] It is remarkable that this very point became the target of both the criticism and praise of other proponents of archaic *sophia*, in a back-and-forth of denial and/or support that may be read, in the context of the competition for wisdom, as other opinions about the best way to conquer it.

It is also possible that Alcmaeon, by dedicating his writing to members of the Pythagorean school, also meant to stress his autonomy from the wisdom claimed by their teacher by ascribing *to the gods* the direct knowledge of all things; according to this hypothesis, reclaiming the dignity of *tekmairesthai* would mean rejecting the kind of doctrines (both theological and cosmological) that find authority in an *ipse dixit*.[24] At any rate, Heraclitus's fragments present more explicit, even harsher polemical overtones. We have already seen how, in frag. 40, Heraclitus accuses Pythagoras, Hesiod, Xenophanes, and Hecataeus of *polumathiē*, that is, knowledge designed as an accumulation of notions assimilated from others instead of being the fruit of a personal interpretation of the signs gathered from *phusis*. We have also seen, in another fragment, that Pythagoras is the target of particular execration for having built this accumulated knowledge with a fraudulent and "bad art" (*kakotechniē*; frag. 129). These passages, as well as another in which we are led to understand that Heraclitus allegedly called Pythagoras an "originator of deceptions" (frag. 81), invite us to think that the person being targeted in frag. 28 is again Pythagoras, even though he is not mentioned by name:

> The most renowned one of them all (*ho dokimōtatos*) knows and treasures apparent things; but surely Justice shall condemn the makers and witnesses of lies.

With this polemic, which is matched in aggressiveness only by the one in which he charges at *magoi* and purifiers (frags. 14 and 15), Heraclitus targets not the contents of Pythagoras's thought (which are not expressly criticized in

---

[22] See Ferrari 2004, who starts with interesting remarks about the Pindaric notion of wisdom.

[23] See above, 120–21.

[24] This hypothesis appears in Vlastos 1953, 344n5.

the fragments we possess) but the exceptional fame of his intellectual persona, which he identifies with a knowledge that is not merely false but also mendacious. It is very likely that for Heraclitus, also given his different ideas regarding immortality and the soul, the "mother" of all of Pythagoras's lies was the self-legitimizing reference to metempsychosis.[25]

In this light let us now analyze the entertaining scene in which Xenophanes ridicules a believer in reincarnation. In this case, too, the allusion may be to Pythagoras himself (frag. 7; Diogenes Laertius, who provides the citation, is convinced of this):

> He once happened to walk by when a puppy was being beaten, and,
>   they say, he felt compassion and said these words:
> "Stop striking, because it is the soul of a dear friend
> that I recognized upon hearing him cry out."

These verses were surely meant to cause immediate amusement, but they also express the judgment of a "disillusioned" thinker on a belief that he deems barely "plausible." Moreover, one can glean here a strategy for presenting knowledge; Xenophanes is also telling us that no plausible content can be credited a fortiori to someone who introduces it as an emanation of his reincarnated self.

Yet Pythagoras is not isolated in the tower of his wisdom. He has on his side Empedocles, at least, who makes the perfectly analogous, opposite move when he eulogizes the figure of a wise man (we are probably dealing here, too, with Pythagoras) whose reincarnation gives him a power of knowledge spanning a long series of past lives (frag. 129):

> Among those was a man who knew exceptional things (*eidōs*),
> endowed with immense richness of mind,
> and capable of all sorts of wise actions;
> and when he reached out with all the strength of his mind (*pasēisi*
>   *prapidessin*)[26]
> easily did he glean all existing things, one by one
> in the span of ten and even twenty human lives.

---

[25] On the modalities and targets of Heraclitus's polemic, see also above, 99–101, and Gemelli Marciano 2002, 96–103. On Heraclitus's conception of the soul, see above, 114–16.

[26] The term *prapides* is noteworthy. In Homer it refers to a part of the chest—analogous to *phrēn*—that is a seat of sense perception, emotions, and intelligence; in Hippocrates and Plato the meaning of the term becomes specialized for the diaphragm. The same word appears in frag. 110 (line 1), where Empedocles invites Pausanias to rely on this organ in order to reach a state of contemplation "with pure exercises" (line 2). Gernet (1981 [1945], 359–60) saw this as an echo of a meditation practice based on the regulation of breathing through contraction and release of the diaphragm, and Kingsley gave this observation its due value (2002, 400–1). See also Frontisi-Ducroux 2002.

Of course, Empedocles, too, furthers his own cause. As we have seen, he presents himself as the last incarnation of a *daimōn* who has fallen from an original state of blessedness and, after a long cathartic journey, has come into possession of extraordinary cognitive and magical powers; he, too, just like Pythagoras, aspires to the fame of a *Wundermann*. By praising Pythagoras (or a similar figure), he enlists himself in the ranks of those wise men who claim to be inspired by the gods, among whom we also find Parmenides.

But now we pause on Empedocles and Parmenides, who ascribe a divine source to their *sophia* and, what is more, adopt the formal trappings of epic poetry. After all that we have argued regarding the relationship between poetry and philosophy, distinguishing them by their appealing to determined images of knowledge, should we group these two thinkers among the poets rather than the philosophers? In other words, is it legitimate to trace in the poetic form of their discourse a *philosophical intention*? This is the last, particularly thorny issue that demands our attention.

The Truth Revealed in Song

Let us turn first to Parmenides's poem to try and outline its formal structure and its likely communicative context. It almost goes without saying that the often lengthy fragments that have come down to us (thanks mostly to Sextus Empiricus, who cites the proem, and to Simplicius in his commentaries to Aristotle's *On the Heavens* and *Physics*) present us with a text that is not at all suitable to be memorized due to its peculiar style and argumentative structure. Thus, we should imagine that it was written down, not only—as is more obvious—during composition but also for transmission and conservation. Parmenides's thought was soon disseminated to places far from its place of origin, as shown by the fact that Empedocles (as, later, Anaxagoras and the atomists) brings forth an account of becoming that responds both to Parmenides's theory and to the attacks on it, incurred by the latter's denial of movement and multiplicity—and it is possible that the unidentified authors of these attacks were the target of Zeno's arguments, which reiterate the unity and immobility of Being through a *reductio ad absurdum* of the rivals' hypotheses.[27] This does not exclude the possibility of there having been an initial phase of oral transmission, when Parmenides himself was reciting his writings before an audience.

What sort of audience would this have been? A passage in Plato's *Sophist* might be pointing us in the right direction, and the instance is even more significant because superfluous, from a theoretical point of view, in the context

---

[27] See Solmsen 1971 for an accurate analysis of the relationship between Zeno and Parmenides's theory, which culminates in an invitation to downscale the student's dependence on his teacher.

of the dialogue. Here the Eleatic Stranger, to whom Plato assigns the discussion of the Parmenidean arguments on Being, remembers that the "great" Parmenides presented his thought to him and other young listeners (*paisin hēmin*) "every time both in prose and in verse" (237a, followed by a quotation of the first two lines of frag. 7: "for never shall this be proved, that things that are not are / but you, keep your thought away from this route of investigation"). If we trust Plato,[28] youngsters were present at these readings and, though they may not have been the only listeners, they likely had a learning attitude. Moreover, Parmenides did not fail to comment on or clarify, in a more "daily" language, the sense of the verses after reading them,[29] if only to answer questions from the audience, according to a modality of aural fruition still reflected in Zeno's discussion of his teacher's book in Plato's *Parmenides*.[30]

Thus, it is likely that Parmenides's audience was more limited, or at any rate different in composition, than the one for traditional poetry, but we cannot be sure of this, since he clearly thinks of, and represents himself, as a wise *poet*, writing in hexameters and using the style and vocabulary of epic poetry. However, it is also true that this formal structure is used to express highly original speculative contents. A case in point is the term *eukuklēs* ("well rounded"), which is formular in Homer and used by Parmenides in frag. 1 to refer to an abstract concept like *Alētheiē* (Truth), to denote its completeness (frag. 1, line 29, cited below).[31] The expressive effects of these linguistic forays are often too convoluted,[32] but they do not necessarily reflect Parmenides's intention to distance himself from a certain poetic tradition.[33] Nor did he intend, by adopting versification, to depart from the prose of the Milesians, as the latter was far from having established itself as the language "of philoso-

---

[28] Of course, Plato may be projecting anachronistically onto Parmenides's Elea a situation that was familiar to him in Athens. But I think there is no evidence that Plato *misunderstood* Parmenides's intentions. Similarly, and more generally, one cannot say with certainty (as do interpreters like Kingsley) that from Plato onward Parmenides's discourse on Being was given a philosophical sense that it *could not have had* in its own right.

[29] Naturally, these "extemporaneous" comments have not been preserved in the text; the report in *Suda* (in the entry on Parmenides) that Parmenides also wrote in prose is clearly extrapolated from the passage in Plato's *Sophist*.

[30] See above, 80–81.

[31] That is, if we accept the variant *eukukleos* (another legitimate possibility would be the variant *eupeitheos*, which would emphasize the persuasive character of truth). The image of a "well-rounded" sphere, a symbol of perfection, is applied to Being itself in frag. 8, line 43.

[32] See Wöhrle 1993a for a thorough analysis of Parmenides's work on Homeric and Hesiodic motifs, formulas, epithets, and versification.

[33] As opposed to Wright 1998, who regards the peculiar versification strategies of Parmenides as representative of the author's will to break away from the epic tradition; cf. Osborne 1998.

phy" par excellence.[34] Rather, the epic mode appeared "naturally" available
to Parmenides as the most suited to convey especially serious subjects. In particular, the use of the hexameter signals (as it will in Empedocles) that the
author himself is godlike; it is worth remembering that the Greek gods expressed themselves through poets as well as oracles, and the latter were also
composed in verse, almost exclusively dactylic hexameter.[35]

In conclusion, the reasons for Parmenides's formal choice are inseparable
from the object of his thought, presented as a transcendent truth revealed by
a goddess. The proem, contained in the long frag. 1, recounts vividly and in
detail how she welcomed Parmenides after a journey that brought him in an
unusual manner to the boundaries of the human world. It is worth quoting
this intriguing fragment in its entirety:

> The mares that carry me as far as my spirit might go
> were bringing me onwards, after having led me and set me upon the
>   renowned road
> of the goddess, which takes through all the towns the man who knows
>   (*eidota phōta*).
> It was there that I was being carried: for on it the much-knowing
>   mares were carrying me,
> straining the chariot, and maidens led the way.
> The axle in the naves emitted the whistle of a pipe
> as it was heated (for it was pressed hard by two whirling wheels,
> one on each side), while the maidens of the Sun
> hastened to bring me, having just left the palace of Night,
> toward the light, and having pushed back the veils from their heads
>   with their hands.
> There is the gate of the paths of Night and Day:
> a lintel and a stone threshold frame it,
> and great sky-reaching doors close it:
> and much-punishing Justice holds the alternate keys.
> The maidens, addressing her with soft words,
> skillfully persuaded her to push back for them the bolted bar
> quickly from the gate; and when it flew open
> the gate made through the doorposts an immense void (*chasm'
>   achanes*),

---

[34] That the choice of verse implies a detachment from philosophical prose is argued,
for instance, by Cherniss 1977, 20; by contrast, see above, 82–84. Granger (2008, 1–2, 17–
18) comes closer to my position here, in that he argues that Parmenides's formal choice
contrasts the tendency of a good number of "new" intellectuals (Pherecydes, Hecataeus,
Acusilaus, Alcmaeon) to record in prose form an empirical and rationalistic inquiry, independent from superhuman sources of knowledge.

[35] As noted in Most 1999b, 353.

swinging in turn in their sockets the two bronze pivots
fastened with pegs and rivets. Right through
the maidens guided the chariot and horses straight along the way.
And the goddess welcomed me kindly, took my right hand
in her own hand, and thus began to speak, addressing me:
Young man (*kour'*), companion of immortal charioteers,
who have come to our home by the mares that bear you,
welcome [or, rejoice!]; for it is no evil destiny that has sent you to
    travel
this road (for indeed it is far from the paths of humans),
but Right and Justice. It is necessary that you learn all things,
both the unshaken heart of well-rounded [or: well-convincing] truth
and the opinions of mortals, in which there is no true belief.
But nevertheless you will learn this too: how all the things that seem
must be plausible, forever pervading all things.

Hesiod's *Theogony* is certainly a model that Parmenides has in mind, not
only with respect to certain topographic details of the journey, which recall
Hesiodic (and Homeric) descriptions of the underworld (in particular, the
chasma in frag. 1 is reminiscent of the one that opens over Tartarus in the
Theogony, line 733; and in the *Theogony*, too, we find a house of Night at
whose door the paths of Day and Night take turns) but also—and especially—
in the structure of the narrative of his initiation.[36] Parmenides recounts, as an
experience that actually took place (like Hesiod's encounter with the Muses),
a journey he made on a chariot drawn by flying mares, off the path beaten by
humans, to a portal where, at the limits of the world, Day and Night follow
one another every day. Dike herself holds the keys to this portal and, per-
suaded by the daughters of the Sun, who have accompanied their protégé,
opens the door to an abyss. Once he has crossed the threshold, an unnamed
goddess welcomes him, takes him by his right hand, and tells him that a privileged, yet just, destiny has brought him there, where one normally arrives
after death (at the hands of an "evil fate"). This apostrophe is followed by the
proclamation of a speech on the truth of Being and also on the opinions
which mortals are accustomed to build around it. This distinction between
alētheia and *doxa* reprises, and modifies, the distinction between truth and
falsehood enunciated by Hesiod's Muses. The corrective consists in opposing
the true speech with a speech that is not only mendacious but formulated
with ambitions of truth, and whose failure is brought about by mortals' habit
of self-deceit. Moreover, it is remarkable that the goddess promises to explore

---

[36] See Cerri 1995 for a careful comparison with the representation of the underworld
in Homer and Hesiod. For an analysis of the relationship with Hesiod in relation to the
formal configuration of the proem, see the ever-useful Schwabl 1963.

the deceitful opinions on the sensible world in her own *teaching*, with the clear objective of turning her pupil from error. Fragment 2, which must have followed, if not immediately after frag. 1, within the next few lines after the end of the proem, states that the path of truth and persuasion is the one that "is," while the one that "is not" does not bring knowledge, and must therefore be avoided; yet both are "conceivable paths of inquiry." Coherently with this promise, the poem will fork into two parts, conventionally entitled *Alētheia* and *Doxa*; the latter will contain the exposition of a "plausible" model for explaining Being, lest any "mortal thought derail" Parmenides (frag. 8, lines 60–61).[37] The apostrophe uttered by Parmenides's goddess shows no trace of the ambiguity of Hesiod's Muses; in this game of truth and falsehood, the cards will be revealed; there is no cheating.

The references to Hesiod with which the proem is interspersed show other significant points of departure that converge at the moment of revelation to accentuate Parmenides's active role.[38] Right away in the first line we find the personal pronoun in the accusative, *me* (which is then repeated several times, while in Hesiod it appears only at line 24), which puts the greatest emphasis on the figure of the poet; we read in the same line that he has been brought this far by the force of his *thumos*—his passion for knowledge, we might say. To be sure, Parmenides is the addressee of a revelation, but he presents this revelation as the result of a personal inquiry. An indication of this is given by the long series of stops he makes prior to arriving before the goddess, whose welcome speech then develops in the space of relatively few lines. Conversely, at the beginning of the *Theogony*, the arrival of the Muses is introduced by a long preamble in which the goddesses themselves approach the poet, who realizes his privileged position from a quasi-aggressive apostrophe before receiving the symbolic gift of the laurel branch and an inspired voice.

It may seem curious that, whereas Hesiod wants to have *his* voice heard, and starts his theogonic song with a sudden change of scene (with the likely proverbial expression of line 35: "but why should I talk about a rock or a stone?"), the speech of Parmenides's goddess unravels without a break and *coincides* with the contents of the poem itself. One would be tempted to conclude that Parmenides's persona is set aside in giving the floor to a superior authority. But if we consider the context of performance, in which the wise man strove to present his personal experience and the revelation that ensued, we must maintain that it was still *his* voice that was being echoed, and that the listeners ended up seeing *themselves* in the "you" to whom the goddess is speaking (frags. 2, line 1; 6, lines 2–3; 7, lines 2–3, etc.; an analogous shift of

[37] I leave aside here the possibility that Parmenides may have postulated a "third way" of inquiry, as well as the idea, just as controversial, that he may have given minimal epistemic value to the cosmology contained in the second part of the poem.

[38] As has been pointed out by Tulli 1993 and 2000. See also Diller 1946, 142.

identity may also take place in reading a long reported speech, if said speech is so long as to run for most of the written text).

But if we want to grasp the meaning of Parmenides's self-presentation as an inspired wise man we cannot, at this point, limit ourselves to a comparison with the Hesiodic model, important though it is. In other words, we must admit that the imagery in the proem adumbrates an itinerary of mystery initiation, and that Parmenides is describing a mystic experience, in which a religious truth is revealed that is similar to the one achieved by *mustai* or followers of mystery cults (which were flourishing in Magna Graecia) after a series of ritual stages. The expression "the man who knows" with which Parmenides describes himself at line 3, and the term of endearment *kouros* with which the goddess addresses him at line 24 may in fact derive from the context of initiation.

Let us try to unravel the implications of this possibility. Since antiquity, and for a long time in the history of modern studies, Parmenides's journey has been interpreted as a journey from darkness into the light, symbolizing the transition from a condition of ignorance to one of full knowledge. In the past few decades, however, another interpretive line has prevailed that both effectively explains some topographical details and gives more emphasis to the modalities of representation of archaic wisdom. According to this interpretation (largely propelled by a fundamental article by Burkert) Parmenides instead configures a *katabasis*, that is, a descent into a dark region reminiscent of the underworld, where he attains *alētheia*, through clairvoyant powers (similarly to Epimenides, Aristeas, and Pythagoras himself).[39] This perspective has recently been enriched by the parallel studies of Giovanni Cerri and Peter Kingsley, who have seen the proem as the description (containing elements of the Homeric *nekuia* and the Hesiodic Tartarus) of a geography of Hades and/or of a place at the limits of the world where opposites (Day and Night, sky and earth) meet. Moreover, Cerri and Kingsley, still independently of one another, have proposed an identification of Parmenides's goddess, which, although it will never be certain (there is no reason to exclude the possibility that her identity is deliberately unspecified), seems much more convincing than those proposed so far; she may be Persephone, queen of the underworld, depicted in many vases from Magna Graecia as tendering her right

[39] See Burkert 1969, but also Gilbert 1907, and a hint of this interpretation can be found in Gernet 1981 [1945], 349. The last fruit of this research trend is Gemelli Marciano 2008, with useful bibliography. I would also like to stress the possible comparison between the topography of the proem and the otherwordly itinerary described in the Orphic tablets. Both the initiated/deceased in the tablets and Parmenides are presented with a forking road; one path leads to salvific knowledge, while the other, which is to be avoided, is trodden by the uninitiated. Cf. Morrison 1955, Sassi 1988b, and Pugliese Carratelli (1988), who proposes to identify the goddess as Mnemosyne; see also Cassio 1996 for the demonstration of a "linguistic solidarity" between Parmenides and the texts of the tablets.

hand to either Heracles or Orpheus, who have remarkably arrived to the underworld while still alive. She is called simply *thea* because she need not be mentioned by name, being the queen of Hades, but also because as such she *must* be shrouded by sacral silence.[40]

There is general agreement today regarding the religious configuration of the proem and the truth proclaimed in it.[41] However, scholars are divided when it comes to drawing conclusions. Some maintain that Parmenides uses a set of images recognizable by his public in order to bestow more authority upon himself, perhaps in competition—in the area of Magna Graecia—with mystery religions or the teachings of Pythagoras;[42] others argue that he is executing a sophisticated strategy for emotional involvement.[43] But can we be certain that Parmenides (and his audience) was detached enough from the world of mystery religions and initiation rites to appropriate them and propose them again in *metaphorical* terms? Should we not consider the historical context in which his philosophy of Being originates and admit that what he is recounting is an actual *lived* experience?

The problem is that the interpreters who currently advocate for a "literal" reading of the proem (Kingsley and Gemelli Marciano) are also those who deny most vehemently the philosophical quality of Parmenides's poem.[44] There is no discrepancy, they argue, between the tone of the proem and that of the following discourse on Being, since this discourse is meant to lure the bystanders away from a partial knowledge of things and toward the mystical understanding of a reality that should be regarded as a whole, in an experience of death and rebirth that the wise man has incubated and brought to

[40] Cf. Cerri 1995 and 1999, 96–110, Kingsley 1999, 104ff and 272–73, Kingsley 2003, 217ff, 272–73 and 578, and Seaford 2004, 264. I have dealt with this issue elsewhere (Sassi 2006c, 112–13), with further references to the historical context of Elea/Velia.

[41] The perplexity expressed by Granger (2008, 7ff) relates to the vagueness that has been noted in both the geography of the proem and its main (anonymous) characters; we may argue that this vagueness is in line with an account of a visionary, sometimes dreamlike experience.

[42] See, for instance, Blank 1982, 168, 177. Laks (2003, 21) sees Parmenides's enterprise as a "transposition" (a rather attractive category, which he borrows from Gernet; cf. Laks 1998, 280).

[43] See, for instance, Robbiano (2006), who acutely examines (thus preserving the philosophical potential of Parmenides's poem) what she regards as a rhetorical strategy aimed at drawing the public to a learning process that is also an *identification* with Being. Conversely, Morgan (2003, 67–68) argues that the mythological construction of the proem has the (metalinguistic) goal of drawing attention to its own falsehood. Interpretations such as these, though acute, reflect the assumption that Parmenides's world is a world of *logos*, where *muthos* is now reduced to a mere reference from which to depart or to a linguistic tool. No explicit statement by Parmenides authorizes this assumption; this is why I prefer to work from the hypothesis of an *active* contact between Parmenides and his traditional references.

[44] See in particular Kingsley 2003 and Gemelli Marciano 2008.

fruition, and that he intends to reproduce in the listeners through the magic of speech. An implication of this approach is that whatever philosophical meaning has been given to the words of Parmenides is the product of a rationalistic deformation for which the major blame must be assigned to Aristotle, and which has lasted from Aristotle until now.

This reading of Parmenides, which we may call "hyporational," is as unilateral as the "hyperrational" one of scholars who make him the founder of logic, or at least of ontology, completely ignoring the cultural context in which his philosophy was shaped (in general, they do not consider the proem or reduce it to an allegory).[45] It ignores or denies, for instance, not only that the statements about Being do not have the features that we would expect of the mystic view of a divine object but also, more specifically, that the teaching of the goddess is carried out in an argumentative sequence supported by a large use of inferential particles.

This is not the place for a detailed analysis of the long and complex demonstration (frag. 8) of the prerogatives that can be attributed to Being without violating the law of noncontradiction (according to which one cannot say that something both is and is not). Suffice it to say that attributing to Parmenides a certain ability to formulate some principles of reasoning (among which is the law of noncontradiction, which will be theorized by Aristotle) does not imply that because of this he is a full-blown logician. And furthermore, the goddess's insistence on the need to *actively* listen to her claims cannot be underestimated; that is, divine warrant does not mean that statements should not be checked with care. Consider for instance, in frag. 7, the admonishment to resist the superficial testimony of the eyes, of the ears, and of ordinary language, and also to evaluate the correctness of the distinction articulated, polemically, between the different paths of inquiry:

> For never shall this be proved, that things that are not are
> but you, keep your thought away from this route of investigation
> and do not let much-experienced habit force you down onto this road,
> to wield an aimless eye and an echoing ear
> and tongue—but evaluate with the *logos* the much-disputed refutation
> spoken by me.

It is likely that the *logos* on which the listener's judgment must rely is not his personal "reasoning" but rather the actual "speech" of the goddess; in other

---

[45] As an example (a list of names would be endless), see Owen 1960. Curd (2002, 118–19) calls "hyperrational" the anachronistic aim to find in Presocratic thought elements of rationality and method that are only conceivable after the scientific revolution, and defines an approach such as Peter Kingsley's as "hyporational." I would like to attempt a mediation, however difficult, between the two positions.

words, he will have to follow the series of arguments that will be developed (in frag. 8) about immutability, indestructibility, and the eternity of Being. In order to go down this road, in any case, the individual will have to knowingly commit to a learning process, resisting the automatism of sense perception that would set him upon the path of investigation taken by men who "know nothing" in their mixing Being and not-Being (frag. 6).[46] As we can see, Parmenides's general approach is not very different from that of Heraclitus, where the *logos* takes up the traits of an inspired revelation, but grasping the truth in it requires nonetheless one's undivided rational engagement.[47]

Understandably, scholars who are more receptive to the "rational" moments of Parmenides's account argue that the figure of the goddess is his "symbol for the capacity of pure reason for getting at truths,"[48] and that this makes Parmenides the champion of a "demythologizing" process. But if this were the case, would it not have been just as easy and straightforward for him to express himself in prose, leaving in the backdrop (as does Alcmaeon, for instance) the gods and their otherworldly spaces? As I already noted, one loses something by giving up the image of a visionary Parmenides, who is distant from the ways of our rationality but in recompense is more concretely immersed in his own time and space. Let us suppose instead (to get past what seems to be a dead end) that *starting from* a search for a religious truth, and *within* a personal experience of revelation, Parmenides made room for *other* objects of knowledge and rational modalities, which he may have come to know in his native Elea, then a flourishing city and active exchange hub of both goods and ideas capable of keeping alive the tradition of Ionian culture (we will remember that Xenophanes traveled here).

The current evidence does not enable us to describe in more detail this process, which, moreover, cannot be comprehended in terms of (our) categories of rationality versus irrationality. Yet this seems to be the only way to identify as the same person the Parmenides of the proem and the author of an

---

[46] For the interpretation of frag. 7, I follow Lesher 1984, a study which, though widely cited, contains ideas that still need to be appreciated and explored (I am referring in particular to the identification of an effective play on the image of a chariot game, a metaphor of the difficulty of commanding the path of investigation with certainty, and without going off-track). See also Lesher 1999, 238–39 and, for a different reading of frag. 7 (yet complementary in emphasizing the exercise of critical reason required by the goddess), Cordero 1990.

[47] See Curd 2002, 124–25 and 133–35. On Heraclitus, see above, 98ff and 148. Cornford does not hesitate to see in Parmenides a "prophet" of logic, believing that a "metaphysical" thought "at work on the abstract concepts of being and unity" (1952, 117, 118) is quite compatible with inspiration. These considerations are found in a chapter devoted to "The Philosopher As Successor of the Seer-Poet" (107–26), where the emphasis is on the unity of religious and scientific vision in Parmenides, Pythagoras, Empedocles, and Heraclitus (another passage from the same work is cited below, 168).

[48] Granger 2008, 16.

elaborate reflection on Being and its requirements of knowability, whose theoretical importance has been sanctioned in the subsequent developments of philosophical thinking. What is more, this also enables us to situate Parmenides within a broader framework of discourses on knowledge than that of a religious circle; a framework that also includes the Ionian inquiry into nature. In fact, Parmenides's reflections on the characteristics of Being prove to be quite meaningful if read against the Ionian problem of the *archē* of Becoming. He seems to be concerned with formulating the criteria necessary to ascertain what genuinely exists and therefore is a principle of Becoming; and the so-called pluralists, in resorting to a plurality of *archai* that meet the requirements of eternity and immutability (such as Empedocles's "roots," Anaxagoras's "seeds," and Democritus's atoms), will unequivocally end up using the same criteria posited by Parmenides.[49]

According to this construction, Parmenides was rather bold in deciding to divulge his particular truth beyond the esoteric context within which it was revealed to him. His self-presentation as a poet-sage, his use of the "meter of the gods," and his references to the Homeric and Hesiodic tradition, then, may have served to protect the author and his work from being viewed as a somewhat "scandalous" enterprise. Among other things, this perspective would corroborate a recent, enticing reading of the proem by Franco Ferrari, according to which we are indeed dealing here with a descent into the underworld, but the reference to the "road rich in songs" trodden by Parmenides, as well as the details described in the first ten lines of the proem, do not refer to the path that brought him there. Rather, they describe the journey he has made after the revelation, on the truth-*propagating* chariot of poetry.[50]

Between Muses and Other Gods

Empedocles, too, uses poetry as the most effective soundbox for his authorial voice. Having received a rhapsodic education based on listening and memorizing traditional (mostly epic) literature, he molds a vocabulary that is rich in Homeric, and partly Hesiodic, lexemes and yet includes a number of per-

---

[49] We have already mentioned Empedocles in this respect; see above, 130–31. Curd 1998 has emphasized this line of development with a painstaking and convincing analysis, but she ends up suggesting (reductively, in my view) that cosmology and science are Parmenides's only interests.

[50] See Ferrari 2007, 97–114. The idea that the poem was disseminated into the circuits of archaic poetry may be supported by the hypothesis (see D'Alessio 1995) that the Parmenidean image of the chariot of poetry may have influenced Pindar in his sixth *Olympic*, datable to 476–468 BCE; we might surmise that Parmenides's poem was written before Pindar's ode if we accept Apollodorus's chronology, according to which Parmenides reached *akmē* around 500 BCE, as opposed to the one emerging from Plato's *Parmenides* (see above, 80–81), which would suggest a later date.

sonal coinages and unexpected formulae, with highly original effects (the manipulation of formulaic diction indicates that the possibility of memorizing the text now plays a rather secondary role).[51]

Unlike the case of Parmenides, Empedocles's poetic flair was already appreciated in antiquity, as shown by his elevation to didactic poet par excellence and Lucretius's model in *On the Nature of Things*.[52] It is also interesting that Aristotle is clearly intrigued by the peculiar mix of science and poetry found in Empedocles. In fact, in the first pages of *Poetics* (1447b 13–18) he observes that Empedocles has nothing in common with Homer (who is rightly called a poet) except that they both write in verse, and then he tries to set the record straight by defining Empedocles as "*more* of a natural philosopher than a poet" (*phusiologos mallon ē poiētēn*). One should note, however, that Aristotle here is concerned with denying that the type of verse used is an appropriate criterion to distinguish the various forms of poetry (while he thinks that such a criterion should be the kind of *mimesis* employed by an author). This explains why, conversely, in other works Aristotle often mentions Empedocles as an important representative of the art of poetry, e.g., for his use of metaphor, which belongs precisely to the poet's toolkit and not the scientist's (see for instance the comment to the description of the sea as "the earth's sweat" in *Meteorology* II, 3, 357 a 24 = 31 A 25 and B 55 DK).[53] Empedocles is mentioned again in the *Rhetoric* (III, 5, 1407a 32–39) as an instance of a poet who, with ambiguous sentences, elicits from his audience illusionistic effects similar to those produced by soothsayers.[54]

It will not be surprising, at this point, that the initial section of the poem *On Nature* can be reconstructed (as in Diels's arrangement of the fragments) along the lines of traditional didascalic poetry. The apostrophe to the pupil Pausanias (frag. 1) likely occurred at the beginning of the poem, even if not precisely in the first line (since the fragment contains a particle of transition,

---

[51] On Empedocles's language, see at least Gemelli Marciano 1990 and Bordigoni 2004 (in particular 257–63 for the reworking of epic formulae).

[52] On the relationship between Lucretius and Empedocles, cf. Cherniss 1977, 21–23, and Sedley 1998, 2–34.

[53] See also Aristotle, *Poetics* 1457b 13–26 (= 31 B 138, 143, 152). Apart from Aristotle's devaluation of the heuristic power of metaphor, one should note that Empedocles's images, rooted as they are in analogical reasoning, are perfectly tailored to his account of the cosmos; cf. Lloyd 1996, 327–29 and Wright 1998, 20–22.

[54] As noted by Palumbo 2007, 85 in her careful analysis of Aristotle's judgment on Empedocles as poet, this passage bears the echo of the Platonic and Aristotelian condemnation of "deceitful sophistry," but also of the identification of ambiguity as the "register of poetry." If we remember that in the construction of the first book of *Metaphysics*, on the contrary, the linguistic quality of philosophy is clearness (see above, 25–26), it will become even more evident that Empedocles is especially resistant to Aristotle's criteria for defining philosophical thought. Let us also remember that Aristotle, in *Sophist*, frag. 65 Rose, indicates Empedocles as the "inventor" of rhetoric.

dē); in any case, it has a good precedent in Hesiod's dedication to his brother Perses (in *Works and Days*) and in that of Theognis's elegies to Cyrnus. Its traditional flavor leads one to think that in this case, too, as in the others, the mention of a personal relationship between teacher and pupil does not at all exclude the presence of a wider audience (and the same can be said, incidentally, for the dedication of Alcmaeon's writing).[55]

Here we could ask ourselves whether it may be useful to apply the notion of "pseudo-intimacy" minted by Ruth Scodel to explain a problem in archaic Greek lyric in order to understand the modalities of communication in the writing *On Nature*: why do poems that seem to be addressed to a small group of friends survive the death of their author and are even broadly circulated? Poets such as Archilochus and Alcaeus, she argues, are anything but uninterested in audiences different from those present at the first performance of their texts; for these "secondary" audiences, the phrases that refer to the immediate, more intimate occasion nevertheless retain their role of eliciting a sense of pseudo-confidentiality in the listener, who feels as if he or she is part of an elite environment.[56] Moreover, the compositional technique of the rhapsodes already resorted to a direct address to an anonymous interlocutor in order "to make the audience feel like they were physically present before the scene being described."[57] We can surmise that Empedocles's "you" (and, I believe, even the "you" of Parmenides's goddess) similarly aspires to engage other users of the text in other potential times and places, beyond the direct addressee, and to elicit in them a sense of a privileged call.[58] It is clear that this possibility, combined with Empedocles's references to a consolidated poetic tradition (among which is the invocation to the Muse, about which more below), is a decisive factor against those who believe that the *peri phuseōs* was an esoteric writing strictly functional for Pausanias's initiation; on the contrary, this thesis fails to explain how and why the poem enjoyed such precocious and widespread dissemination[59] and was transmitted by the countless citations of ancient authors, so that we did not need to wait for fortunate excavations of tombs (as in the case of the Gold Tablets or the Derveni papyrus) for it to come down to us.[60]

[55] See Obbink 1993, 70–76 and 79n61.

[56] See Scodel 1996, 60.

[57] Cf. Velardi 2004, 208. This usage is attested five times in the *Iliad*.

[58] If not virtually all of humankind; this is precisely how Bollack explains the problematic occurrence of verbal forms in the first person plural (2001, 183–84).

[59] Let us remember that the earliest mention of Empedocles (more fully explored here, 176ff) is contained in chapter 20 of the Hippocratic writing *On Ancient Medicine* (last decades of the fifth century BCE).

[60] The esoteric thesis I refute here (without rejecting *in toto* the idea of Empedocles as a "seer"; see above, 129ff) is already suggested by Kahn 1960 (1974), 431–32 and then put forth by Kingsley 1995, 347–76; Kingsley 2002, 347–48; Kingsley 2003, 322–25; Gemelli Marciano

Moreover, it is plausible that the dedication, or in any case the first section of the poem, was followed by the general lament for the human condition contained in frag. 2. Here, with the pessimistic tones that pervade much archaic Greek lyric, men are represented in a situation of extreme existential precariousness, grappling with a restlessness that prevents them from rising above the grief of the moment and gaining an understanding of "all things."[61] The last few lines of the fragment, however, introduce a moderately optimistic attitude that, as we shall see in a moment, prepares for the enunciation of a learning program. This is the invitation to the pupil, addressed in the second person singular, to remain secluded from the ignorant multitude in order to learn "not beyond the heights reached by mortal intelligence." In the following fragment (whose contiguity with the preceding one is pointed out by Sextus Empiricus, who quotes both) this promise is accompanied by an invocation to the Muse in which the goddess is asked to facilitate a discourse that *does not aim* to bridge the gap between human and divine knowledge, for absolute truth is accessible only to the gods, and those who aspire to obtain it are "fools."[62] Rather, Empedocles wants to suggest to his addressee (and again,

---

2001, 205–207; Gemelli Marciano 2006, 664ff. It is also accepted by Primavesi 2001, 5. In tackling the problem of the circulation of Empedocles's writing, Kingsley 1995, 357, claims that the poem was not necessarily kept secret, since it was already protected by its being incomprehensible to the uninitiated; even so, I fail to see a reason for the text's first *exit* from the initiatic context, not to mention (and this is, after all, Kingsley's premise) that the entire story of its reception becomes the result of an enormous misunder-standing.

[61] See Calzolari 1984 for a reading of frags. 2 and 3 focused on the disparagement of human knowledge that is typical of poetic tradition in the sense that we have tried to convey; also see above, 144–45 (the adjective *ephēmerios* at frag. 3.4 is a key term for this reading). Elsewhere (Sassi 2015) I made the additional point that Empedocles transforms the poetic *topos* of the precariousness of the human condition and its dependence on the gods within the framework of a theory of knowledge where cognitive processes still depend on the impact of external perceptions and events on the body. Humans, however, still have (or are to develop) a steady cognitive ability rooted in the very mixture (*krasis*) of the elements constituting their bodies.

[62] It is unclear to whom Empedocles is alluding here. Diels was the first to surmise that Empedocles is referring to Parmenides, who presents himself as the depositary of an absolute truth communicated to him directly by the goddess, and this conjecture has been reprised with valid arguments by Calzolari 1984. One should certainly consider the objection by Trépanier (2004, 58) that an accusation of *maniē* seems "far too strong for the man to whom Empedocles' thought owed so much"; but I would not exclude the possibility that Empedocles, concerned as he is here with gaining the favor of his listener(s), is trying to remain competitive on the foundations of knowledge, even with a wise man whose influence he profoundly acknowledges in other respects. The other objection by Trépanier, according to whom the genitive plural seems to indicate a plurality of individuals, appears even less convincing if we remember that in any case Parmenides was not the only one to claim a direct relationship with truths revealed to him in ultramundane contexts. It is far more difficult to speculate (as does Trépanier) that Empedocles is alluding to a foolishness *of his own* consisting of some act of ritual transgression.

at line 9, he switches to the second person) the possibility of an intelligent coordination of the indications provided by the apparatus of the senses (frag. 3):

> But, gods, avert from my tongue the madness (*maniēn*) of these,
> and from pious lips draw forth a pure stream.
> And you, much-wooed white-armed maiden Muse,
> I entreat: of those things that it is lawful for creatures of a day
>   (*ephēmerioisin*) to hear,
> send them forth, driving your well-reined chariot from the house of
>   Piety.
> Nor will the flowers of glorious honor force you
> to take them up from mortals on condition of saying more than is holy
> in rashness—and then sit on the summits of wisdom (*sophiē*).
> Come now, observe with all your resources how each thing is clear,
> not holding any sight in greater trust than hearing
> nor noisy hearing above the evidence of the tongue,
> nor withhold trust from any of the other limbs, wherever
> there is a channel for understanding, but grasp each thing in whatever
>   way it is clear.[63]

In frag. 131, too, Empedocles addresses an "immortal" goddess (who is here
named *Kalliōpeia*, the "beautiful-voiced" Muse) in the traditional form of the
rhapsodic hymn, reminding her that she has already intervened alongside
him to help the wretched mortals (*ephēmeriōn*; line 1), and enlisting her help
once more for the "beautiful speech" (*agathon logon*) on the "blessed gods"
that he is about to formulate. This announcement of a religious subject led
Diels to place the fragment in the section dedicated to the other writing, *Katharmoi* (whose contents are hotly debated). Yet the discourse contained in the
"physical" writing, too, as Charles Kahn rightly sensed and as ultimately confirmed by the Strasbourg papyrus, is pervaded by a religious inspiration that
would well justify mention of the gods. Fragment 131, then, may be a reprisal
of the invocation to the Muse in frag. 3, although its position within the poem
is not easy to determine.[64] In both passages, in any case, Empedocles stresses
that he is summoning the Muse as a *mediator* between divine and human
knowledge, but also—we might say—between traditional contents and the
new, unheard-of ones he sets out to propose. The choice to adhere to the po-

---

[63] Cerri 2001 has a fine commentary on frag. 3; see also Cerri 2004. Most 2007, 291–92
makes an interesting connection with the proem of Hesiod's *Theogony*.

[64] Cf. Kahn 1960 (1974), 429–30; Obbink 1993, 59–64 (also for other allusions of
Empedocles to the Muse, e.g., frag. 4); and Trépanier 2004, 57–59 (although the scholar
assumes that Empedocles was the author of a single poem, which I find tempting but unlikely; see above, 129).

etic tradition, in other words, serves not only as a guarantee of truth but also as protection for the author from possible accusations of impiety. Empedocles must have been aware that he was running that risk for, on one hand, his discourse on nature (and the soul) plays a strategic role in his fierce battle against the ritual of animal sacrifice and the communal consumption of the sacrificial victim, which was part and parcel of Greek religious tradition; on the other hand, the framework within which the discourse on nature is developed assigns a supreme (and hence divine) cosmological role not only to the force of Love but also to that of Strife—a negative and certainly unexpected one.[65]

But Empedocles also relies on other guarantees of truth. Let us remember that in frag. 115 he describes himself as an exiled *daimōn* fallen on earth.[66] In citing the passage, Plutarch reports that Empedocles "uttered it as prelude at the beginning of his philosophy" (*On Exile*, 17, 607c), and this seems to indicate that it served as a self-presentation aimed at emphasizing the author's stature as a wise man. But at the beginning of which of the two writings did this fragment appear? Diels places frag. 115 in the *Katharmoi* section; however, once it was agreed that there were demonological elements in the writing *On Nature*, scholars had good grounds for arguing that the fragment in question belonged to the latter work.[67] In this fragment, then, by emulating the same Pythagoras that he so admires for his ability to extend his mind beyond the limits of a single life,[68] Empedocles brings forth his semidivine status as further proof of his vast cosmogonic and zoogonic knowledge, and of the knowledge of magic that is intimately tied to the acquaintance with nature and bestows upon the author-*magos* a power to intervene in the workings of the elements as well as in men's grievances, diseases, and old age (frag. 111).

I am inclined to accept the attribution of the fragment to the writing *On Nature* with the accompanying caveats, given the persisting difficulty of reconstructing the sequence of the contents and even the general structure of the two poems.[69] Fragment 112, which surely belongs to *Purifications*, is a better candidate for serving as a preamble to this writing, being more in keeping

---

[65] The first point has been observed by Wildberg 2001, 55; the second by Broadie 1999, 218.

[66] See above, 130–31.

[67] See Martin-Primavesi 1999, 113–14; Curd 2001, 31; Gemelli Marciano 2001, 223–29; and Gemelli Marciano 2002, 106, 109. By contrast, see Bollack 2001, 175.

[68] In frag. 129, quoted above, 150.

[69] For instance, Primavesi 2001, relying precisely on the esoteric character ascribed to the writing *On Nature*, has insisted on assigning frag. 115 to the cathartic poem on the grounds that it reflects an "exoteric" daimonology; Trépanier 2004, on the other hand, places it at the beginning of the *only* poem written by Empedocles according to his working hypothesis. My argument is intentionally limited to the relationship between the passages that have a justificatory-proemial function.

with its general character and with the conditions of transmission, and it also contrasts with the self-presentation in frag. 115. The book of *Purifications* may have contained, as its title seems to indicate, a description of a series of ritual acts of purification.[70] We can imagine Empedocles reciting this text while setting himself up as an *iatromantis*, a doctor-soothsayer hailed by the crowds for his curing powers. It is likely that the target of this propagandistic operation was broader than in the cases hitherto analyzed, and that it coincided with the entire population of the city to which Empedocles arrived, as an itinerant wise man, to reveal his portentous powers, or even with a Panhellenic gathering; indeed, an ancient witness, Dicaearchus (in Athenaeus, XIV, 620 D = 31 A 12 DK), reports the poem's great success at Olympia, where it was recited by the rhapsode Cleomenes. In fact, frag. 112 represents the best text with which to debut at such occasions:

> O friends who in the great city on the mouth of the blond Akragas
> dwell on top of the citadel, caring for noble deeds,
> respectful havens for strangers, unacquainted with evil,
> I salute you! An immortal god, no longer mortal,
> I come to you honored among all, as is appropriate,
> crowned with ribbons and garlands of flowers.
> And by those to whom I come in the flourishing cities,
> men and women, I am revered; they follow me
> in throngs of thousands, to know the road to gain,
> the ones in need of prophecies, the others for ailments
> of all sorts have asked to hear a healing voice,
> long pierced by harsh pains.

We can imagine the crowds before whom Empedocles declaims his poem while recalling—and reenacting in his performance—his triumphal entry into other cities, where he has already brought his divine and thaumaturgic presence. Some additional doubts have been raised, however, concerning the "friends (*philoi*)" at the beginning of the fragment, a usage not attested before; is this a reference, as it seems, to Empedocles's fellow citizens of Akragas, and not to gods? More important, its function is unclear if Empedocles is using it before an audience in a different city.[71] Starting from this observation, Eva Stehle has proposed an entirely new reading supported by painstaking and convincing arguments, and demonstrated that Empedocles is actually referring to the gods, thus anticipating with the appellation *philoi* his announcement that he has become a god himself after victoriously climbing the ladder of living beings; at the same time, this appellation serves the purpose

---

[70] According to the minimal, yet plausible, hypothesis by Sedley 1998, 4–5.
[71] The possible doubts are summarized by Trépanier 2004, 48–49.

of declaring the author's origins by evoking the deities inhabiting the summit of his native Akragas (the summit is the normal position of temples in Greek cities; we might surmise that Empedocles accompanied his declamation by pointing emphatically to far-off altitudes); furthermore, benevolence toward mortals and protection of exiles are all suitable attributes of the gods.[72]

If we accept this interpretation, the interplay of tradition and innovation emerging from frag. 112 becomes more complex and, if possible, even more interesting. Indeed, if the first few lines contain an apostrophe to the gods, we may recognize in them the typical structure of a rhapsodic invocation. This invocation, however, serves to further showcase the persona of Empedocles who, claiming to have become a god himself, "shifts, before their eyes as it were, from a human along with them who invokes the gods to a god intimate with gods, to whom they can appeal."[73]

At any rate, here, at the intersection of highest contrast between frag. 112 and the contents of frag. 115, is an invitation to place the two texts in two different writings. In frag. 115 Empedocles presents himself as a *daimōn* who has come a long way, almost to the end of his ascent from the lowest forms of life, while in frag. 112 he portrays himself as a full-blown *theos* who has already completed and transcended the cycle of transmigrations, as outlined in frag. 146:

and in the end they are seers, hymn singers and doctors
and come as princes among humans on earth,
and from there they blossom up as gods, highest in honors.

In other words, Empedocles may have considered himself a *daimōn* who, thanks to his *sophia*, attained the status of *theos* at the peak of his career. Based on the argument hitherto developed, it is possible to suggest that the two poems of Empedocles, if not easily distinguishable in terms of contents, are at least different when it comes to the modalities of self-presentation contained in them. Admittedly, in the end we just have reprised an updated and corrected version of the old "biographical" pattern ascribing the difference between the two writings to different times of composition. But at least we have not applied the modern category of conversion from reason to religion; on the contrary, under the premise of a coherent religious view, we have followed the development not of the contents of Empedocles's knowledge but of his authorial persona.

[72] See Stehle 2005. Apart from this hypothesis, the accurate commentary on this fragment by Bollack 2003, 52–57 remains invaluable.

[73] Stehle 2005, 261. On the relationship between the belief in metempsychosis and the claim to have become a god that appears in the first lines of frag. 112, see above, 133ff.

The Specialization of Reason

As Cornford rightly pointed out in his extraordinary *Principium Sapientiae*,[74] in the archaic period the traits of the philosopher emerge through a gradual process of differentiation from the poet on one hand and the soothsayer on the other, starting from an initial figure of seer and purifier incarnated in the prodigious characters of Pherecydes, Epimenides, Abaris, and Aristeas. According to Cornford, this thread extends to wise men such as Pythagoras, Parmenides, and Empedocles (and, in his interpretation, also Heraclitus), who give to their own message the force of a religious faith, thus inaugurating a powerful dogmatic trend in Greek philosophy. In this trend of "philosophic wisdom" Cornford saw a depth that, in his eyes, was absent from strictly naturalistic doctrines (starting with the Ionian cosmologies, which he confined to the mythical sphere).[75] Again, it is worth using Cornford's words to illustrate his intuition:

> The great pre-Socratic thinkers of this type [i.e., divinely inspired] have not, each of them, two distinct versions of the universe—a religious one for Sundays and a scientific one for weekdays. Each has a single, unitary vision, embracing all that he believes about reality, all that he would call wisdom. In the Italian tradition the fundamental impulse is religious and moral, not mere intellectual curiosity which might lead to the acceptance of any type of conclusion about the nature of the world.[76]

During the same time that this framework was taking shape, the problem of the "origins of philosophy" was sparking the interest of Louis Gernet, a scholar with dramatically different training but equal acumen. Gernet also put the emphasis on the notion of metaphysical truth, attainable only through divination and well represented by those seers who, like Epimenides, were also repositories of theological and cosmological knowledge; moreover, he singled out Pythagoras and Empedocles as the heirs of this inspired attitude (which, through them, will eventually reach Plato). Gernet's intuition would later influence Marcel Detienne's book *Masters of Truth*, where poets inspired by the Muse, seers, and "kings of justice" appear as the holders of the effective ex-

---

[74] On which see above, 11. I prefer not to evoke here—as has often been done in the wake of Cornford and Dodds—the category of shamanism, whose application to the historical and cultural context of archaic Greece is interesting theoretically but also rather problematic.

[75] This construction privileges the empiricism of the Hippocratic doctors as a worthy opponent of the wisdom trend.

[76] Cornford 1952, 109. From this passage emerges the fortunate notion of an "Italic philosophy" characterized by a religious inclination, as opposed to an "Ionian philosophy" devoted to empirical inquiry. On the history and limits of this historiographic pattern, see Sassi 1994 and 2011.

pression of a religious truth, and thus as full-fledged protagonists of the "pre-history" of the truth that Parmenides finally discovers as a philosopher.[77]

Detienne's framework hinges on a close tie between the Greek noun for truth, *alētheia*, and the role of memory; in the unsteadiness of a world that is essentially still oral, truth, Detienne argues, is the content that the soothsay-er's words rescue from the oblivion (*lēthē*) into which it constantly risks fall-ing. In insisting on this point, the scholar takes a stance against the Heideg-gerian interpretation of *alētheia* as *Unverborgenheit* ("unconcealment"), where the privative *a*- is applied to the root **leth* of the verb *lanthanō*, which means "to conceal" and, in middle voice, "to hide oneself" or "to escape." This most influential interpretation, which makes truth a quality of being rather than of theories about its nature, notoriously goes along with the idea that Plato and Aristotle inaugurate a transition to a conception of truth as correspondence (i.e., correctness of the assertions *about* beings), and thus a manipulation of Being that belongs to *technē* rather than to "true" philosophy. Against this view, Detienne rightly claims back for archaic Greek culture the problemati-zation of truth as an attribute of *the discourse* on reality.[78] However, he be-lieves that said culture resists a rational distinction of what is true and what is false and is, instead, governed by a "logic of ambiguity" that can only be neutralized by a divinely inspired discourse. If religious truth finally becomes a "rational notion" with Parmenides, who starts "the imperious demand for noncontradiction," this happens thanks to the "secular" opposition between two theses and two parties, which, in parallel, becomes part and parcel of the decision-making processes in the polis.[79]

In this axiomatic and rather brief conclusion, Detienne overlooks the fact that Parmenides's arguments are developed precisely *within* a religious con-ception of truth.[80] In fact, his entire framework suffers from a reductive op-position between religion and rationality; not only does it leave out authors such as Hecataeus, Alcmaeon, or Xenophanes, who before Parmenides re-flected on the problem of knowledge without any concern about revelation; it also neglects the archaic poets' interest for the rational organization of their discourse, which is revealed in their negotiating with the Muse(s).[81] We may

---

[77] See Gernet 1945. Detienne 1967 cites many of Gernet's studies, but the debt is more clearly acknowledged in Detienne (1994, 8–9).

[78] The criticism toward Heidegger is explicit in Detienne (1994, 20–22).

[79] See Detienne 1996 [1967], 136 (with a reference to Jean-Pierre Vernant).

[80] A brevity also questioned by Caveing (1969, 95–97), although within a positive as-sessment of Detienne's general construction. Caveing emphasizes the need to consider other intellectual venues (for instance, mathematics, with its development of techniques of demonstration) to explain the "need for reason" that emerged with Parmenides. Admit-tedly, according to Detienne (1996 [1967], 130) Parmenides's attitude as a soothsayer is the result of a *mise en scène*.

[81] A fundamental study by Cole (1983) has shown that archaic Greek poetry attests both the sense of a "remembered" truth (the only one found in Homer) and that of a truth

now turn back to Gernet and observe that he, unlike Detienne (or Cornford), did not emphasize unilaterally the importance of the "transpositions of a mystical past onto philosophy proper" that he diagnosed in Pythagoras, Parmenides, or Empedocles,[82] and he was well aware that he was focusing on just one aspect of a much broader and more complex problem.[83] After everything we have said thus far, we may well agree on this point, and try to reformulate it by stating that the *cohabitation* (sometimes even in the same author; consider Parmenides and Empedocles) of study of nature and eschatology, religiosity and empiricism is a characteristic trait of the philosophy "of the beginnings," even if it does not define it as a homogeneous whole.

The most accurate depiction of this situation has been ultimately given by Jean-Pierre Vernant, who reflected on it in the wake of both Cornford and Gernet. According to Vernant, the terrain of the earliest phases of Greek thought is not a field of clear opposition between rationality and reflective intelligence on one hand, religion and mysticism on the other. Instead it should be regarded as a "field of multiple rationalities," of intellectual processes that vary depending on the author or the subject under investigation but are nonetheless recognizable as such.[84] Let us add, *in limine*, that Empedocles somehow represents the culmination, but also the point of nonreturn, of this complexity. Indeed, if we consider the panorama of Greek culture in the last decades of the fifth century, what is more striking to us is the very disappearance of the figure of the inspired wise man,[85] which goes hand in hand with the separation of natural inquiry and eschatology.[86] At the same time, not by chance, another aspect that until now had accompanied the presentation of knowledge starts to disappear, namely, that search for the expressive register best suited to a certain context, whose outcomes were as diverse as the "judi-

---

that "does not escape." In any case (and this is the crucial point) one can detect in this literature several allusions both to a subjective dimension of knowledge (*contra* Heidegger) and to a rational organization of the authorial discourse (*contra* Detienne).

[82] Gernet 1945, 350. I suspect that Gernet was tacitly borrowing from Diès 1913, who introduced it for Plato, the fortunate idea of a "transposition" of notions from mysticism to philosophy (see above, 125n36). The absence of a direct reference on Gernet's part is understandable—as Riccardo Di Donato has pointed out to me—in a work lacking a bibliographical apparatus, written by Gernet in the isolation of his Algerian period (1921–48).

[83] See ibid., 359.

[84] See Vernant 1996, 207–8. Gernet's influence on Vernant need not be demonstrated, but cf. at least Sassi 2007, 194n7. For the critical attention of Vernant to Cornford's work, see above, 15n36 and 48n26 and Sassi 2007, 202ff.

[85] The Derveni author does not belong to this category, since he presents his doctrines as the outcome of his exegesis of the theogonic poem attributed to Orpheus. On the contrary, Empedocles, as Betegh 2001, 67 put it, "is not the *exēgetēs* of the divine poet; he himself is the divine poet."

[86] The two paths will unite again in Plato's *Timaeus*, that is, exactly where the cosmological and eschatological aspects of the soul converge (see above, 137).

cial" style of Anaximander's prose, Xenophanes's rhapsodic compositions, Heraclitus's oracular language, and the religious solemnity of Parmenides's and Empedocles's hexameters. We may trace these developments (following Vernant and Lloyd's "paradigm")[87] to the publicization and secularization of decision-making taking place in the Greek cities (especially in cases of full-blown democracy, as at Athens, which, not coincidentally, stands out in this period as the center of Greek cultural production). But here I prefer to refrain from searching for an exhaustive explanation and stop at a descriptive level, trying to trace an outline of some important changes in the modalities of writing and authorial self-presentation that take place in this period and signal the emergence of a new (and more standardized) style of rationality.

The most evident symptom of the transformation that took place in the last decades of the fifth century BCE, then, is the establishment of prose as the main expressive medium for a discourse that aims to draw attention to its internal reasons, without relying on the external sources of authority invoked in the poetical tradition. This is not only true of philosophy; we should not forget that the first extended prose narrative of Greek literature is Herodotus's *Histories*, whose composition began around 450 BCE and stretched over thirty years.[88] At any rate, prose is chosen by Zeno and Melissus, who insist, albeit in different ways, on the ontological aspect of Parmenides's thought and consistently work on a kind of argumentative writing. A prose that tends to be rich in elaborate syntactical structures in unison with a linguistic inquiry that prefers precision over metaphors and evocative expressions is again chosen, for instance, by the Pythagoreans Philolaus and Archytas (a contemporary and friend of Plato), Anaxagoras, and Diogenes of Apollonia, Leucippus and Democritus.[89]

A new awareness of the advantages of a clear and structured organization of contents transpires from the incipit of the writing of Diogenes of Apollonia:

> I believe (*dokei moi*) that at the beginning of every speech (*logou*) one should provide an indisputable point of departure, and that the expression should be simple and solemn.

This declaration of clarity is in (likely premeditated) contrast with the allusive patina overlaying the proems of authors such as Heraclitus, Parmenides, or Empedocles who, conversely, aim to create an enigmatic and suspenseful

[87] See above, 65ff.

[88] On the play of distance and detachment from the poetical tradition, concerning both form and contents, put in place by Herodotus, see Marincola 2006.

[89] On the qualities of prose, see above, 82ff. For a careful analysis of the style of the authors mentioned above, cf. Schick 1955b, 123–35; Schick 1955–56; and Nieddu 1993. It should be noted that Anaxagoras and Diogenes still offer solemn overtones in their descriptions of the *archē*, which is a sign of a persistent attention to the effects of an oral teaching.

atmosphere.[90] This can be explained by the different nature of their audience; whereas their predecessors strived to elicit curiosity and eagerness for new contents among listeners accustomed to traditional poetry, Diogenes of Apollonia has before him, in the literate environment of Athens, an audience that is predisposed to learn about his particular opinions on nature during an articulate and clear lesson, in spite of its solemn character, which underscores the importance of the subject. It is also remarkable that Diogenes announces his intentions in the first person, without referring to a special investiture of authority. It is due to the same attitude that his fragments (as well as those of Anaxagoras) do not feature a direct polemic against rival figures; an attitude of dogmatic confidence of an author who relies exclusively on the strength of his own reasoning.

It should be noted that entrusting a sequence of arguments to a written text does not prevent its being read out loud later, partially or in its entirety. In this period, the oral dimension of performance has certainly not disappeared; on the contrary, it acquires new vitality and competitive strength. At least in that "marketplace of ideas" that is Athens (whose situation is in any case better documented than for other Greek cities), the growing production of written texts goes along with the habit of reading in large public spaces; significantly, this practice is called *epideixis*, a term that emphasizes the aspect of "displaying" or "exhibiting" (which, in fact, coincides with "publishing") the argumentative skills implemented in the texts.[91]

This climate is marked by the advent of the Sophists, who emerge as professional teachers of rhetorical techniques to be used as powerful tools in the political and cultural debate. This also explains other developments of the communication modes of philosophical and scientific knowledge. Consider the Hippocratic doctors, representatives of a discipline pervaded by a strong professional awareness, who often say "I" (in no less decisive tones than Diogenes of Apollonia) when introducing a personal opinion or a new theory on health and disease that they discovered on their own. To give but one example, in the writing *On Ancient Medicine* the suggestion (presented as profoundly innovative) of an extremely individualized approach to the patient and to the search of the best remedy is enforced through constantly resorting to the pronoun *egō* (thirty times) and, in general, to verb forms in the first person (another twenty). Herodotus uses the first person 1,087 times, which is the sign of a similar attitude. It is especially remarkable that, both in the Hippocratic writings and in Herodotus's *Histories*, a more aggressive authorial presence is

---

[90] Cf. Mansfeld 1995, Gemelli Marciano 2002, 86–88, and Gemelli Marciano 2007a, 29–33. Corradi 2007 interestingly suggests that Protagoras's fragment on man-as-measure may have also been placed at the beginning of the author's writing (a suggestion that invites to see in this text, too, the programmed rejection of divinely inspired knowledge).

[91] See Thomas 2003.

accompanied by a growing focus on methodological questions, such as the role of empirical observation and the evaluation of symptoms/testimonies as proof of an argument.[92] In short, we can see arising from this complex of factors a new image of knowledge and of its source (the internal *ratio* of the discourse). While this image pervades the most disparate areas of knowledge, authors are free to make personal use of it, by resorting to *their own* reflections within *their own* field.

A less continuous but no less important development takes place in the second half of the fifth century BCE. For a certain period the division between the various areas of wisdom remains rather blurry, with the resulting intersection of subjects and expressive media that we observed already in the first phase of the archaic period.[93] A case in point is offered by a work as difficult to classify as that of Empedocles (whose death must be dated around 435 BCE), but there are more. Consider, for instance, Ion of Chios, born between 490 and 480 BCE, who traveled through the Greek world, including Athens (Chios fell under Athenian hegemony), from about 465 to 430 BCE. He is an author of tragedies and sympotic poems, as well as prose writings of local history and mythography, biography and philosophy; his work, in other words, illustrates his versatility, and it may well be that the categorization by genre that prevailed in the last decades of the fifth century did not help its reception.[94] Another author active in the second half of the fifth century is Oenopides, also from Chios, an astronomer and mathematician who also tackles such issues as the cosmic principles[95] and the floods of the Nile, connecting the latter to temperatures of the subterranean waters in the region over the seasons (41 A 11 DK).[96]

The phenomenon of the Nile's summer floods was particularly apt to spark the interest of the ancients, especially those who aspired to "stand out for their wisdom" about it. Those are the words of Herodotus, who devotes a long section to this specific theme in the second book of the *Histories*, dedicated to Egypt (ll. 19–27). Here he reports three different hypotheses concerning the phenomenon; he does not mention any names (line 20), but other ancient sources allow us to ascribe the various solutions to such diverse authors as Thales, Hecataeus, Euthymenes of Marseille (a sailor and geographer),

---

[92] Cf. Thomas 1996, Thomas 2000, 235–48, and Luraghi 2006 for Herodotus; van der Eijk 1997, Roselli 2006 for the Hippocratic writers. Obviously, and conversely, this "personalistic" style is in opposition to Aristotle's deliberately impersonal one; see van der Eijk 1997, 115–19.

[93] See above, 29ff.

[94] See Jennings and Katsaros 2007.

[95] Sextus Empiricus (*Outlines of Pyrrhonism*, III, 30 = 41 A 5 DK) ascribes to Oenopis an identification of the *archai* of fire and air that is also reported as an anonymous *doxa* by Lucretius, I, 713.

[96] On the complicated tradition of this *doxa*, see Gemelli Marciano 1993. For a systematic study of the testimonies, see Bodnár 2007.

and Anaxagoras (whose opinion will be reprised by Democritus, 59 A 42, 5; 59 A 91 and 68 A 99 DK). And Herodotus does not fail to give his own explanation where, in singling out the role of evaporation by the sun, he comes close to a *doxa* attributed to Diogenes of Apollonia (64 A 18 DK). In sum, what we have here is a context where the same themes can spark the interest of geographers, historians, doctors, and natural philosophers alike, and which does not happily allow itself to be left at the outskirts of the conventional distinctions between disciplines.[97]

Such a distinction, however, begins to take hold during the last decades of the fifth century, within the framework of cultural transformation that I have been describing. In this phase, when ideas circulate more freely and book production intensifies, the ideal of a total "wisdom," preferably condensed in a single writing, begins to lose ground before the diversified demands of a wider, learned public. This backdrop also explains why Democritus (alone among the Presocratics) authored several writings, each with a specialty (cosmological as well as ethical, mathematical, "musical," and technical).[98] More generally, against this backdrop the different literary genres are finally defined according to specific thematic areas and the language and methods most suitable to them.

To give a notable example, we owe the definition of the field of historiography to Herodotus, who is rightly indicated as its father. For, at the beginning of the *Histories*, he clearly illustrates the goal he has set for his "inquiry" (*historiē*), prompted by the need to prevent time from erasing the memory of human events and the glorious deeds of Greeks and barbarians, as well as to pinpoint the causes of the conflict (the Persian Wars) that brought them against each other. To salvage the memory of a glorious past by writing a work that stems from factual investigation and a great attention to the causes of events; these words bespeak the author's desire to distinguish his own methods and agenda from those of the poets, who shared the same aspiration to preserve cultural memory.

Admittedly, the term *historiē* in Herodotus still retains the meaning, characteristic of Ionian culture, of a generic "intellectual activity" (only in the

---

[97] See Thomas 2000, 136ff and Thomas 2006. There are other instances of "transversality": the long description of the vascular system by Diogenes of Apollonia (reported by Aristotle), whose importance has been pointed out by Lloyd (2006); the presence of zoological terms in both Democritus and medical literature (see Perilli 2007b); the mostly underestimated interest for the study of nature in some Sophists (see Bonazzi 2006 and above, 29–30, for a mention of Antiphon); and the other cases considered by Cambiano 1997. Perhaps most notable, and of broader importance, is that until the end of the fifth century the reflection on causality passes through historiographical and (even more decisively) medical thought before being reverberated onto fourth-century philosophy; see Vegetti 1999 and Jouanna 2005.

[98] See Leszl 2007, 13–14.

fourth century will it start to designate what we now call "history"). This is, for instance, the meaning of the term in frag. 129 of Heraclitus, who criticizes Pythagoras for having carried out a broad yet superficial "inquiry" (*historiē*, here used in a derogatory sense) in the name of an alleged wisdom.[99] It is noteworthy that in another fragment (B 35 DK) Heraclitus deplored, with similarly polemical tones, those "lovers of knowledge" (*philosophous andras*) who think they need to "know many things" (to be *histores*); and here not only the term *histōr* but also *philosophos* (in its first attestation in Greek literature)[100] recur with a generic meaning, which indicates that we are still far from any definition of *historia* or *philosophia* as specific areas of knowledge. It is therefore remarkable that Herodotus so lucidly indicates both the *object* and *objectives* of his particular intellectual activity to distinguish it from the others, thus laying the foundations for the specialized sense that *historia* will acquire shortly thereafter.[101]

In the long run the definition of philosophy, too, will be facilitated, like history in Herodotus, by a need to differentiate the various intellectual roles in the cultural arena. If, however, we were to search already at the end of the fifth century for a narrowing of the notion of *philosophia* in terms of its own object and objectives, we would be disappointed. As we know, we will have to wait for Plato for a reflection on those terms, one that is even more explicit because it serves to discredit the educational value of rhetoric (championed by the Sophists and Isocrates).[102] Before the turn of the century, however, some hints of a definition of the field of philosophy arrive *from outside*, from an author who presents us with one of the earliest attestations of the term *philosophia* in relation to a particular kind of inquiry—the study of nature— as he sets out to distance himself from it.

Such is the case, not by chance, of the author of the Hippocratic writing *On Ancient Medicine*, who, as I have mentioned, is remarkable for the way he exhibits the authorial awareness that is widespread among Hippocratic

[99] For Heraclitus's polemic against *polumathiē*, see above, 149–50.

[100] The anecdote according to which Pythagoras minted the term *philosophia* (Aëtius, I, 3, 8 = 58 B 15 DK) should not be trusted, as it is the fruit of that same retrospective projection of an ideal of speculative life onto exemplary figures of the Preplatonic period that we observed above, 4–5. For the retrospective ascription to Pythagoras of a memorable pairing of philosophical activity and the disinterested contemplation of a religious celebration (*theōria*), see also Sassi 1991; Nightingale 2004, 17–22.

[101] Herodotus's self-image as a historian has been explored in Marincola 2006, Fowler 2006 and Luraghi 2006. Bouvier (1997, 49ff) notes, however, that Herodotus and Thucydides (and Xenophon) seem to work "on their own," without sharing a *common* mission to earn history the status of a recognized discipline; this is also why *historia* takes a long time to mean history "proper" (and it is remarkable that the term never occurs in Thucydides). The process of self-recognition of philosophy, at any rate, will take place later.

[102] For an interesting sociological analysis of the competition for *paideia* in Plato and the Sophists, see Böhme 1986.

writers.[103] In the name of framing an approach as focused as possible on the physical constitution of the patient, our author starts with a polemic against those who scale down the etiological framework of diseases into generic "postulates" (*hupotheseis*) such as hot or cold, wet or dry. These postulates are legitimate (yet unverifiable) whenever one tries to explain "invisible" things like those taking place in the sky or under the earth, but they do not mean anything if applied to a reality, such as the human body, that can be observed (and the art of medicine is, in fact, based on observation). This first chapter attacks a study of nature that aims to encompass human physiology, and it is possible to identify a more precise polemical target in Empedocles, whose medical doctrines hinged upon reducing the human body to a combination of the four cosmic elements, somehow connected to the four qualities mentioned above. This framework also underlies an important tradition of medical thought that developed in southern Italy (with Philistion of Lokris, for example). In any case, Empedocles is singled out later in the text (chapter 20) as one of those doctors and wise men who claim to base their therapeutic approach on a general knowledge of the nature of man—understood as a knowledge of the compositional process by which man has come to be, within a cosmological framework. It is precisely here that the term *philosophia* appears with the function of stigmatizing the abstract character of natural inquiry and contrasting it with medicine, which, being based on experience and a long practice, is well worthy of establishing its dominion over all that concerns human nature:

> Certain doctors and sophists [or "experts"; *sophistai*], say that it is impossible to know what medicine is for anyone who does not know what a man is, and that this is what whoever wants to treat patients correctly must learn thoroughly. But the discourse of those, like Empedocles and others who have written about nature [saying] what a human being is since the beginning, how he originally came to be and of what he was made, well, their discourse ends up in *philosophia*. But I think, first, that all that has been said or written about nature by one of these doctors or sophists pertains to the art of medicine less than it does to painting [or, writing]. I also hold that clear knowledge about nature (*peri phuseōs gnōnai ti saphes*) comes from no other field than medicine.

Here *philosophia* denotes a trend that stands out in the general field of *historia*, thanks to a particular object (nature) and a specific method (the hypo-

---

[103] For an assessment of this attestation of the term *philosophia*, as well as other more or less contemporary ones, see Laks 2001c, 2005a, 2005b, and 2006, 55–81. Laks's acute observations on this delicate transition phase contradict Nightingale's thesis (1995ff) that the birth of philosophy is an artificial construct that we essentially owe to Plato.

thetical one; but we may see in it the reasoning by conjecture that we have emphasized time and again in this book). We should not be be surprised that, for the author of *On Ancient Medicine*, the best representative of this kind of inquiry is Empedocles himself, for whom the interest in the physical nature of the cosmos is inseparable from the problem of saving the soul. The author's polemic is selective, but the selection is not random; the doctor is isolating in the work of Empedocles what he perceives to be the most competitive element on the arena in which his own discipline clashes with *philosophia* for the monopoly on the knowledge of human nature—at the same time one wonders if Empedocles is chosen as a target also for his profession of healer.[104]

With a retrospective glance that prolongs and complicates that of the Hippocratic writer, Plato, in his *Phaedo* (96a), will call *peri phuseōs historia* the important research trend that once attracted a young Socrates (it must be noted that Socrates employs this expression as if it is well in use in his time).[105] And again Aristotle will regard *phusiologia* as the most important component of the thought before Socrates (namely, before the "ethic turn" of philosophy), so as to place his own inquiry on nature in continuity with it.[106] Yet again, that selective construction will not be unjustified. And in conclusion, the fact that the legacy of Presocratic thought has come down to us in an abridged and simplified form, due to the mediation imposed upon it by a world of specialized reason, should not prevent us from appreciating the indications that seeped in through that world, nor from glimpsing behind it an age during which the rationalities were "multiple."

---

[104] I am reprising this image from Pellegrin 2006, 664 (see 664–69 on the "theoretical reputation" of Hippocratic medicine, seen as the "natural enemy" of philosophy in this period). The references to the "study of nature" in *On Ancient Medicine* have been analyzed closely by Vegetti 1998, Heinemann 2000, and Schiefsky 2005b. For a detailed commentary of chapter 20, see Schiefsky (ed.) 2005a, 298ff.

[105] See above, 174–75.

[106] This point has been acutely developed by Leszl 2006.

BIBLIOGRAPHY

Ackerman, R. 1991. *The Myth and Ritual School: J. G. Frazer and the Cambridge Ritualists*. New York: Garland.

Adomenas, M. 1999. "Heraclitus on Religion." *Phronesis* 44: 87–113.

———. 2006. "Plato, Presocratics, and the Question of Intellectual Genre." In Sassi 2006b, 329–53.

Algra, K. 1999. "The Beginnings of Cosmology." In Long 1999b, 45–65.

Allan, W. 2006. "Divine Justice and Cosmic Order in Early Greek Epic." *Journal of Hellenic Studies* 126: 1–35.

Althoff, J., ed. 2007. *"Philosophie und Dichtung im antiken Griechenland: Festschrift für Wolfgang Kullmann." Akten der 7. Tagung der Karl und Gertrud Abel-Stiftung am 10 und 11 Oktober 2002 in Bernkastel-Kues*. Philosophie der Antike Band 23. Stuttgart: Franz Steiner.

Arrighetti, G. 2001. "Fra purificazione e produzione letteraria: La 'Teogonia' di Epimenide." In Gigante et al. 2001, 217–25.

———. 2006. *Poesia, poetiche e storia nella riflessione dei Greci*. Pisa: Giardini.

Arrighetti, G., et al. 1982. *"Aspetti di Hermann Usener filologo della religione." Seminario della Scuola Normale Superiore di Pisa, 17–20 febbraio 1982 (con premesse per una discussione di Arnaldo Momigliano)*. Pisa: Giardini.

Arrighetti, G., and F. Montanari, eds. 1993. *"La componente autobiografica nella poesia greca e latina fra realtà e artificio letterario." Atti del Convegno, Pisa, 16–17 maggio 1991*. Pisa: Giardini.

Arrighetti, G., and M. Tulli, eds. 2000. *"Letteratura e riflessione sulla letteratura nella cultura classica." Atti del Convegno, Pisa, 7–9 giugno 1999*. Pisa: Giardini.

Asper, M. 2001. "‹Stoicheia› und Gesetze: Spekulationen zur Entstehung mathematischer Textformen in Griechenland." In *Antike Naturwissenschaft und ihre Rezeption* XI, edited by J. Althoff, B. Herzhoff, and G. Wöhrle, 73–106. Trier: Wissenschaftlicher Verlag Trier.

———. 2004. "Law and Logic: Towards an Archaeology of Greek Abstract Reason." *AION: Annali dell'Università degli Studi di Napoli "L'Orientale," Dipartimento di Studi del Mondo Classico e del Mediterraneo Antico. Sezione filologico-letteraria* 26: 73–94.

———. 2007. "Medienwechsel und kultureller Kontext: Die Entstehung der griechischen Sachprosa." In Althoff 2007, 67–102.

Assmann, J. 1992. *Das kulturelle Gedächtnis. Schrift, Erinnerung und politische Identität in frühen Hochkulturen*. Munich: Beck. Translated by the author as *Cultural Memory and Early Civilization: Writing, Remembrance, and Political Imagination*. New York: Cambridge University Press, 2011.

Atherton, C., ed. 1998. *Form and Content in Didactic Poetry*. Bari: Levante.

Averincev, S. S. 1971–73. *Atene e Gerusalemme: Contrapposizione e incontro di due principi creativi*. Translated by R. Belletti. Rome: Donzelli.

Balaudé, J.-F. 2006. "Hippias le passeur." In Sassi 2006b, 287–304.

Barnes, J. 1979. *The Presocratic Philosophers*. Vol. 2, *Empedocles to Democritus*. London: Routledge & Kegan Paul.

Baumgarten, R. 1998. *Heiliges Wort und Heilige Schrift bei den Griechen: Hieroi Logoi und verwandte Eischeinungen*. Tübingen: Gunter Narr.

Beall, E. F. 1993. "Hegel and the Milesian 'Origin of Philosophy.'" *Classical and Modern Literature* 13: 241–56.

Beard, M. 2000. *The Invention of Jane Harrison.* Cambridge, MA: Harvard University Press.

Beare, J. I. 1906. *Greek Theories of Elementary Cognition from Alcmaeon to Aristotle.* Oxford: Clarendon Press.

Bernabé, A. 2001. "La 'Teogonia' di Epimenide." In Gigante et al. 2001, 195–225.

——. 2002. "Orphisme et Présocratiques: Bilan et perspectives d'un dialogue complexe." In Laks-Louguet 2002, 205–47.

——. 2004 and 2005. *Poetae Epici Graeci. Testimonia et fragmenta. Pars 2, Orphicorum et Orphicis similium fragmenta.* Edidit Albertus Bernabé. Fasciculus 1, Monachii et Lipsiae: Saur 2004. Fasciculus 2, Monachii et Lipsiae: Saur 2005.

——. 2007. "L'âme après la mort: Modèles orphiques et transposition platonicienne." *Études platoniciennes* (4, *Les puissances de l' âme selon Platon*): 25–44.

Bertelli, L. 2007. *"Nomos, scrittura e identità civica."* In *Unità e disunione dalla polis*, edited by Gennaro Carillo, 23–65. Naples: Sellino.

Berti, E. 1997. *La filosofia del "primo" Aristotele.* Milan: Vita e Pensiero. First published 1962 by CEDAM.

Beta, S., ed.. 2006. *"I poeti credevano nelle loro Muse?" Atti della giornata di studio, Siena, 2 aprile 2003.* Fiesole: Edizioni Cadmo.

Betegh, G. 2001. "Empédocle, Orphée et le papyrus de Derveni." In Morel-Pradeau 2001, 45–70.

——. 2004. *The Derveni Papyrus. Cosmology, Theology and Interpretation.* Cambridge: Cambridge University Press.

——. 2006a. "Eschatology and Cosmology: Models and Problems." In Sassi 2006b, 27–50.

——. 2006b. "Greek Philosophy and Religion." In Gill-Pellegrin 2006, 625–39.

——. 2007. "On the Physical Aspect of Heraclitus' Psychology." *Phronesis* 52: 3–32.

Blank, D. L. 1982. "Faith and Persuasion in Parmenides." *Classical Antiquity* 1: 167–77.

Blumenberg, H. 1987. *Das Lachen der Thrakerin: Eine Urgeschichte der Theorie.* Frankfurt am Main: Suhrkamp. Translated by S. Hawkins as *The Laughter of the Thracian Woman: A Protohistory of Theory.* New York: Bloomsbury Academic, 2015.

Bodei, R. 1982. "Hermann Usener nella filosofia moderna: tra Dilthey e Cassirer." In Arrighetti et al. 1982, 23–42.

Bodnár, I. M. 2007. *Oenopides of Chius: A Survey of the Modern Literature with a Collection of the Ancient Testimonia.* Preprint 327 of the Max Planck Institut für Wissenschaftsgeschichte, Berlin. Accessible at http://www.mpiwg-berlin.mpg.de/Preprints /P327.PDF.

Böhme, G. 1986. "Demarcation As a Strategy of Exclusion: Philosophers and Sophists." In *The Knowledge Society. The Growing Impact of Scientific Knowledge on Social Relations*, 57–66, edited by G. Böhme and N. Stehr. Dordrecht: Reidel.

Bollack, J. 1965–69. *Empédocle. Les Origines. Introduction, édition et commentaire du poème de la nature.* 4 vols. Paris: Les Éditions de Minuit.

——. 1997. *La Grèce de personne: Les mots sous le mythe.* Paris: Éditions du Seuil, Paris.

——. 2001. "'Voir la Haine.' Sur les nouveaux fragments d'Empédocle." *Methodos* 1: 173–85.

——. 2003. *Empédocle: 'Les purifications'; Un projet de paix universelle.* Edited and translated by J. Bollack. Paris: Éditions du Seuil.

Bolton, J. D. P. 1962. *Aristeas of Proconnesus.* Oxford: Clarendon Press.

Bonanate, U. 1974. "I filologi dell'inquietante." *Rivista di Filosofia* 65: 272–308.

Bonazzi M. 2006. "La realtà, la legge e la concordia secondo Antifonte." *Quaderni di storia* 64: 117–39.

Bordigoni, C. 2004. "Empedocle e la dizione omerica." In Rossetti-Santaniello 2004, 199–289.

Borsche, T. 1985. *"Nietzsches Erfindung der Vorsokratiker."* In *Nietzsche und die philosophische Tradition*, vol. 1, edited by J. Simon, 62–87. Würzburg: Königshausen und Neumann.

Boss, Gilbert (ed). 1981. *Métaphysique, histoire de la philosophie: Recueil d'études offert à Fernand Brunner*. 1981. Neuchâtel: À la Baconnière.

Bottéro, J. 1996. "Religiosité et raison en Mésopotamie." In J. Bottéro, C. Herrenschmidt, and J.-P. Vernant 1996, 17–91.

Bottéro, J., C. Herrenschmidt, and J.-P. Vernant. 1996. *L'Orient ancien et nous: L'écriture, la raison, les dieux*. Paris: Albin Michel. Reprinted 1998 by Hachette.

Bottéro, J., and S. N. Kramer. 1989. *Lorsque les dieux faisaient l'homme: Mythologie mésopotamienne*. Paris: Gallimard.

Boudouris, K. J., ed. 1989. *Ionian Philosophy*. Athens: International Association for Greek Philosophy and International Center for Greek Philosophy and Culture.

Bouvier, D. 1997. *"Mythe ou histoire: Le choix de Platon; Réflexions sur les relations entre historiens et philosophes dans l'Athènes classique." Atti del Convegno del Pôle Alpin de Recherches sur les Sociétés Anciennes*. In *Filosofia, storia, immaginario mitologico*, edited by M. Guglielmo and G. F. Gianotti, 41–64. Alessandria: Edizioni dell'Orso.

Brancacci, A. 2002. *"La notion de Présocratique (Introduction, I)."* In *Platon source des Présocratiques: Exploration*, edited by Monique Dixsaut and Aldo Brancacci, 7–12. Paris: Vrin.

Brancacci, A., and P.-M. Morel, eds. 2007. *Democritus: Science, the Arts, and the Care of the Soul. Proceedings of the International Colloquium on Democritus, Paris, 18–20 September 2003*. Leiden: Brill.

Bravo, B. 2002. "D'Homère à Callimaque: Transformation de la fonction des intellectuels dans la Cité qui se transforme." In Wessely 2002, 19–30.

———. 2001. "Un frammento della Piccola Iliade (P.Oxy 2510), lo stile narrativo tardo-arcaico, i racconti su Achille immortale." *Quaderni Urbinati di Cultura Classica* 96 (n.s. 67): 49–114.

———. 2007. "Testi iniziatici da Olbia Pontica (VI e V sec. a.C.) e osservazioni su Orfismo e religione civica." *Palamedes. A Journal of Ancient History* 2: 55–92.

Breglia Pulci Doria, L. 2001. "Osservazioni sulla Teogonia di Epimenide." In Gigante et al. 2001, 279–311.

Bréhier, É. 1913. "Une nouvelle théorie sur les origines de la philosophie grecque." *Revue de Synthèse Historique* 27: 120–30. Reprinted in Bréhier, *Études de philosophie antique*, 33–43. Paris: Presses Universitaires de France, 1955. Reprinted in *Storiografia* I (1997): 311–17, with a foreword by M. M. Sassi.

Bremmer, J. 1983. *The Early Greek Concept of the Soul*. Princeton, NJ: Princeton University Press.

Bresson, A. 2005. *"Les cités grecques et leurs inscriptions."* In *L'écriture publique du pouvoir*, edited by A. Bresson, A.-M. Cocula, and C. Pébarthe, 153–68. Paris: De Boccard.

Brillante, C. 2006. "Le Muse tra verità, menzogna e finzione." In Beta 2006, 27–58.

Brisson, L. 1982. *Platon: les mots et les mythes*. Paris: Maspero.

———. 1990. "Mythes, écriture et philosophie." In Mattéi 1990, 49–58.

———. 1996. *Introduction à la philosophie du mythe*. Vol. 1, *Sauver les mythes*. Paris: Vrin.

Broadie, S. 1999. "Rational Theology." In Long 1999b, 205–25.

Bryan, J. 2012. *Likeness and Likelihood in the Presocratics and Plato*. Cambridge: Cambridge University Press.

Bugno, M., ed. 2005. *Senofane ed Elea tra Ionia e Magna Grecia*. Naples: Luciano.

Burkert, W. 1963. "Iranisches bei Anaximandros." *Rheinisches Museum* 106: 97–134.

——. 1969. "Das Prooimion des Parmenides und die Katabasis des Pythagoras." *Phronesis* 14: 1–30.

——. 1972. *Lore and Science in Ancient Pythagoreanism*. Cambridge, MA: Harvard University Press. Revised translation of *Weisheit und Wissenschaft: Studien zu Pythagoras, Philolaos und Platon*. Nuremberg: Hans Carl Verlag 1962.

——. 1983. "Eraclito nel papiro di Derveni. Due nuove testimonianze." In Rossetti 1983, 37–42.

——. 1987. "Oriental and Greek Mythology: The Meeting of Parallels." In *Interpretations of Greek Mythology*, edited by Jan Bremmer, 10–40. London: Croom Helm.

——. 1992. *The Orientalizing Revolution. Near Eastern Influence on Greek Culture in the Early Archaic Age*. Cambridge, MA: Harvard University Press. Updated English translation, with M. E. Pinder, of W. Burkert 1984, *Die orientalisierende Epoche in der griechischen Religion und Literatur. Sitzungsberichte der Heidelberger Akademie der Wissenschaften. Philosophisch-historische Klasse*.

——. 1994–95. "Orientalische und griechische Weltmodelle von Assur bis Anaximandros." *Wiener Studien* 107–8: 179–86.

——. 1999a. *Da Omero ai Magi: La tradizione orientale nella cultura greca*. Edited by Claudia Antonetti. Venice: Marsilio.

——. 1999b. "The Logic of Cosmogony." In Buxton 1999, 87–106.

Burnet, J. 1892. *Early Greek Philosophy*. London: Adam and Charles Black. Fourth edition 1930.

Burnyeat, M. F. 1997. "Postscript on Silent Reading." *Classical Quarterly* 47: 74–76.

Busch, S. 2002. "Lautes und leises Lesen in der Antike." *Rheinisches Museum* 145: 1–45.

Butti de Lima, P. 2002. *Platone, Esercizi di filosofia per il giovane Teeteto*. Venice: Marsilio.

Buxton, R., ed. 1999. *From Myth to Reason? Studies in the Development of Greek Thought*. Oxford: Oxford University Press.

Calame, C. 1983. *Alcman, Introduction, texte critique, témoignages, traduction et commentaire*. Rome: Edizioni dell'Ateneo.

——. 2002. "Qu'est-ce qui est orphique dans les Orphica? Une mise au point introductive." *Revue de l'histoire des religions* 219: 385–400.

——. 2006. *Pratiques poétiques de la mémoire: Représentations de l'espace-temps en Grèce ancienne*. Paris: Éditions la Découverte.

Calder III, W. M., ed. 1991. "The Cambridge Ritualists Reconsidered." *Proceedings of the First Oldfather Conference, Campus of the University of Illinois at Urbana-Champaign, 27–30 April 1989. Illinois Classical Studies*, Suppl. 2. Atlanta: Scholar Press.

Calzolari, A. 1984. "Empedocle, frr. 2 e 3 Diels-Kranz." *Studi Classici e Orientali* 34: 71–81.

Camassa, G. 1988. "Aux origines de la codification écrite des lois en Grèce." In Detienne 1988, 130–55.

Cambiano, G. 1980. "La sapienza greca di Giorgio Colli." *Rivista di Filosofia* 71: 157–62.

——. 1982. "Patologia e metafora politica. Alcmeone, Platone, Corpus Hippocraticum." *Elenchos* 3: 219–36.

——. ed. 1986. *Storiografia e dossografia nella filosofia antica*. Turin: Tirrenia Stampatori.

——. 1988a. *Il ritorno degli antichi*. Rome-Bari: Laterza.

——. 1988b. "Sapere e testualità nel mondo antico." In Rossi 1988, 69–98.

——. 1996. "Il filosofo." In Settis 1996, 815–47.

——. 1997. *"Unité du savoir et pluralité des savoirs en Grèce ancienne." Actes du colloque des 11–13 janvier 1996, Paris Nanterre University*. In *"L'entreprise encyclopédique,"* edited by J.-B.-F. Mélonio. *Littérales*, 21: 23–44. Reprinted in Cambiano, *Figure, mac-*

chine, sogni. Saggi sulla scienza antica, 1–20. Rome: Edizioni di Storia e Letteratura, 2006.

———. 2002. "Catastrofi naturali e storia umana in Platone e Aristotele." *Rivista Storica Italiana* 114: 694–714.

———. 2013. *I filosofi in Grecia e a Roma*. Bologna: Il Mulino.

Cardona, G. R. 1988. "Il sapere dello scriba." In Rossi 1988, 3–27.

Casadio, G. 1991. *"La metempsicosi fra Orfeo e Pitagora."* In *Orphisme et Orphée en l'honneur de Jean Rudhart*, edited by Philippe Borgeaud, 119–155. Geneva: Librairie Droz.

Casertano, G. 1977. *La nascita della filosofia vista dai Greci (morte o rinascita della filosofia)*. Naples: Il Tripode. Updated second edition 2007. Pistoia: Editrice Petite Plaisance.

———, ed. 2007 *Empedocle tra poesia, medicina, filosofia e politica*. Naples: Loffredo.

Cassio, A. C. 1996. "Da Elea a Hipponion e Leontinoi: Lingua di Parmenide e testi epigrafici." *Zeitschrift für Papyrologie und Epigraphik* 113: 14–20.

Cavallo, G. 1988. "Cultura scritta e conservazione del sapere dalla Grecia antica all'Occidente medievale." In Rossi 1988, 29–67.

Caveing, M. 1969. "À propos d'un livre de Marcel Detienne: La laïcisation de la parole et l'exigence rationnelle." *Raison Présente* 1969 (janvier): 85–98.

Centrone, B. 1996. *Introduzione ai Pitagorici*. Rome: Laterza.

———. 2007. *"Il ruolo di Eraclito nello sviluppo della concezione dell'anima."* In *Gli irraggiungibili confini. Percorsi della psiche nell'età della Grecia classica*, edited by Rita Bruschi, 131–49. Pisa: Edizioni ETS.

Cerri, G. 1995. "Cosmologia dell'Ade in Omero, Esiodo e Parmenide." *La Parola del Passato* 50: 437–67.

———, ed. 1999. *Parmenide di Elea: Poema sulla natura*. Milan: Rizzoli.

———. 2001. "Physikà e Katharmoì di Empedocle." *Aevum Antiquum* 1 (n.s.): 181–96.

———. 2004. "Empedocle, fr. 3 D.-K.: saggio di esegesi letterale." In Rossetti-Santaniello 2004, 83–93.

Chambers, M. 1991. "Cornford's *Thucydides Mythistoricus*." In Calder III 1991, 61–77.

Charles, D. 1970. *Hommages à Marie Delcourt*. Brussels: Latomus.

Cherniss, H. 1935. *Aristotle's Criticism of Presocratic Philosophy*. Baltimore: The Johns Hopkins Press.

———. 1977. "Ancient Forms of Philosophic Discourse: The First Annual George Boas Lecture, 1970, unpublished." In H. Cherniss, *Selected Papers*, 14–35. Leiden: E. J. Brill.

Classen, C. J. 1962. "The Creator in Greek Thought from Homer to Plato." *Classica et Mediaevalia* 23: 1–22.

———. 1965. "Bemerkungen zu zwei griechischen Philosophiehistorikern." *Philologus* 109: 175–81.

———. 1989. "Xenophanes and the Tradition of Epic Poetry." In Boudouris 1989, 31–103.

Cole, T. 1983. "Archaic Truth." *Quaderni Urbinati di Cultura Classica* 52 (n.s. 13): 9–28.

Colli, G. 1977. *La sapienza greca*. Vol. 1, *Dioniso, Apollo, Eleusi, Orfeo, Museo, Iperborei, Enigma*. Milan: Adelphi.

———. 1978. *La sapienza greca*. Vol. 2, *Epimenide, Ferecide, Talete, Anassimandro, Anassimene, Onomacrito*. Milan: Adelphi.

———. 1980. *La sapienza greca*. Vol. 3, *Eraclito*. Milan: Adelphi.

Collins, D. 2004. *Master of the Game. Competition and Performance in Greek Poetry*. Washington, DC: Center for Hellenic Studies / Harvard University Press.

Cordero, N. L. 1990. "La Déesse de Parménide, maîtresse de philosophie." In Mattéi 1990, 207–14.

Cornford, F. M. 1907. *Thucydides Mythistoricus*. London: Arnold.

——. 1912. *From Religion to Philosophy. A Study in the Origins of Western Speculation*. London: Arnold. Reprinted with a Foreword by Robert Ackerman. Princeton, NJ: Princeton University Press, 1991.

——. 1921. "The Unconscious Element in Literature and Philosophy." *Proceedings of the Classical Association* 18 (1921): 104–19. Reprinted in Cornford 1950, 1–13.

——. 1931. *The Laws of Motion in Ancient Thought. An Inaugural Lecture*. Cambridge: Cambridge University Press.

——. 1934. "Innumerable Worlds in Presocratic Philosophy." *Classical Quarterly* 28: 1–16.

——. 1936. "The Invention of Space." In Thomson, J. A. K. and A. Toynbee (eds), *Essays in Honour of Gilbert Murray*, 215–35. London: George Allen & Unwin.

——. 1941. "A Ritual Basis for Hesiod's *Theogony*." In Cornford 1950, 95–116.

——. 1950. *The Unwritten Philosophy and Other Essays*. Cambridge: Cambridge University Press. Reprinted 1967.

——. 1952. *Principium Sapientiae. The Origins of Greek Philosophical Thought*. Cambridge: Cambridge University Press. Reprinted 1973.

Corradi, M. 2007. "Protagoras dans son contexte: L'homme mesure et la tradition archaïque de l'incipit." *Métis* 5 (n.s.): 185–204.

Couprie, D. L., R. Hahn, and G. Naddaf. 2003. *Anaximander in Context: New Studies in the Origins of Greek Philosophy*. Albany: State University of New York Press.

Cozzo, A. 2001. *Tra comunità e violenza. Conoscenza, logos e razionalità nella Grecia antica*. Milan: Carocci.

Crippa, S. 2004. "*Figures du σιβυλλαίνειν*." In *La Sibylle: Parole et représentation*, edited by M. Bouquet, 99–108. Rennes: Presses Universitaires de Rennes.

Curd, P. 1998. *The Legacy of Parmenides. Eleatic Monism and Later Presocratic Thought*. Princeton, NJ: Princeton University Press. Reprinted 2004.

——. 2001. "A New Empedocles? Implications of the Strasburg Fragments for Presocratic Philosophy." *Proceedings of the Boston Area Colloquium in Ancient Philosophy* 17: 27–49.

——. 2002. "The Presocratics as Philosophers." In Laks-Louguet 2002, 115–38.

D'Alessio, G. B. 1995. "Una via lontana dal cammino degli uomini (Parm. frr. 1+6 D.-K.; Pind. *Ol.* VI 22–27; *Pae.* VIIb 10–20)." *Studi Italiani di Filologia Classica* 88: 143–81.

Deichgräber, K. 1962. "*Rhytmische Elemente im Logos des Heraklit*." *Abhandlungen der Geistes- und Sozialwissenschaftlichen Klasse. Akademie der Wissenschaften und der Literatur, Wiesbaden* 1962, n. 9, Akademie (tip. L. C. Wittich), Mainz.

Derron, P., ed. 2015. "*Cosmologies et cosmogonies dans la littérature antique: Huit exposés suivis de discussions et d'un épilogue*." *Entretiens sur l'Antiquité Classique* 61. Vandoeuvres: Fondation Hardt pour l'Étude de l'Antiquité Classique.

Desclos, M.-L., and F. Fronterotta, eds. 2013. *La sagesse "présocratique": Communication des savoirs en Grèce archaïque; Des lieux et des hommes*. Paris: Armand Colin.

Detienne, M. 1967. *Les maîtres de vérité dans la Grèce archaïque*. Paris: Maspero. Translated by J. Lloyd as *The Masters of Truth in Archaic Greece*. New York: Zone Books 1996.

——. 1988. *Les savoirs de l'écriture en Grèce ancienne*. Lille: Presses Universitaires de Lille.

——. 1989. *L'écriture d'Orphée*. Paris: Gallimard. Translated by J. Lloyd as *The Writing of Orpheus. Greek Myth in Cultural Context*. Baltimore and London: The Johns Hopkins University Press 2003.

——. 1994. *En ouverture: Retour sur la bouche de la vérité*. In Detienne 1967, 5–31. Reprinted 1994 by Pocket.

Dewald, C., and Marincola, J., eds. 2006. *The Cambridge Companion to Herodotus*. Cambridge: Cambridge University Press.

Di Benedetto, V., ed. 2004. *Euripide, "Le Baccanti."* Milan: Rizzoli.

Di Donato, R. 2005. "Senofane poeta: la critica della tradizione." In Bugno 2005, 47–54.

Diels, H., ed. 1879. *Doxographi Graeci*. Berlin: De Gruyter, 1958. Originally published 1879 by Georg Reimers.

———. ed. 1903. *Die Fragmente der Vorsokratiker*. Berlin: Weidmann. Sixth edition edited By W. Kranz, 1951–52 (3 vols).

Diès, A. 1913. *"La transposition platonicienne." Annales de l'Institut Supérieur de Philosophie de Louvain* 2: 267–308. Reprinted in Diès, *Autour de Platon*, 400–49. Paris: Les Belles Lettres, 1972.

Dilcher, R. 1995. *Studies in Heraclitus*. Hildesheim: Olms.

Dilke, O. A.W. 1982. *Greek and Roman Maps*. London: Thames and Hudson.

Diller, H. 1946. *"Hesiod und die Anfänge der griechischen Philosophie." Antike und Abendland* 2: 140–51. Reprinted in *Hesiod*, edited by Ernst Heitsch, 688–707. Darmstadt: Wissenschaftche Buchgesellschaft.

Dodds, E. R. 1951. *The Greeks and the Irrational*. Berkeley-London: University of California Press.

Dougherty, C., and L. Kurke, eds. 1993. *Cultural Poetics in Archaic Greece: Cult, Performance, Politics*. Cambridge: Cambridge University Press.

Drozdek, A. 2007. *Greek Philosophers As Theologians: The Divine Arche*. Aldershot: Ashgate.

Edmonds, R. G. 1999. "Tearing Apart the Zagreus Myth: A Few Disparaging Remarks on Orphism and Original Sin." *Classical Antiquity* 18: 35–73.

———. 2004. *Myths of the Underworld Journey: Plato, Aristophanes and the Orphic Gold Tablets*. Cambridge: Cambridge University Press.

Effenterre, H. van, and F. Ruzé. 1995. *Nomima: Recueil d'inscriptions politiques et juridiques de l'archaïsme grec*. Rome: École Française de Rome.

Eisenstadt, S. N., ed. 1986. *The Origins and Diversity of Axial Age Civilizations*. Albany: State University of New York Press.

Elkana, Y. 1981. *A Programmatic Attempt at an Anthropology of Knowledge*. Dordrecht and London: Reidel.

———. 1986. "The Emergence of Second-Order Thinking in Classical Greece." In Eisenstadt 1986, 40–64.

Engmann, J. 1991. "Cosmic Justice in Anaximander." *Phronesis* 36: 1–26.

Epimenide cretese. 2001. Naples: Luciano.

Everson, S. 1991. *Psychology*. Vol. 2, *Companions to Ancient Thought*. Cambridge: Cambridge University Press.

Ferrari, F. 2004. *"La sapienza acerba e il dio-tutto: Pindaro e Senofane." Prometheus* 30: 139–47. Reprinted in Ferrari 2007, 83–90.

———. 2007. *La fonte del cipresso bianco. Racconto e sapienza dall' 'Odissea' alle lamine misteriche*. Turin: UTET.

Ferrari, F., and L. Prauscello. 2008. "Demeter Chthonia and the Mountain Mother in a New Gold Tablet from Magoula Mati." *Zeitschrift für Papyrologie und Epigraphic* 162: 203–11.

Ferrari, G. R. F. 1984. "Orality and Literacy in the Origin of Philosophy." *Ancient Philosophy* 4: 194–205.

Festugière, A-J., ed. and trans. 1948. *Hippocrate. L'Ancienne Médecine*. Paris: Klincksieck. Reprinted in 1979 by Arno Press.

Finkelberg, M. 1998. *The Birth of Literary Fiction in Ancient Greece*. Oxford: Clarendon Press.

Föllinger, S. 2007. *"Die Funktion von Nicht-Wissen in der frühgriechischen Literatur."* In Althoff 2007, 53–65.

Ford, A. 2002. *The Origins of Criticism. Literary Culture and Poetic Theory in Classical Greece*. Princeton, NJ: Princeton University Press.

Foster, B. R. 2005. "Transmission of Knowledge." In Snell 2005, 261–68.

Fowler, R. L. 2000. *Early Greek Mythography*. Oxford: Oxford University Press.

———. 2006. "Herodotus and His Prose Predecessors." In Dewald-Marincola 2006, 29–45.

Fränkel, H. 1925. "Xenophanesstudien, II: Der Empirismus des Xenophanes und seine Erkenntniskritik (Fgt. 34)." *Hermes* 60: 174–92. Reprinted in Fränkel 1960, 335–49.

———. 1946. "Man's 'Ephemeros' Nature according to Pindar and Others." *Transactions of the American Philological Association* 77: 131–45. Reprinted in Fränkel 1960, 23–39 as "ΕΦΗΜΕΡΟΣ *als Kennwort für die menschliche Natur*."

———. 1962. *Dichtung und Philosophie des frühen Griechentums: Eine Geschichte der griechischen Epik, Lyrik und Prosa bis zur Mitte des fünften Jahrhunderts von Homer bis Pindar*. Munich: Beck. Translated by Hadas and Willis as *Early Greek Poetry and Philosophy:A History of Greek Epic, Lyric, and Prose to the Middle of the Fifth Century*. Oxford: Blackwell 1972.

———. 1955. *Wege und Formen frühgriechischen Denkens. Literarische und philosophiegeschichtliche Studien*. Munich: Beck.

Frankfort, H., H. Frankfort, J. A. Wilson, T. Jacobsen, and W. A. Irwin. 1946. *Before Philosophy: The Intellectual Adventure of Ancient Man; An Essay on the Speculative Thought in the Ancient Near East*. Chicago: The University of Chicago Press.

Frede, D. 2004. *"Die Orphik—Mysterienreligion oder Philosophie?"* In *Der Orpheus Mythos von der Antike bis zur Gegenwart*, edited by C. Maurer Zenck, 229–45. Frankfurt-Berlin: Peter Lang.

Frede, M. 1986. "Philosophy and Medicine in Antiquity." In *Human Nature and Natural Knowledge*: *Essays Presented to Marjorie Grene on the Occasion of Her Seventy-Fifth Birthday*, edited by A. Donagan, A. N. Perovich, Jr., M. V. Wedin, and D. Reidel, 211–32; reprinted in Frede, *Essays in Ancient Philosophy*, 225–42. Oxford: Clarendon Press, 1987.

———. 2004. "Aristotle's Account of the Origins of Philosophy." *Rhizai* 1: 9–44.

Freudenthal, G. 1986. "The Theory of the Opposites and an Ordered Universe: Physics and Metaphysics in Anaximander." *Phronesis* 31: 197–228.

Fronterotta, F. 2007. *"Che effetto fa essere un pipistrello? Il problema mente-corpo nel Timeo platonico."* In *Interiorità e anima: La psychè in Platone*, edited by M. Migliori, L. M. Napolitano, and V.-A. Fermani, 89–108. Milan: Vita e Pensiero.

Frontisi-Ducroux F. 2002. "Avec son diaphragme visionnaire, Ἰδυίῃσι πραπίδεσσι," 'Iliade' XVIII, 481: À propos du bouclier d'Achille." *Revue des Études Grecques* 115: 463–84.

Fuhrmann, M. 1966. *"Obscuritas: Das Problem der Dunkelheit in der rhetorischen und literarästhetischen Theorie der Antike."* In *Poetik und Hermeneutik*. Vol. 2, *Immanente Äesthetik. Äesthetische Reflexion: Lyrik als Paradigma der Moderne*, edited by Wolfgang Iser, 47–71. Munich: Fink.

Funghi, M. S., and G. W. Most. 1995. *"Commentarium in Alcmanem, edizione e commento."* In *Corpus dei Papiri Filosofici Greci e Latini: Testi e lessico nei papiri di cultura greca e latina, parte III, Commentari*, 3–13. Florence: Olschki.

Furley, D. J. 1987. *The Greek Cosmologists*. Vol. 1, *The Formation of the Atomic Theory and Its Earliest Critics*. Cambridge: Cambridge University Press.

Furley, D. J., and R. E. Allen. 1970. *Studies in Presocratic Philosophy*, vol. 1. London: Routledge & Kegan Paul.

———. 1975. *Studies in Presocratic Philosophy*, vol. 2. London: Routledge & Kegan Paul.

Gadamer, H-G. 1993. *L'inizio della filosofia occidentale: Lezioni raccolte da Vittorio De Cesare*. Milan: Guerini e Associati.

Gagarin, M. 1974. "*Dike* in Archaic Greek Thought." *Classical Philology* 69: 186–97.

——. 1981. *Drakon and Early Athenian Homicide Law*. New Haven, CT: Yale University Press.

——. 1986. *Early Greek Law*. Berkeley: University of California Press.

——. 2002. "Greek Law and the Presocratics." In *Presocratic Philosophy: Essays in Honour of Alexander Mourelatos*, edited by V. M. Caston and D. W. Graham, 19–24. Aldershot: Ashgate.

——. 2004. "Writing Athenian Law." In Law, *Rhetoric and Comedy in Classical Athens: Essays in Honour of Douglas M. MacDowell*, edited by D. L. Cairns and R. A. Knox, 15–31. Swansea: The Classical Press of Wales.

García Quintela, M. V. 1996. "Le livre d'Anaximandre et la société de Milet." *Métis* 11: 37–68.

Gavrilov, A. K. 1997. "Reading Techniques in Classical Antiquity." *Classical Quarterly* 47: 56–73.

Gehrke, H.-J. 1988. "*Die Geburt der Erdkunde aus dem Geiste der Geometrie. Überlegungen zur Entstehung und zur Frühgeschichte der wissenschaftlichen Geographie bei den Griechen.*" In *Gattungen wissenschaftlicher Literatur in der Antike*, edited by W. Kullmann, J. Althoff, and M. Asper, 163–92. Tübingen: Gunter Narr.

——. 1995. "*Der Nomosbegriff der Polis.*" In *Nomos und Gesetz: Ursprünge und Wirkungen des griechischen Gesetzesdenkens*, edited by O. Behrends and W. Sellert, 13–35. Göttingen: Vandenhoeck.

Gemelli Marciano, M. L. 1990. *Le metamorfosi della tradizione: Mutamenti di significato e neologismi nel 'Peri Physeos' di Empedocle*. Bari: Levante.

——. 1993. "Ein neues Zeugnis zu Oinopides von Chios bei Iohannes Tzetzes: Das Problem der Nilschwelle." *Museum Helveticum* 50: 79–93.

——. 2001. "Le 'demonologie' empedoclee: Problemi di metodo e altro." *Aevum Antiquum* 1 (n.s.): 205–35.

——. 2002. "Le contexte culturel des Présocratiques: adversaires et destinataires." In Laks-Louguet 2002, 83–114.

——. 2005. "Senofane: interpretazioni antiche e contesto culturale; La critica ai poeti e il cosiddetto 'monismo.'" In Bugno 2005: 63–76. Extended German version in Rechenauer 2005, 118–34.

——. 2006. Review of Kingsley 2003. *Gnomon* 78: 657–71.

——. 2007a. "Lire du début: Remarques sur les incipit des écrits présocratiques." *Philosophie Antique* 7: 7–37.

——, ed. and trans. 2007b. *Die Vorsokratiker. Band I, Thales, Anaximander, Anaximenes, Pythagoras und die Pythagoreer, Xenophanes, Heraklit*. Düsseldorf: Artemis & Winkler.

——. 2008. "Images and Experience: At the Roots of Parmenides' 'Aletheia.'" *Ancient Philosophy* 28: 21–48.

Gernet, L. 1945. "Les origines de la philosophie." *Bulletin de l'enseignement public du Maroc* 183: 1–12. Reprinted in Gernet, *Anthropologie de la Grèce antique*, 239–258. Paris: Maspero, 1968. Reprinted as "The Origins of Greek Philosophy." In Gernet, *The Anthropology of Ancient Greece*, translated by J. Hamilton, S. J. Nagy, and B. Nagy, 352–64. Baltimore: The Johns Hopkins University Press, 1981.

Gigante, M. et al. 2001. *Epimenide cretese*. Naples: Luciano.

Gilbert, O. 1907. "Die Daimon des Parmenides." *Archiv für Geschichte der Philosophie* 20: 25–45.

Gill, C. 2001. "La 'psychologie' présocratique: Quelques questions interprétatives." In Morel-Pradeau 2001, 169–89.

Gill, M. L., and P. Pellegrin, eds. 2006. *A Companion to Ancient Philosophy*. Malden: Blackwell.

Giordano-Zecharya, M. 2003. *Tabellae auris: Musica e memoria nella trasmissione della lirica monodica*. In *Rysmós. Studi di poesia, metrica e musica greca offerti dagli allievi a Luigi Enrico Rossi per i suoi settant'anni*, edited by R. Nicolai, 73–92. Rome: Quasar.

Giuliano, F. M. 2000. "Filosofia versus poesia: Platone davanti a un'antica disputa." In Arrighetti-Tulli 2000, 377–400. Reprinted in Giuliano, *Studi di letteratura greca*, 216–39. Pisa: Giardini, 2004.

Goldhill, S. 2002. *The Invention of Prose*. Oxford: Oxford University Press.

Gomperz, T. 1893 and 1902. *Griechische Denker: Eine Geschichte der antiken Philosophie*. Leipzig: Veit.

Goody, J. R. 1977. *The Domestication of the Savage Mind*. Cambridge: Cambridge University Press.

———. 1987. *The Interface between the Written and the Oral*. Cambridge: Cambridge University Press.

———. 2000. *The Power of the Written Tradition*. Washington, DC: Smithsonian Institution Press.

Goody, J. R., and I. Watt, 1962–63. "The Consequences of Literacy." *Comparative Studies in Society and History* 5: 304–45. Reprinted in J. R. Goody (ed.), *Literacy in Traditional Societies*, 27–68. Cambridge: Cambridge University Press, 1968.

Gorman, V. B. 2001. *Miletos, the Ornament of Ionia: A History of the City to 400 B.C.* Ann Arbor: University of Michigan Press.

Gostoli, A. 2005. "La critica dei miti tradizionali in Senofane e nella lirica coeva." In Bugno 2005, 55–61.

Graf, F., and J. Barnes. 1979. Review of Colli 1977 and Colli 1978. *Classical Review* 29: 239–53.

Graf, F. and S. Iles Johnston. 2007. *Ritual Texts for the Afterlife. Orpheus and the Bacchic Gold Tablets*. London-New York: Routledge.

Graham, D. W. 2006. *Explaining the Cosmos: The Ionian Tradition of Scientific Philosophy*. Princeton, NJ: Princeton University Press.

Granger, H. 2004. "Argumentation and Heraclitus' Book." *Oxford Studies in Ancient Philosophy* 25: 1–17.

———. 2008. "The Proem of Parmenides' Poem." *Ancient Philosophy* 28: 1–20.

Gregory, A. 2007. *Ancient Greek Cosmogony*. London: Duckworth.

———. 2013. *The Presocratics and the Supernatural: Magic, Philosophy and Science in Early Greece*. London and New York: Bloomsbury.

Guthrie, W. K. C. 1950. Introductory Memoir to Cornford 1950, vii–xix.

———. 1952. *Orpheus and Greek Religion: A Study of the Orphic Movement*. London: Methuen. First edition 1935.

Hahn, R. 2001. *Anaximander and the Architects: The Contributions of Aegyptian and Greek Architectural Technologies to the Origins of Greek Philosophy*. Albany: State University of New York Press.

Hankinson, R. J. 1998a. *Cause and Explanation in Ancient Greek Thought*. Oxford: Clarendon Press.

———. 1998b. "Divination, Religion and Science: Divine and Human in the 'Hippocratic Corpus.'" *Apeiron* 31: 1–34.

Harris, W. V. 1989. *Ancient Literacy*. Cambridge, MA: Harvard University Press.

Hartog, F. 1996. *Mémoire d'Ulysse, Récits sur la frontière en Grèce ancienne*. Paris: Gallimard. Translated by J. Lloyd as *Memories of Odysseus: Frontier Tales from Ancient Greece*. Chicago: University of Chicago Press 2001.

Havelock, E. A. 1963. *Preface to Plato*. Cambridge, MA: Harvard University Press.

———. 1966. "Pre-literacy and the Pre-Socratics." *Bulletin of the Institute of Classical Studies* 13: 44–67. Reprinted in Havelock, *The Literate Revolution in Greece and Its Cultural Consequences*, 220–60. Princeton, NJ: Princeton University Press, 1982.

———. 1983. "The Linguistic Task of the Presocratics." In Robb 1983b, 7–82.

———. 1996. *Alle origini della filosofia greca*. Translated by L. Lomiento. Edited by T. Cole. Posthumous Italian translation of the manuscript *The Preplatonic Thinkers of Greece: A Revisionist History*.

Heinemann, G. 2000. "Natural Knowledge in the Hippocratic Treatise 'On Ancient Medicine.'" In *Antike Naturwissenschaft und ihre Rezeption*, vol. 10, edited by J. Althoff, B. Herzhoff, and G. Wöhrle, 13–41. Trier: Wissenschaftlicher Verlag Trier.

Heitsch, E. 1966. "Das Wissen des Xenophanes." *Rheinisches Museum* 109: 193–235.

Henrichs, A. 2003. "Writing Religion: Inscribed Texts, Ritual Authority, and the Religious Discourse of the Polis." In Yunis 2003b, 38–58.

Hershbell, J. P. 1983. "The Oral-Poetic Religion of Xenophanes." In Robb 1983b, 125–33.

Hölkeskamp, K.-J. 1992. "Arbitrators, Lawgivers and the 'Codification of Law' in Archaic Greece: Problems and Perspectives." *Métis* 7: 49–81.

———. 1999. *Schiedsrichter, Gesetzgeber und Gesetzgebung im archaischen Griechenland*. Stuttgart: Franz Steiner.

Hölscher, U. 1953. "Anaximander und der Anfang der Philosophie." *Hermes* 81: 257–77 and 385–418. Reprinted in *Um die Begriffswelt der Vorsokratiker*, edited by H.-G. Gadamer, 95–176. Darmstadt:Wissenschaftliche Buchgesellschaft. Reprinted in Hölscher 1968, 9–89. Translated as "Anaximander and the Beginnings of Greek Philosophy." In Furley-Allen 1970, 281–322.

———. 1968. *Anfängliches Fragen: Studien zur frühen griechischen Philosophie*. Göttingen: Vandenhoeck und Ruprecht.

———. 1974. "Paradox, Simile and Gnomic Utterance in Heraclitus." In Mourelatos 1974, 229–38. Translated from Hölscher 1968, 136–41, 144–48, and 459–69.

Hornung, E. 1987. "L'Égypte, la philosophie avant les Grecs." *Les Études Philosophiques* 2–3: 113–25.

Horton, R. 1967. "African Traditional Thought and Western Science." *Africa* 37: 50–71, 155–87.

Huffman, C. A. 2002. "*Polyclète et les Présocratiques*." In Laks-Louguet 2002, 303–27.

———. 2007. "Philolaus and the Central Fire." In *Reading Ancient Texts*. Vol. 1, *Presocratics and Plato: Essays in Honour of Denis O'Brien*, edited by S. Stern-Gillet and K. Corrigan, 57–94. Leiden: Brill.

Humphreys, S. C. 1975. "'Transcendence' and Intellectual Roles: The Ancient Greek Case." *Daedalus* 104.2: 91–118. Reprinted in Humphreys, *Anthropology and the Greeks*, 209–41. London: Routledge & Kegan Paul, 1978.

———. 1986. "Dynamics of the Greek Breakthrough: The Dialogue between Philosophy and Religion." In Eisenstadt 1986: 92–110. Reprinted in Humphreys, *The Strangeness of Gods: Historical Perspectives on the Interpretation of Athenian Religion*, 51–76. Oxford: Oxford University Press, 2004.

———. 1996. "From Riddle to Rigour: Satisfactions of Scientific Prose in Ancient Greece." In *Proof and Persuasion: Essays on Authority, Objectivity and Evidence*, edited by S. Marchand and E. Lunbeck, 3–24. Turnhout: Brepols.

Hussey, E. 1999. "Heraclitus." In Long 1999b, 88–112.

———. 2006. "The Beginnings of Science and Philosophy in Archaic Science." In Gill-Pellegrin 2006, 3–19.

Inwood, B. 2001. *Empedocles. A Text and Translation with an Introduction*. Revised Edition. Toronto: University of Toronto Press.

Ioli, R. 2003. "Senofane B 34 DK e il conoscere." *Giornale Italiano di Filologia* 55.2: 199–219.

Jacob, C. 1988. "Inscrire la terre habitée sur une tablette: Réflexions sur la fonction de la carte géographique en Grèce ancienne." In Detienne 1988, 273–304.

Jaeger, W. 1928. "Über Ursprung und Kreislauf des philosophischen Lebensideal." *Sitzungsberichte der Preussischen Akademie der Wissenschaften, Phil.-Hist. Klasse* 1928: 390–421], translated as "On the Origin and Cycle of the Philosophic Ideal of Life." In Jaeger 1948, 426–61.

——. 1936. *Paideia*. Vol. 1, *Die Formung des griechischen Menschen*. Berlin and Leipzig: De Gruyter. Translated by G. Highet as *Paideia: The Ideals of Greek Culture*. New York: Oxford University Press, 1986.

——. 1947. *The Theology of the Early Greek Philosophers*. Oxford: Oxford Clarendon Press.

——. 1948. *Aristotle: Fundamentals of the History of His Development*. Translated, with the author's corrections, by R. Robinson. Oxford: Clarendon Press.

Jennings, V., and Katsaros, A. 2007. *The World of Ion of Chios*. Leiden and Boston: Brill.

Johansen, T. K. 1999. "Myth and Logos in Aristotle." In Buxton 1999, 279–91.

Jouanna, J. 2005. "Cause and Crisis in Historians and Medical Writers of the Classical Period." In van der Eijk 2005, 3–27.

Kahn, C. H. 1960. "Religion and Natural Philosophy in Empedocles' Doctrine of the Soul." *Archiv für Geschichte der Philosophie* 42: 3–35. Reprinted with corrections and Retractations in *Essays in Ancient Greek Philosophy*, edited by J. P. Anton-G. L. Kustas, 3–38. Albany: State University of New York Press, 1971. Reprinted in Mourelatos 1974, 426–66.

——. 1979. *Art and Thought of Heraclitus: An Edition of the Fragments with Translation and Commentary*. Cambridge: Cambridge University Press.

——. 1983. "Philosophy and the Written Word: Some Thoughts on Heraclitus and the Early Greek Uses of Prose." In Robb 1983b, 110–24.

——. 2002. Review of Hahn 2001. *Ancient Philosophy* 22: 143–52.

——. 2003. "Writing Philosophy: Prose and Poetry from Thales to Plato." In Yunis 2003b, 139–61.

Kingsley, P. 1995. *Ancient Philosophy, Mystery and Magic: Empedocles and the Pythagorean Tradition*. Oxford: Oxford University Press.

——. 1999. *In the Dark Places of Wisdom*. Inverness, California: Golden Sufi Center.

——. 2002. "Empedocles for the New Millennium." *Ancient Philosophy* 22: 333–413.

——. 2003 *Reality*. Inverness, California: Golden Sufi Center.

Kirk, G. S. 1960. "Popper on Science and the Presocratics." *Mind* 69: 318–39. Reprinted in Furley-Allen 1970, 154–77.

——. 1961. "Sense and Common-sense in the Development of Greek Philosophy." *Journal of Hellenic Studies* 81: 105–17.

Kirk, G. S., J. E. Raven, and M. Schofield. 1983. *The Presocratic Philosophers: A Critical History with a Selection of Texts*. 2nd ed. Cambridge: Cambridge University Press.

Knox, B. M. W. 1968. "Silent Reading in Antiquity." *Greek, Roman, and Byzantine Studies* 9: 421–35.

Körner, R. 1993. *Inschriftliche Gesetzestexte der frühen griechischen Polis*. Edited by K. Hallof. Cologne: Böhlau.

Kouloumentas, S. 2007. "The Derveni Papyrus on Cosmic Justice." *Rhizai* 4: 105–32.

Kouremenos, T., G. M. Parássoglou, and K. Tsantsanoglou, eds. 2006. *The Derveni Papyrus*. Florence: Olschki.

Krischer, T. 2006. "Die natürlichen Vorausgebungen der griechischen Kulturenfaltung." *Hermes* 134: 379–83.

Kullmann, W., and J. Althoff, eds. 1993. *Vermittlung und Tradierung von Wissen in der griechischen Kultur*. Tübingen: Gunter Narr.

Kurke, L. V. 2007. "Archaic Greek Poetry." In Shapiro 2007, 141–68.

Laks, A. 1998. "Les Origines de Jean-Pierre Vernant." *Critique* 54: 268–82. Reprinted in Laks 2006, 83–122.

———. 1999. "Soul, Sensation, and Thought." In Long 1999b, 250–70.

———. 1999-2000. *"Naissance d'intellectuels: Le cas de la philosophie grecque."* In Wessely 1999-2000, 5–18.

———. 2001a. "Comment s'écrit l'histoire des débuts? À propos des Présocratiques." *Internationale Zeitschrift für Philosophie* 2: 153–72.

———. 2001b. "Écriture, prose et les débuts de la philosophie grecque." *Methodos* 1: 131–51.

———. 2001c. " 'Philosophes Présocratiques.' Remarques sur la construction d'une catégorie de l'historiographie philosophique." In Most 2001: 293–311. Reprinted in Laks-Louguet 2002, 17–38.

———. 2003. "Phénomènes et références: Éléments pour une réflexion sur la rationalisation de l'irrationnel." *Methodos* 3: 9–33.

———. 2004. *"Aristote, l'allégorie et les débuts de la philosophie."* In *L'Allégorie de l'Antiquité à la Renaissance*, edited by B. Pérez-Jean and P. Eichel-Lojkine, 211–20. Paris: Champion. Reprinted in Laks 2007, 237–46.

———. 2005a. "Die Entstehung einer (Fach)Disziplin: Der Fall der Vorsokratischen Philosophie." In Rechenauer 2005, 19–39.

———. 2005b. "Remarks on the Differentiation of Early Greek Philosophy." In *Philosophy and the Sciences in Antiquity*, edited by R. W. Sharples, 8–22. Aldershot: Ashgate.

———. 2006. *Introduction à la "philosophie présocratique*. Paris: Presses Universitaires de France. Translated by G. Most as *The Concept of Presocratic Philosophy Its Origin, Development, and Significance*. Princeton: Princeton University Press 2018.

———. 2007. *Histoire, doxographie, vérité: Études sur Aristote, Théophraste et la philosophie présocratique*. Louvain-La-Neuve: Peeters.

———. 2008. "Le génie du rapprochement et les limites de la similitude: À propos d'Anaximandre." *Agenda de la pensée contemporaine* 10: 113–25.

Laks, A., and C. Louguet, eds. 2002. *Qu'est-ce que la philosophie présocratique? / What Is Presocratic Philosophy?* Lille: Presses Universitaires de Septentrion.

Laks, A., and G. W. Most, eds. 1997. *Studies on the Derveni Papyrus*. Oxford: Clarendon Press.

———. 2016: *Early Greek Philosophy*. 9 vols. Cambridge, MA: Harvard University Press.

Lambert, W. G. 1968. "Myth and Ritual As Conceived by the Babylonians." *Journal of Semitic Studies* 13: 104–12.

Ledbetter, G. M. 2003. *Poetics before Plato: Interpretation and Authority in Early Greek Theories of Poetry*. Princeton, NJ: Princeton University Press.

Lesher, J. H. 1984. "Parmenides' Critique of Thinking. The *poludēris elenchos* of Fragment 7." *Oxford Studies in Ancient Philosophy* 2: 1–30.

———, ed. and trans. 1992. *Xenophanes of Colophon: Fragments*. Toronto: University of Toronto Press.

———. 1999. "Early Interest in Knowledge." In Long 1999b, 225–49.

Leszl, W., ed. 1982. *I Presocratici*. Bologna: Il Mulino.

———. 1985. "Origine od origini di filosofia e scienza." *Quaderni di Storia* 11: 169–72.

———. 1989. "Zeller e i presocratici." *Annali della Scuola Normale Superiore di Pisa*, 3rd s. (19.3): 1143–87.

——. 2006. "Aristotle on the Unity of Presocratic Philosophy: A Contribution to the Reconstruction of the Early Retrospective View of Presocratic Philosophy." In Sassi 2006b, 355–80.

——. 2007. "Democritus' Works: From Their Titles to Their Contents." In Brancacci-Morel 2007, 11–76.

——. 2011. "From Hegel to Zeller." In Primavesi-Luchner 2011, 309–333.

Lewis, J. D. 2006. *Solon the Thinker: Political Thought in Archaic Athens.* London: Duckworth.

Lightfoot, J. L. 2007. *The Sibylline Oracles. With Introduction, Translation, and Commentary on the First and Second Books.* Oxford: Oxford University Press.

Lincoln, B. 1999. *Theorizing Myth: Narrative, Ideology, and Scholarship.* Chicago: University of Chicago Press.

Lloyd, G. E. R. 1966. *Polarity and Analogy: Two Types of Argumentation in Early Greek Thought.* Cambridge University Press, Cambridge.

——. 1967. "Popper versus Kirk: A Controversy in the Interpretation of Greek Science." *The British Journal for the Philosophy of Science* 18: 21–38. Reprinted in Lloyd 1991, 100–120.

——. 1970. *Early Greek Science: Thales to Aristotle.* London: Chatto & Windus.

——. 1979. *Magic, Reason and Experience: Studies in the Origin and Development of Greek Science.* Cambridge: Cambridge University Press.

——. 1982. "The Debt of Greek Philosophy and Science to the Ancient Near East." *Pedilavium* 14: 1–19. Reprinted in Lloyd 1991, 278–98.

——. 1987. *The Revolutions of Wisdom: Studies in the Claims and Practice of the Ancient Greek Science.* Berkeley: University of California Press.

——. 1990. *Demystifying Mentalities.* Cambridge: Cambridge University Press.

——. 1991 *Methods and Problems in Greek Science.* Cambridge: Cambridge University Press.

——. 1992. "The Invention of Nature." In *The Concept of Nature,* edited by J. B. Torrance, 1–24. Oxford: Clarendon Press, 1992. Reprinted in Lloyd 1991, 417–34.

——. 1996a. *Adversaries and Authorities: Investigations into Ancient Greek and Chinese Science.* Cambridge: Cambridge University Press.

——. 1996b. *"Images et modèles du monde."* In *Le savoir grec: Dictionnaire critique,* edited by J. Brunschwig and G. E. R. Lloyd with P. Pellegrin, 57–75. Paris: Flammarion.

——. 2002a. *The Ambitions of Curiosity: Understanding the World in Ancient Greece and China.* Cambridge: Cambridge University Press.

——. 2002b. "Ancient Science and Modern Justice." In *Le style de la pensée: Recueil de textes en hommage à Jacques Brunschwig,* edited by M. Canto and P. Pellegrin, 502–21. Paris: Les Belles Lettres.

——. 2002c. "Le pluralisme de la vie intellectuelle avant Platon." In Laks-Louguet 2002, 39–54.

——. 2003. *In the Grip of Disease. Studies in Ancient Greek Imagination.* Oxford-New York: Oxford University Press.

——. 2005. *The Delusions of Invulnerability: Wisdom and Morality in Ancient Greece, China and Today.* London: Duckworth.

——. 2006. "Diogenes of Apollonia: Master of Ducts." In Sassi 2006b, 237–57.

Lloyd, G. E. R., and N. Sivin. 2002. *The Way and the Word. Science and Medicine in Early China and Greece.* New Haven, CT: Yale University Press.

Long, A. A. 1999a. "The Scope of Early Greek Philosophy." In Long 1999b, 1–21.

——, ed. 1999b. *The Cambridge Companion to Early Greek Philosophy.* Cambridge: Cambridge University Press.

Luraghi, N. 2006. "Meta-*historiē*: Method and Genre in the 'Histories.'" In Dewald-Marincola 2006, 76–91.

Luzzatto, M. J. 1992. "Grecia e vicino Oriente: tracce della 'Storia di Ahiqar' nella cultura greca tra VI e V secolo a. C." *Quaderni di storia* 36: 5–84.

Machinist, P. 1986. "On Self-Consciousness in Mesopotamia." In Eisenstadt 1986, 183–202.

Maltomini, F. 2004. *"Sulla trasmissione dei 'Detti dei Sette Sapienti.'"* In *Aspetti di letteratura gnomica nel mondo antico*, edited by M. S. Funghi, 1–24. Florence: Olschki.

Manetti, G. 1997. "The Language of the Sibyls." *Euphrosyne* 25 (n.s.): 237–50.

——. 1998. *"Strategie del discorso oracolare: la scrittura." Atti del Convegno, Macerata—Norcia settembre 1994.* In *Sibille e linguaggi oracolari: Mito Storia Tradizione.* edited by I. Chirassi Colombo and T. Seppilli, 53–74. Pisa: Istituti Editoriali e Poligrafici Internazionali (longer version of Manetti 1997).

Mansfeld, J. 1967. "Heraclitus on the Psychology and Physiology of the Sleep and on Rivers." *Mnemosyne* 20: 1–29.

——. 1983. "Cratylus 402a–c: Plato or Hippias?" In Rossetti 1983, 43–55. Reprinted in Mansfeld 1990, 84–96.

——. 1984. "Mito scienza filosofia: Una questione di origini." *Quaderni di storia* 20: 43–67. Reprinted in Mansfeld 1990, 1–21.

——. 1985. "Aristotle and Others on Thales, or the Beginnings of Natural Philosophy (with Some Remarks on Xenophanes)." *Mnemosyne* 38: 109–29. Reprinted in Mansfeld 1990, 126–46.

——. 1989. "Fiddling the Books (Heraclitus B 129)." In Boudouris 1989, 229–34. Reprinted in Mansfeld 1990, 443–48.

——. 1990. *Studies in the Historiography of Greek Philosophy.* Assen-Maastricht: Van Gorcum.

——. 1995. "Insight by Hindsight: Intentional Unclarity in Presocratic Proems." *Bulletin of the Institute of Classical Studies* 40: 225–32.

Marincola, J. 2006. "Herodotus and the Poetry of the Past." In Dewald-Marincola 2006, 13–28.

Martin, A., and O. Primavesi, eds. 1999. *L'Empédocle de Strasbourg (P. Strasb. gr. Inv. 1665-1666).* Berlin and New York: De Gruyter.

Martin, J. 2003. *"Bedingungen der frühgriechischen Philosophie."* In *Philosophie und Lebenswelt in der Antike*, edited by K. Piepenbrink, 22–35. Darmstadt: Wissenschaftliche Buchgesellschaft.

Martin, R. P. 1993. "The Seven Sages as Performers of Wisdom." In Dougherty-Kurke 1993, 108–28.

Matson, W. I. 1954–55. "Cornford and the Birth of Metaphysics." *Review of Metaphysics* 8: 443–54.

Mattéi, J.-F., ed. 1990. *La naissance de la raison en Grèce. Actes de Congrès de Nice, Mai 1987.* Paris: Presses Universitaires de France.

Maul, S. 2015. "Kosmologie und Kosmogonie in der antiken Literatur: Das sog. babylonische Weltschöpfungsepos Enûma eliš." In Derron 2015, 15–49.

Meier, C. 1986. "The Emergence of an Autonomous Intelligence among the Greeks." In Eisenstadt 1986, 65–91.

Mele, A. 2001. "Il corpus epimenideo." In Gigante et al. 2001, 227–78.

Miller, M. H. 1977. "La logique implicite de la cosmogonie d'Hésiode." *Revue de Métaphysique et de Morale* 82: 433–56.

——. 2001. "'First of all': On the Semantics and Ethics of Hesiod's Cosmogony." *Ancient Philosophy* 21: 251–76.

Miralles, C. 1996. "Poeta, saggio, sofista, filosofo: L'intellettuale nella Grecia antica." In Settis 1996, 849–82.

Mogyoródi, E. 2000. "Thales and the Beginnings of Greek Philosophical Speculation: Problems of Interpretation." *Acta antiqua Academiae Scientiarum Hungaricae* 40: 335–48.

Momigliano, A. 1986. "Ancient Biography and the Study of Religion in the Roman Empire." *Annali della Scuola Normale Superiore di Pisa* 16.1 (3rd s.): 25–44. Reprinted in Momigliano, *Ottavo contributo alla Storia degli Studi Classici e del Mondo Antico*, 193–210. Rome: Edizioni di Storia e Letteratura, 1987.

Morel, P.-M., and J. F. Pradeau, eds. 2001. *Les anciens savants: Études sur les philosophies préplatoniciennes*. Strasburg: Cahiers Philosophiques de Strasbourg.

Morgan, C. 2003. *Early Greek States Beyond the Polis*. London: Routledge.

Morgan, K. A. 2000. *Myth and Philosophy from the Presocratics to Plato*. Cambridge: Cambridge University Press.

Morrison, J. S. 1955. "Parmenides and Er." *Journal of Hellenic Studies* 75: 59–68.

Most, G. W. 1987. "Alcman's 'Cosmogonic' Fragment." *Classical Quarterly* 37: 1–19.

——. 1993. "Hesiod and the Textualization of Personal Temporality." In Arrighetti-Montanari 1993, 73–92.

——. 1995. "*Pòlemos pànton patér: Die Vorsokratiker in der Forschung der Zwanziger Jaher.*" In *Altertumwissenschaft in den 20er Jahren. Neue Fragen und Impulse*, edited by H. Flashar and S. Vogt, 87–114. Stuttgart: Franz Steiner.

——. 1999a. "From Logos to Mythos." In Buxton 1999, 25–50.

——. 1999b. "The Poetics of Early Greek Philosophy." In Long 1999b, 332–62.

——. 2001. *Historicization=Historisierung*. Vol. 5, *Aporemata*. Göttingen: Vandenhoeck & Ruprecht.

——. 2003. "Ancient Philosophy and Religion." In Sedley 2003, 300–22.

——, ed. and trans. 2006. *Hesiod. Theogony, Works and Days, Testimonia*. Cambridge, MA: Harvard University Press.

——. 2007. "ἄλλος δ' ἐξ ἄλλου δέχεται: Presocratic Philosophy and Traditional Greek Epic." In *Wege zu einer mythisch-rituellen Poetik bei den Griechen*, edited by A. Bierl, R. Lämmle, and K. Wesselmann, 271–302. Berlin and New York: De Gruyter.

Mourelatos, A. P. D., ed. 1974. *The Presocratics. A Collection of Critical Essays*. New York: Anchor Press.

Murray, P. 1999. "What Is a Mythos for Plato?" In Buxton 1999, 251–62.

——. 2005. "The Muses: Creativity Personified?" In *Personification in the Greek World: From Antiquity to Byzantium*, edited by E. Stafford and J. Herrin, 147–59. Ashgate: Aldershot.

Nestle, W. 1923. *Die Nachsokratiker*. Jena: Diederichs (2 vols).

——. 1940. *Vom Mythos zum Logos. Die Selbstentfaltung des griechischen Denkens von Homer bis auf die Sophistik und Sokrates*. Stuttgart: Kröner.

Nieddu, G. F. 1984. "Testo, scrittura, libro nella Grecia arcaica e classica: Note e osservazioni sulla prosa scientifico-filosofica." *Scrittura e civiltà* 8: 213–61. Reprinted in Nieddu 2004, 71–120.

——. 1993. "*Neue Wissenformen, Kommunikationstechniken und schriftliche Ausdrucksformen in Griechenland im sechsten und fünften Jh. v. Chr.: Einige Beobachtungen.*" In Kullmann-Althoff 1993, 151–66. Italian text reprinted, revised, and expanded, in Nieddu 2004, 121–36.

——. 2004. *La scrittura "madre delle Muse." Agli esordi di un nuovo modello di comunicazione culturale*. Amsterdam: Hakkert.

Nightingale, A. W. 1995. *Genres in Dialogue: Plato and the Construct of Philosophy*. Cambridge: Cambridge University Press.

——. 2000. "Sages, Sophists, and Philosophers: Greek Wisdom Literature." In Taplin 2000, 156–91.

——. 2001. "On Wandering and Wondering. ⟨Theoria⟩ in Greek Philosophy and Culture." *Arion* 9 (ser. 3): 23–58.

——. 2004. *Spectacles of Truth in Classical Greek Philosophy:* Theoria *in Its Cultural Context.* Cambridge: Cambridge University Press.

——. 2007. "The Philosophers in Archaic Greek Culture." In Shapiro 2007, 169–98.

Nussbaum, M. C. 1972a. "ΨΥΧΗ in Heraclitus, I." *Phronesis* 17: 1–16.

——. 1972b. "ΨΥΧΗ in Heraclitus, II." *Phronesis* 17: 153–70.

Obbink, D. 1993. "The Addressees of Empedocles." *Materiali e Discussioni* 31: 51–98.

——. 1997. "Cosmology As Initiation vs. the Critique of Orphic Mysteries." In Laks-Most 1997, 39–54.

O'Brien, D. 1969. *Empedocles' Cosmic Cycle: A Reconstruction from the Fragments and Secondary Sources.* Cambridge: Cambridge University Press.

O'Grady, P. F. 2002. *Thales of Miletus. The Beginnings of Western Science and Philosophy.* Burlington: Ashgate.

Ong, W. J. 1982. *Orality and Literacy. The Technologizing of the Word.* London and New York: Methuen.

Osborne, C. 1987a. "Empedocles Recycled." *Classical Quarterly* 37: 24–50.

——. 1987b. *Rethinking Early Greek Philosophy. Hippolytus of Rome and the Presocratics.* Ithaka (N.Y.): Cornell University Press.

——. 1998. "Was Verse the Default Form for Presocratic Philosophy?" In Atherton 1998, 23–35.

——. 2005. "Sin and Moral Responsibility in Empedocles' Cosmic Cycle." In *The Empedoclean Cosmos. Structure, Process, and the Question of Cyclicity*, edited by A. Pierris, 283–308. Patras: Institute for Philosophical Research.

Owen, G. E. L. 1960. "Eleatic Questions." *Classical Quarterly* 10: 84–102. Reprinted in Furley-Allen 1975, 48–81.

Padel, R. 1992. *In and Out of Mind: Greek Images of the Tragic Self.* Princeton, NJ: Princeton University Press.

Palmer, J. A. 2000. "Aristotle on the Ancient Theologians." *Apeiron* 32: 181–205.

Palumbo, L. 2007. "Empedocle e il linguaggio poetico." In *Empedocle tra poesia, medicina, filosofia e politica*, edited by G. Casertano, 83–107. Naples: Loffredo.

Patzer, A. 1986. *Der Sophist Hippias als Philosophiehistoriker.* Freiburg-München: Verlag Karl Alber.

Pébarthe, C. 2006. *Cité Démocratie et Écriture: Histoire de l'alphabétisation d'Athènes à l'époque classique.* Paris: De Boccard.

Pellegrin, P. 2006. "Ancient Medicine and Its Contribution to the Philosophical Tradition." In Gill-Pellegrin 2006, 664–85.

Pellizer, E. 1990. "Outlines of a Morphology of Sympotic Entertainment." In *Sympotica: A Symposium on the Symposion*, edited by O. Murray, 177–84. Oxford: Oxford Clarendon Press.

Perilli, L. 2007a. "*Conservazione dei testi e circolazione della conoscenza in Grecia.*" In *Biblioteche del mondo antico: Dalla tradizione orale alla cultura dell'Impero*, edited by A. M. Andrisano, 36–71. Rome: Carocci.

——. 2007b. "Democritus, Zoology and the Physicians." In Brancacci-Morel 2007, 143–307.

Petit, A. 1992. "La tradition critique dans le Pythagorisme ancien: Une contribution au 'miracle grec.'" In Thivel 1992, 101–15.

Philippson, P. 1936. *Genealogie als mythische Form: Studien zur Theogonie des Hesiod.* Oslo: Brøgger.

Piano, V. 2016. Il papiro di Derveni tra religione e filosofia. Florence: Olschki.

Pierris, A. L. 2007. *Mystery and Philosophy.* Vol. 2, *The Emergence of Reason from the Spirit of Mystery.* Patras: Institute for Philosophical Research.

Popper, K. R. 1958-59. "Back to the Presocratics." *Proceedings of the Aristotelian Society* 49:1-24. Revised in Popper 1963, 136-53 and reprinted in Furley-Allen 1970, 130-53.

———. 1963. *Conjectures and Refutations. The Growth of Scientific Knowledge.* London: Routledge & Kegan Paul.

———. 1998. *The World of Parmenides. Essays on Presocratic Enlightenment.* London: Routledge.

Primavesi, O. 2001. "La daimonologia della fisica empedoclea." *Aevum antiquum* 1 (n.s.): 3-68.

Primavesi, O., et al. 2001. "Sul nuovo Empedocle, Forum." *Aevum antiquum* 1 (n.s.): 3-259.

Primavesi, O. and K. Luchner, eds. 2011. *The Presocratics from the Latin Middle Ages to Hermann Diels.* Stuttgart: Franz Steiner.

Pugliese Carratelli, G. 1988. "La θέα di Parmenide." *La Parola del Passato* 43: 337-46.

———. 2001. *Le lamine d'oro orfiche. Istruzioni per il viaggio oltrremondano degli iniziati greci.* Milan: Adelphi.

Ragone, G. 2005. "Colofone, Claro, Notio. Un contesto per Senofane." In Bugno 2005, 9-45.

Rangos, S. 2007. "Latent Meaning and Manifest Content in the Derveni Papyrus." *Rhizai* 4: 35-75.

Rappe, G. 2001. "*Wiedergeburt als Mnemotechnik zur Anthropologie bei Empedokles und Platon.*" In *Wiedergeburt und kulturelles Erbe,* edited by W. Schweidler, 61-85. Sankt Augustin: Academia Verlag.

Rechenauer, G., ed. 2005. *Frühgriechisches Denken.* Göttingen: Vandenhoeck & Ruprecht.

Riedweg, C. 1995. "Orphisches bei Empedokles." *Antike und Abendland* 41: 34-59.

———. 1997. " 'Pythagoras hinterliess keine einzige Schrift'—ein Irrtum? Anmerkungen zu einer alten Streitrage." *Museum Helveticum* 54: 65-92.

Rivier, A. 1956. "Remarques sur les fragments 34 et 35 de Xénophane." *Revue de Philologie* 30: 37-61. Reprinted in A. Rivier, *Études de littérature grecque,* 337-67. Geneva: Droz.

Robb, K. 1983a. "Preliterate Ages and the Linguistic Art of Heraclitus." In Robb 1983b, 153-206.

———. ed. 1983b. *Language and Thought in Early Greek Philosophy.* Illinois: La Salle.

Robbiano, C. 2006. *Becoming Being: On Parmenides' Transformative Philosophy.* Sankt Augustin: Academia Verlag.

Rochberg, F. 2005. "Mesopotamian Cosmology." In Snell 2005, 333-52.

Romeyer-Dherbey, G. 1999. "'*Mais quand brille un rayon accordé par le dieu': Le kairos chez Pindare.*" In G. Romeyer-Dherbey, *La parole archaïque,* 5-13. Paris: Presses Universitaires de France.

Roochnik, D. 1985. "The First Philosopher (and the Poet)." *Classical and Modern Literature* 6: 39-54.

Roselli, A. 2006. "Strategie espositive nei trattati ippocratici: Presenza autoriale e piano espositivo in Malattie IV e in Fratture e Articolazioni." In Sassi 2006b, 259-83.

Rossetti, L. ed. 1983. *Atti del Sympsium Heracliteum 1981.* Rome: Edizioni dell'Ateneo.

———. 1992. "Ésope et le 'Miracle' du paradoxe à l'aube de la civilisation grecque." In Thivel 1992, 69-79.

Rossetti, L., and Santaniello, C., eds. 2004. *Studi sul pensiero e sulla lingua di Empedocle.* Bari: Levante.

Rossi, L. E. 1992. "*L'ideologia dell'oralità fino a Platone.*" In *Lo spazio letterario della Grecia antica* I 1: 77-106, edited by G. Cambiano, L. Canfora, and D. Lanza. Rome: Salerno Editrice.

Rossi, P., ed. 1988. *La memoria del sapere: Forme di conservazione e strutture organizzative dall'antichità a oggi*. Rome-Bari: Laterza.

Roussel, M. 1990. "Rationalité et vocabulaire mystique: À propos de certains termes ayant une origine ou une connotation religieuse, en usage chez les présocratiques." In Mattéi 1990: 153–64.

Rowe, C. 1983. "Archaic Thought in Hesiod." *Journal of Hellenic Studies* 103: 124–35.

Rudberg, G. 1948. "Xenophanes Satiriker und Polemiker." *Symbolae Osloenses* 26: 126–33.

Santoni, A. 1983. "Temi e motivi di interesse socio-economico nella leggenda dei 'Sette Sapienti.'" *Annali della Scuola Normale Superiore di Pisa* 13.1 (3rd s.): 91–160.

Sassi, M. M. 1978. *Le teorie della percezione in Democrito*. Florence: La Nuova Italia.

——. 1980. "Cosmologie ioniche: modelli e sviluppo." *La Parola del Passato* 35: 81–103.

——. 1982a. "Dalla scienza delle religioni di Usener ad Aby Warburg." In Arrighetti et al. 1982, 65–92.

——. 1982b. "Xenophan. B 16 e Herodt. 4,108: Una nota sul significato di πυρρός." *Rivista di Filologia e di Istruzione Classica* 110: 391–93.

——. 1986. "La freddezza dello storico: Christian Gottlob Heyne." *Annali della Scuola Normale Superiore di Pisa*, 16.1 (3rd s.): 105–26.

——. 1987. "*Tra religione e scienza: il pensiero pitagorico*." In *Storia della Calabria*, vol I.1: *La Calabria Antica*, edited by G. Cingari, 565–87. Reggio Calabria: Gangemi.

——. 1988a. *La scienza dell'uomo nella Grecia antica*. Turin: Bollati Boringhieri. Translated by P. Tucker as *The Science of Man in Ancient Greece*. Chicago: Chicago University Press.

——. 1988b. "Parmenide al bivio. Per un'interpretazione del proemio." *La Parola del Passato* 43: 383–96.

——. 1991. "*Il viaggio e la festa. Note sulla rappresentazione dell'ideale filosofico della vita*." In *Idea e realtà del viaggio. Il viaggio nel mondo antico*, edited by G. Camassa and S. Fasce, 17–36. Genoa: ECIG.

——, ed. and trans. 1993. *Platone. Apologia di Socrate. Critone*. Milan: Rizzoli.

——. 1994. "*La filosofia 'italica': genealogia e varianti di una formula storiografica*." In A. C. Cassio and P. Poccetti, eds. *Forme di religiosità e tradizioni sapienziali in Magna Grecia*. Atti del convegno, Napoli "L'Orientale", Dipartimento di Studi del Mondo Classico e Mediterraneo Antico. Sezione filologico-letteraria (16), 29–53.

——. 1996. "La storia del pensiero." In Settis 1996, vol. 1, 743–69.

——. 2002. "La naissance de la philosophie de l'esprit de la tradition." In Laks-Louguet 2002, 55–81.

——. 2005b. "Poesie und Kosmogonie: der Fall Alkman." In Rechenauer 2005, 63–80.

——. 2006a. "Anassimandro e la scrittura della 'legge' cosmica." In Sassi 2006c, 3–26.

——, ed. 2006b. *La costruzione del discorso filosofico nell'età dei Presocratici / The Construction of Philosophical Discourse in the Age of Presocratics*. Pisa: Edizioni della Normale.

——. 2006c. "*Stili di pensiero ad Elea: Per una contestualizzazione degli inizi della filosofia*." In *Velia: Atti del quarantacinquesimo convegno di studi sulla Magna Grecia, Taranto-Marina di Ascea 21–25 settembre 2005*, 95–114. Taranto: Istituto per la Storia e l'Archeologia della Magna Grecia.

——. 2007. "Ordre cosmique et 'isonomia': En repensant Les origines de la pensée grecque de Jean-Pierre Vernant." *Philosophie antique* 7: 187–216.

——. 2011. "*Ionian Philosophy and Italic Philosophy: From Diogenes Laertius to Diels*." In *The Presocratics from the Latin Middle Ages to Hermann Diels*, edited by O. Primavesi and K. Luchner, 19–44. Stuttgart: Franz Steiner.

——. 2013a. "*La logique de l'eoikos et ses transformations: Xénophane, Parménide, Platon*." *Philosophie antique* 13: 13–35.

———. 2013b: "Where Epistemology and Religion Meet. What Do(es) the God(s) Look Like?" *Rhizomata* 1: 283–307.

———. 2015. *Indagine su Socrate. Persona filosofo cittadino.* Turin: Einaudi.

———. 2016. "Parmenides and Empedocles on *Krasis* and Knowledge." *Apeiron* 5: 1–19.

Scarpi, P., ed. 2002. *Le religioni dei misteri.* 2 vols. Milan: Mondadori.

Schefer, B. 2000. "Nur für Eingewehite!: Heraklit und die Mysterien." *Antike und Abendland* 46: 46–75.

Schenkeveld, D. M. 1992. "Prose Usages of Akouein 'To Read.'" *Classical Quarterly* 42: 129–41.

Schibli, H. S. 1990. *Pherekydes of Syros.* Oxford: Clarendon Press.

Schick, C. 1955a. "Appunti per una storia della prosa greca. *I.* La lingua delle iscrizioni." *Rivista di Filologia e Istruzione Classica* 32: 361–90.

———. 1955b. "Studi sui primordi della prosa greca." *Archivio Glottologico Italiano* 40: 89–135.

———. 1955–56. "Appunti per una storia della prosa greca. La lingua dei filosofi naturalisti ionici del V secolo: Anassagora, Diogene di Apollonia, Democrito." *Atti dell'Accademia delle Scienze di Torino* 90: 462–96.

Schiefsky, M. J., ed. and trans. 2005a. *Hippocrates' "On Ancient Medicine."* Leiden: Brill.

———. 2005b. "'On Ancient Medicine' on the Nature of Human Beings." In van der Eijk 2005, 69–85.

Schlesier, R. 1994. *Kulte, Mythen und Gelehrte. Anthropologie der Antike seit 1800.* Frankfurt: Fischer, Frankfurt.

Schmalzriedt, E. 1970. *"Peri Physeos": Zur Frühgeschichte der Buchtitel.* Munich: Fink.

Schnapp-Gourbeillon, A. 2002. *Aux origines de la Grèce (XIII-VIII siècles avant notre ère): La genèse du politique.* Paris: Les Belles Lettres.

Schofield, Malcom. 1991. "Heraclitus' Theory of Soul and Its Antecedents." In Everson 1991, 13–34.

Schwabl, H. 1962. *"Weltschöpfung."* In *Pauly-Wissowa Realencyclopädie der classischen Altertumswissenschaft* Suppl. IX, coll. 1433–1582, edited by K. Ziegler.

———. 1963. "Hesiod und Parmenides: Zur Formung des parmenideischen Prooimions (28 B 1)." *Rheinisches Museum* 106: 134–42.

Scodel, R. 1996. "Self-Correction, Spontaneity, and Orality in Archaic Poetry." In *Voice into Text: Orality and Literacy in Ancient Greece,* edited by I. Worthington, 59–79. Leiden: Brill.

———. 2001. "Poetic Authority and Oral Tradition in Hesiod and Pindar." In *Speaking Volumes: Orality and Literacy in the Greek and Roman World,* edited by J. Watson, 109–37. Leiden : Brill.

———. 2002. *Listening to Homer. Tradition, Narrative, and Audience.* Ann Arbor: University of Michigan Press.

Seaford, R. 1986. "Immortality, Salvation and the Elements." *Harvard Studies in Classical Philology* 90: 1–26.

———. 2004. *Money and the Early Greek Mind: Homer, Philosophy, Tragedy.* Cambridge: Cambridge University Press.

Sedley, D. 1998. *Lucretius and the Transformation of Greek Wisdom.* Cambridge: Cambridge University Press.

———, ed. 2003. *The Cambridge Companion to Greek and Roman Philosophy.* Cambridge: Cambridge University Press.

———. 2007. *Creationism and Its Critics in Antiquity.* Berkeley: University of California Press.

Seligman, P. 1978. "Soul and Cosmos in Presocratic Philosophy." *Dionysius* 2: 5–17.

Settis, S. 1973. "Policleto fra 'sophia' e 'mousike.'" *Rivista di Filologia e di Istruzione Classica* 101: 303–17.

———. 1993. *"La trattatistica delle arti figurative."* In *Lo spazio letterario della Grecia antica* I, 2, 469–98, edited by G. Cambiano, L. Canfora, and D. Lanza. Rome: Salerno Editore.

———, ed. 1996. *Noi e i Greci.* Vol. 1, *Greci: Storia cultura arte società.* Turin: Einaudi.

Shapiro H. A., ed. 2007. *The Cambridge Companion to Archaic Greece.* Cambridge: Cambridge University Press.

Sharp, K. 2006. "From Solon to Socrates: Proto-Socratic Dialogues in Herodotus." In Sassi 2006b, 81–102.

Sider, D. 1997. "Heraclitus in the Derveni Papyrus." In Laks-Most 1997, 129–48.

Snell, B. 1926. "Die Sprache Heraklits." *Hermes* 61: 353–81.

———. ed. 1938. *Leben und Meinungen der Sieben Weisen. Griechische und lateinische Quellen erläutert und übertragen von B. Snell.* Munich: Heimeran Verlag.

———. 1944. "Die Nachrichten über die Lehren des Thales und die Anfänge der griechischen Philosophie und Literaturgeschichte." *Philologus* 96: 170–82. Reprinted in Snell 1966, 119–128. Reprinted in *Sophistik*, edited by C. J. Classen, 478–90. Darmstadt: Wissenschaftliche Buchgesellschaft.

———. 1947. *Die Entdeckung des Geistes: Studien zur Entstehung des europäischen Denkens bei den Griechen.* Hamburg: Classen und Goverts. Translated by T. G. Rosenmeyer as *The Discovery of the Mind: The Greek Origins of European Thought.* Oxford: Blackwell 1953.

———. 1966. *Gesammelte Schriften.* Göttingen: Vandenhoeck und Ruprecht.

Snell, D. C., ed. 2005. *A Companion to the Ancient Near East.* Malden: Blackwell.

Solmsen, F. 1949. *Hesiod and Aeschylus.* Ithaca: Cornell University Press.

———. 1950. "Chaos and 'Apeiron.'" *Studi Italiani di Filologia Classica*, 24 (n.s.): 235–48; reprinted in Solmsen, *Kleine Schriften*, vol. 1, 68–91. Hildesheim: Georg Olms.

———. 1971. "The Tradition about Zeno of Elea Re-Examined." *Phronesis* 16: 116–41. Reprinted in Mourelatos 1974, 368–93.

Stannard, J. 1965. "The Presocratic Origin of Explanatory Method." *The Philosophical Quarterly* 15: 193–206.

Stehle, E. 2005. "The Addressees of Empedokles, 'Katharmoi' Fr. B 112: Performance and Moral Implications." *Ancient Philosophy* 25: 247–72.

Strauss Clay, J. 2003. *Hesiod's Cosmos.* Cambridge: Cambridge University Press.

———. 2015. "Commencing Cosmogony and the Rhetoric of Poetic Authority." In Derron 2015, 105–47.

Svenbro, J. 1988. *Phrasikleia. Anthropologie de la lecture en Grèce ancienne.* Paris: La Découverte.

Tannery, P. 1930. *Pour l'histoire de la science hellène de Thalès à Empédocle.* Paris: Gauthiers-Villars. First published 1887 by Alcan.

Taplin O., ed. 2000. *Literature in the Greek and Roman Worlds: A New Perspective.* Oxford: Oxford University Press.

Thivel, A. 1992. *Le miracle grec. Actes du II colloque sur la pensée antique organisé par le C.R.H.I., Nice, 18–20 Mai 1989.* Paris: Les Belles Lettres.

Thomas, Rosalind. 1996. "Written in Stone? Liberty, Equality, Orality and the Codification of Law." In *Greek Law in Its Political Setting: Justifications not Justice*, edited by L. Foxhall and A. D. E. Lewis, 3–31. Oxford: Clarendon Press.

———. 2000. *Herodotus in Context. Ethnography, Science, and the Art of Persuasion.* Cambridge: Cambridge University Press.

———. 2003. "Prose Performance Texts: Epideixis and Written Publication in the Late Fifth and Early Fourth Centuries." In Yunis 2003b, 162–88.

——. 2005. "Writing, Law, and Written Law." In *The Cambridge Companion to Ancient Greek Law*, edited by M. Gagarin and D. J. Cohen, 41–60. Cambridge: Cambridge University Press.

——. 2006. "The Intellectual Milieu of Herodotus." In Dewald-Marincola 2006, 60–75.

Thomson, G., 1953. "From Religion to Philosophy." *Journal of Hellenic Studies* 73: 77–83.

——. 1955. *The First Philosophers. Studies in Ancient Greek Society.* London: Lawrence and Wishart.

Tortorelli Ghidini, M. 2006. *Figli della terra e del cielo stellato: Testi orfici con traduzione e commento.* Naples: D'Auria.

Trépanier, S. 2004. *Empedocles: An Interpretation.* New York: Routledge.

Tulli, M. 1993. "La coscienza di sé in Parmenide." In G. Arrighetti and F. Montanari 1993, 141–62.

——. 2000. "Esiodo nella memoria di Parmenide." In G. Arrighetti and M. Tulli 2000, 65–81.

Turrini, G. 1977. "Contributo all'analisi del termine 'eikos', I: L'età arcaica." *Acme* 30: 541–58.

Valeri, V. 1995. *"Miti cosmogonici e ordine." Parole Chiave* 7/8: 93–110. Reprinted in Valeri, *Uno spazio tra sé e sé, L'antropologia come ricerca del soggetto,* 163–80. Rome: Donzelli.

van der Eijk, P. J. 1997. "Towards a Rhetoric of Ancient Scientific Discourse: Some Formal Characteristics of Greek Medical and Philosophical Texts." In *Grammar as Interpretation: Greek Literature in its Linguistic Contexts,* edited by E. J. Bakker, 77–129. Leiden : Brill.

——, ed. 2005. *Hippocrates in Context: Papers Read at the XIth International Hippocrates Colloquium, Newcastle upon Tyne, 27–31 August 2002.* Leiden: Brill.

van Dongen, E. 2007. "Contacts Between Pre-classical Greece and the Near East in the Context of Cultural Influences: An Overview." In *Getrennte Wege? Kommunikation, Raum und Wahrnehmung in der Alten Welt,* edited by A. Luther, R. Rollinger, and J. Wiesehöfer, 13–49. Frankfurt: Verlag Antike.

Vegetti, M. 1992. *"Anima e corpo."* In *Il sapere degli antichi,* II, *Introduzione alle culture antiche,* edited by M. Vegetti, 201–28. Turin: Bollati Boringhieri.

——. 1996a. *"Iatromantis."* In *I signori della memoria e dell'oblio: Figure della comunicazione nella cultura antica,* edited by M. Bettini, 65–81. Florence: La Nuova Italia.

——. 1996b. "L'io, l'anima, il soggetto." In Settis 1996, 431–67. Reprinted in Vegetti 2007, 43–80.

——. 1998. *"Empedocle 'medico e sofista.' 'Antica Medicina 20'".* In *Text and Tradition: Studies in Ancient Medicine and Its Transmission, presented to J. Kollesch,* edited by K.-D. Fischer, D. Nickel, and P. Potter, 289–99. Leiden, Boston, and Cologne: Brill.

——. 1999. "Culpability, Responsibility, Cause: Philosophy, Historiography, and Medicine in the Fifth Century." In Long 1999b, 271–89. Reprinted in Vegetti 2007, 93–109.

——. 2007. *Dialoghi con gli antichi.* Selected writings edited by S. Gastaldi, F. Calabi, S. Campese, and F. Ferrari. Sankt Augustin: Academia Verlag.

Velardi, R. 2004. "Parola e immagine nella Grecia antica (e una pagina di Italo Calvino)." *AION: Annali dell'Università degli Studi di Napoli "L'Orientale," Dipartimento di Studi del Mondo Classico e del Mediterraneo Antico. Sezione filologico-letteraria* 26: 191–219.

Verbeke, G. 1961. "Philosophie et conceptions préphilosophiques chez Aristote." *Revue Philosophique de Louvain* 49: 405–30.

Verdenius, W. J. 1960. "Traditional and Personal Elements in Aristotle's Religion." *Phronesis* 5: 56–70.

——. 1966. "Der Logosbegriff bei Heraklit und Parmenides, I." *Phronesis* 11: 81–98.

Vernant, J.-P. 1957. *"Du mythe à la raison: La formation de la pensée positive dans la Grèce archaïque." Annales (E.S.C.)* 12: 183–206. English translation in Vernant 1982, 354–98.

——. 1962. *Les origines de la pensée grecque.* Paris: Presses Universitaires de France. Translated as *The Origins of Greek Thought.* Ithaca: Cornell University Press, 1982.

——. 1965. *Mythe et pensée chez les Grecs: Études de psychologie historique.* Paris: Maspero. Translated by J. Lloyd, with J. Fort as *Myth and Thought among the Greeks.* London: Routledge & Kegan Paul 1983.

——. 1970. "Thétis et le poème cosmogonique d'Alcman." In *Hommages à Marie Delcourt,* 219–33. Bruxelles: Latomus.

——. 1987. "Greek Religion." In *Encyclopedia of Religion,* vol. 6, edited by M. Eliade. London and New York: Macmillan. Reedited in French with an introduction by the author, as *"Mythe et religion en Grèce ancienne."* Paris: Éditions du Seuil, Paris, 1990.

——. 1996. "Écriture et religion civique en Grèce." In J. Bottéro, C. Herrenschmidt, and J.-P. Vernant 1996, 189–223.

Vetta, M., ed. 1983. *Poesia e simposio nella Grecia antica.* Rome-Bari: Laterza.

Vidal-Naquet, P. 2000. *"Raison et déraison dans l'histoire."* Foreword to *Thucydide: "La Guerre du Péloponnèse."* Edited and translated by D. Roussel. Paris: Gallimard. Also in P. Vidal-Naquet, *"Les Grecs, les historiens, la démocratie: Le grand écart."* 84–110. Paris: La Découverte.

Vlastos, G. 1946. "Solonian Justice." *Classical Philology* 61: 65–83.

——. 1947. "Equality and Justice in Early Greek Cosmologies." *Classical Philology* 42: 156–78. Reprinted in Furley-Allen 1970, 59–91.

——. 1952. "Theology and Philosophy in Early Greek Thought." *Philosophical Quarterly* 2: 97–123. Reprinted in Furley-Allen 1970, 92–129.

——. 1953. "Isonomia." *American Journal of Philology* 74: 337–66.

——. 1955. Review of Cornford 1952. *Gnomon* 27: 65–76. Reprinted with the title "Cornford's *Principium Sapientiae*" in Furley-Allen 1970, 42–55.

——. 1975. *Plato's Universe.* Seattle: University of Washington Press.

Voelke, A.-J. 1981. *"Aux origines de la philosophie grecque: La cosmogonie d'Alcman."* In *Métaphysique, histoire de la philosophie: Recueil d'études offert à F. Brunner,* 13–24. Neuchâtel: La Baconnière.

——. 1984. "Vers une compréhension renouvelée des origines de la philosophie grecque: la cosmogonie d'Alcman." *Desmos* 7: 11–14.

——. 1985. "La naissance de la philosophie selon Giorgio Colli." *Revue de Théologie et de Philosophie* 3: 208–13.

von Fritz, K. 1971. *"Der Ursprung der Wissenschaft bei den Griechen."* In *Grundprobleme der Geschichte der antiken Wissenschaft,* 1–326. Berlin: De Gruyter.

von Staden, H. 1992. "Affinities and Elisions. Helen and Hellenocentrism." *Isis* 83: 578–95.

Warren, J. 2007. *Presocratics: Natural Philosophers before Socrates.* Berkeley and Los Angeles: University of California Press.

Wesenberg, B. 1984. *"Zu den Schriften griechischer Architekten."* In *Bauplanung und Bautheorie der Antike* 4: *Diskussionen zur archäologischen Bauforschung,* 39–47. Berlin: Deutsches Archäologisches Institut.

Wessely, A., ed. 2002. *Intellectuals and the Politics of the Humanities.* Budapest: Collegium Budapest.

West, M. L. 1963. "Three Presocratic Cosmologies (Alcman, Pherecydes, Thales)." *Classical Quarterly* 13: 154–76.

——. 1967. "Alcman and Pythagoras." *Classical Quarterly* 61 (n.s. 17): 1–15.

——. 1971. *Early Greek Philosophy and the Orient.* Oxford: Oxford University Press.

West, M. L., ed. 1966. *Hesiod, Theogony*. Oxford: Clarendon Press.

Wildberg, C. 2001. "Commentary on Curd (2001)." *Proceedings of the Boston Area Colloquium in Ancient Philosophy* 17: 50–56.

Wöhrle, G. 1992. "Zur Prosa der milesischen Philosophen." *Würzburger Jahrbücher* N.F. 18: 33–47.

———. 1993a. "War Parmenides ein schlechter Dichter? Oder: zur Form der Wissensvermittlung in der frühgriechischen Philosophie." In Kullmann-Althoff 1993, 167–80.

———. 1993b. *"Xenophanes' parodistische Technik."* In *Literaturparodie in Antike und Mittelalter*, edited by W. Ax and R. F. Glei, 13–25. Trier: Wissenschaftlicher Verlag Trier.

Wright, R. 1998. "Philosopher Poets: Parmenides and Empedocles." In Atherton 1998, 1–22.

Xella, P. 2006. "Prima delle Muse. Maestri, scribi e cantori nel vicino Oriente pre-classico." In Beta 2006, 13–26.

Yunis, H. 2003a. "Writing for Reading: Thucydides, Plato, and the Emergence of the Critical Reader." In Yunis 2003b, 189–212.

———, ed. 2003b. *Written Texts and the Rise of Literate Culture in Ancient Greece*. Cambridge: Cambridge University Press.

Zaicev, A. 1993. *Das griechische Wunder. Die Entstehung der griechischen Zivilisation*. Konstanz: Universitätsverlag Konstanz.

Zhmud, L. 1992. "Orphism and Graffiti from Olbia." *Hermes* 120: 159–68.

———. 2012. *Pythagoras and the Early Pythagoreans*. Translated by K. Windle and R. Ireland. Oxford and New York: Oxford University Press.

Abaris, 51, 168
Ackerman, Robert, 9n18
Acusilaus of Argos, 59–60
Adomenas, Mantas, 21n48, 43n20
Aelian, 121
Aeschylus, xx
Aëtius, 114n11, 175n100
Agathemerus, 90
Ahiqar, 79
Alcaeus, xix, 96, 162
Alcmaeon of Croton, xx, 29, 68, 71–72,
    82n34, 141, 146–49, 159, 162, 169
Alcman, xix, 29, 53–57, 78
Algra, Keimpe, 62n51
Alighieri, Dante, 10
Allan, William, 15n35
Amphidamas, 32, 47
Anacreon, 96
Anaxagoras, xx, 2, 21, 29, 48, 61, 67, 80,
    83, 116, 130n51, 137n64, 151, 160,
    171–72, 174
Anaximander, xii, xvi, xix, 3, 12–13, 15,
    24n54, 35, 37–48, 50–54, 56, 58, 60–63,
    68, 75, 78, 81–93, 99–100, 106–7, 111,
    137, 140, 171
Anaximenes, xix, 3, 37, 39n10, 40n14, 41,
    43, 44, 50, 52, 60, 61, 61n49, 62, 63,
    75, 78, 83, 100, 111, 114, 114n11, 116,
    118, 136
Antiphon the Sophist, xx, 30, 174n97,
Apollodorus of Athens, 160n50
Archilochus, xx, 57, 100, 162
Archytas of Tarentum, xx, 72, 171
Aristagoras of Miletus, 90
Aristeas of Proconnesus, 51, 119, 119n23,
    120–21, 156, 168
Aristophanes, xx
Aristotle, ix, xii–xvi, 2, 4, 5, 5n7, 6, 19,
    21–24, 24n55, 25, 25n58, 26–31, 36, 38,
    40, 41, 43, 44, 48, 49, 49n27, 49n28, 50,
    51, 52, 53, 55, 56, 61, 61n49, 63, 64, 72,
    78, 85n46, 90, 97n68, 102, 111, 112, 113,
    120, 127, 128, 128n44, 134n60, 137, 138,

151, 158, 161, 161n53, 161n54, 169,
    173n92, 174n97, 177
Arrighetti, Graziano 49n29, 144n9
Asper, Markus, 83n37, 84n42
Athenaeus of Naucratis, 166
Averincev, Sergej Sergeevič, 70, 71n13

Balaudé, Jean-François, 25n57
Barnes, Jonathan, 6n9, 128
Bathyllus, 72, 146
Baumgarten, Roland, 105n88, 123n30
Beall, E. E., 2n2
Beard, Mary, 9n17
Bernabé, Alberto, 50n30, 122n29, 125n35,
    125n36
Bertelli, Lucio, 76n25
Berti, Enrico, 28n61
Betegh, Gábor, 67n6, 116n18, 118, 118n22,
    119, 123n32, 129n45, 133n58, 137n65,
    170n85
Blank, David L., 157n42
Blumenberg, Hans, 4n5
Bodei, Remo, 8n13
Bodnár, István, 173n96
Böhme, Gernot, 175n102
Bollack, Jean, 131n52, 134, 134n61,
    162n58, 165n67, 167n72
Bolton, James D. P., 119n23
Bonanate, Ugo, 9n18
Bonazzi, Mauro, 174n97
Bordigoni, Carlitria, 161n51
Borsche, Tilman, 8n13
Bottéro, Jean, 7n10, 58, 58n41
Bouvier, David, 175n101
Brancacci, Aldo, 2n2
Bravo, Benedetto, 65n2, 82n35, 103n82,
    124, 124n34
Breglia Pulci Doria, Luisa, 50n30
Bréhier, Émile, 11n22
Bremmer, Jan, 121n26
Bresson, Alain, 76n25
Brillante, Carlo, 142n6
Brisson, Luc, 19, 20n47, 71n15

Broadie, Sarah, 43n20, 165n65

Brodsky, Joseph, 142

Brotinus, 72, 146,

Brucker, Johann J., 5

Bryan, Jenny, 147n18

Buddha, xv

Burkert, Walter, xiii, xv, 16, 16n38, 17,
  17n39, 17n41, 18, 18n43, 18n44, 25,
  38, 39n10, 98n69, 109n97, 123n29,
  156, 156n39

Burnet, John, 6

Burnyeat, Myles F., 80n32

Busch, Stephan, 80n32

Butti de Lima, Paulo, 4n5

Calame, Claude, 54n34, 123, 124n33, 127

Calder III, William Musgrave, 9n18,
  10n18

Calzolari, Alessandro, 163n61, 163n62

Camassa, Giorgio, 76n25

Cambiano, Giuseppe, xiii, 6n9, 22n51,
  29n64, 62, 62n52, 68n7, 108n93

Cardona, Giorgio Raimondo, 73n18,
  75n21

Casadio, Giovanni, 128n42

Casertano, Giovanni, 22n51

Cassio, Albio Cesare, 156n39

Cassirer, Ernst, 8, 18

Cavallo, Guglielmo, 108n92

Caveing, Maurice, 169n80

Centrone, Bruno, 118n21

Cerri, Giovanni, 154n36, 156, 157n40,
  164n63

Chadwick, John, 74

Chambers, Mortimer, 10n19

Cherniss, Harold, xii, xiii, 24n53, 24n54,
  83n39, 153n34, 161n52

Chersiphron, 84

Cicero, Marcus Tullius, 2

Classen, Carl Joachim, 25n57, 56n39,
  96n65

Cleisthenes, xx

Clement of Alexandria, 5

Cleomenes (king of Sparta), 90

Cleomenes (rhapsode), 166

Cole, Thomas, 169n81

Colli, Giorgio, 5, 6, 6n9

Collins, Derek, 94n61

Confucius, xv

Cordero, Nestor Luis, 159n46

Cornford, Francis MacDonald, xiii, xv, 9,
  9n16, 9n18, 10, 10n20, 11, 11n22, 11n23,
  11n24, 12, 12n26, 13, 13n28, 14, 14n31,
  14n32, 14n33, 14n34, 15, 15n36, 16, 17, 18,
  19, 35, 35n3, 37, 48n25, 63n53, 159n47,
  168, 168n74, 168n76, 170, 170n84

Corradi, Michele, 172n90

Couprie, Dirk L., 85n44

Cozzo, Andrea, 19n46

Crippa, Sabina, 105n88

Croesus, 29n63, 77

Curd, Patricia, xi, 130n50, 130n51, 148n20,
  148n21, 158n45, 159n47, 160n49,
  165n67

Cyrnus, 162

D'Alessio, Giovan Battista, 160n50

Darius (Persian king), xix

Darwin, Charles, 10, 40n13

Deichgräber, Karl, 103n79

Demetrius of Phaleron, 27, 79

Democedes of Croton, 72

Democritus of Abdera, xx, 3, 61n49, 83,
  136-37, 160, 171, 174

Descartes, René, 112

Detienne, Marcel, 76, 76n25, 123n30,
  144n9, 168, 169, 169n77, 169n78,
  169n79, 169n80, 170, 170n81

Di Benedetto, Vincenzo, 123n30

Di Donato, Riccardo, 96n64, 170n82

Diagoras of Melos, 67

Dicaearchus of Messana, 166

Diels, Hermann, xi, xiii, 3n3, 5, 6, 8,
  23n52, 30, 43, 95n63, 129, 161, 163n62,
  164, 165

Diès, Auguste, 125n36

Dilcher, Roman, 102n77

Diller, Hans, 36n8, 155n38

Diodorus Siculus, 128

Diogenes Laertius, xiii, 2, 5, 27, 79, 81, 82,
  83, 94, 103, 107, 108, 113, 121, 129, 150

Diogenes of Apollonia, xx, 40n14, 136, 137,
  137n64, 171, 171n89, 172, 174, 174n97

Dodds, Eric R., xiii, 13n28, 121n26, 168n74

Draco, xix, 76

Drozdek, Adam, 43n20

Durkheim, Émile, 10

Eberhard, Johann Augustus, 1n1

Edmonds, Radcliffe G., 124n33, 125n35

Eisenstadt, Shmuel Noah, xv

Elkana, Yehuda, 75n21, 141, 141n4

Empedocles, xii, xiii, xvi, xx, 3, 11, 20, 21,
29, 36, 43, 61, 73, 78, 82n34, 83, 121,
128n41, 129, 129n46, 130, 130n50,
130n51, 131, 132, 133, 133n56, 133n58,
134, 135n63, 136, 137, 137n64, 141, 150,
150n26, 151, 153, 159n47, 160, 160n49,
161, 161n51, 161n52, 161n53, 161n54,
162, 162n59, 162n60, 163, 163n60,
163n61, 163n62, 164, 164n64, 165,
165n69, 166, 167, 168, 170, 170n85,
171, 173, 176, 177

Engmann, Joyce, 89n53

Epicharmus, 52

Epimenides, xix,6, 27, 49, 49n28, 50,
50n30, 51, 57, 59, 156, 168

Eratosthenes of Cyrene, 90

Euripides, xx, 77

Euthymenes of Marseille, 173

Everson, Stephen, 137n64

Ferrari, Franco, 78n28, 124n33, 127n40,
149n22, 160, 160n50

Festugière, André-Jean, 30n67,

Finkelberg, Margalit, 142n6

Föllinger, Sabine, 145n14

Ford, Andrew, 91n58, 96n64, 139n1

Foster, Benjamin R., 75n21

Fowler, Robert L., 59, 59n46, 175n101

Fränkel, Hermann, 36n8, 55, 55n37, 145,
145n13, 147n16

Frankfort, Henri, 7n11, 75n22

Frankfort, Henriette Antonia, 7n11, 75n22

Frede, Dorothea, 120n24

Frede, Michael, xvii, 5n7, 26n59, 29n66

Freudenthal, Gad, 41n15

Fritz, Kurt von, 39n12, 47n60, 93n59

Fronterotta, Francesco, xvi, 137n65

Frontisi-Ducroux, Françoise, 150n26

Fuhrmann, Manfred, 98n70, 105n88

Funghi, Maria Serena, 53n33

Furley, David J., 58n42

Gagarin, Michael, 76n25, 87n50, 89n53

García Quintela, Marco Virgilio, 91n57

Gavrilov, Alexander K., 80n32

Gehrke, Hans-Joachim, 89n52, 93n59

Gemelli Marciano, Maria Laura, xiii, xiv,
4n4, 72, 72n16, 98n69, 132, 132n54,

135n62, 150n25, 156n39, 157, 157n44,
161n51, 163n60, 165n67, 172n90,
173n95

Gernet, Louis, 150n26, 156n39, 157n42,
168, 169n77, 170, 170n82, 170n83,
170n84

Gilbert, Otto, 156n39

Gill, Christopher, 116n17

Giordano-Zecharya, Manuela, 78n27

Giuliano, Fabio Massimo, 140n2

Goldhill, Simon, 83n38

Gomperz, Theodor, 6

Goody, Jack R., 73, 73n18, 74, 75, 76

Gorgias, xx, 20, 77

Gorman, Vanessa B., 91n57

Gostoli, Antonietta, 96n64

Graf, Fritz, 6n9, 124n33, 126

Graham, Daniel, xi, 24n54

Granger, Herbert, 101n74, 106n89,
153n34, 157n41, 159n48

Gregory, Andrew, 39n12, 43n20

Guthrie, William Keith Chambers, 9n16,
10n18, 125n35

Hahn, Robert, 85n44

Hankinson, Robert James, 25n56, 46n22,
61n49, 63n53, 113n10

Harris, William V., 74n20, 76

Harrison, Jane, 9

Hartog, François, 69, 69n9

Havelock, Eric A., 78, 78n28, 93, 93n60

Hecataeus of Miletus, xx, 3, 29, 59, 65, 71,
73, 82n34, 83, 92, 93, 93n59, 100, 147,
148, 149, 153n34, 169, 173

Hegel, Georg Wilhelm Friedrich, xv, 2,
2n2, 5, 113

Heidegger, Martin, 169, 169n78, 170n81

Heinemann, Gottfried, 167n104

Heitsch, Ernst, 147n16

Henrichs, Albert, 74n20, 123n30

Heraclitus of Ephesus, xii, xvi, xx, 3, 5, 18,
19, 20, 40n14, 43, 43n20, 44, 45, 47, 52,
73, 81, 83, 86, 86n47, 98, 99, 99n71,
100, 101, 101n74, 102, 102n76, 103,
104n84, 105, 105n87, 106, 107, 108,
109, 109n97, 111, 112, 114, 114n11, 115,
115n13, 116, 116n17, 117, 118, 118n21,
128, 130, 137, 144n12, 148, 148n21, 149,
150, 150n25, 159, 159n47, 168, 171, 175,
175n99

Herder, Johann, 8
Herodotus, xx, 4, 5, 7n10, 29n63, 33, 58,
    69, 77, 80, 90, 92, 93, 93n59, 119,
    119n23, 121, 122, 128n42, 171, 171n88,
    172, 173n92, 174, 175, 175n101
Hershbell, Jackson P., 96n65
Hesiod, xii, xvi, xix, 6, 7n10, 12, 13, 14, 15,
    17, 21, 22, 22n50, 25, 26, 29, 32, 33, 34,
    35, 35n5, 36, 36n8, 37, 39n11, 39n12,
    41, 42, 44, 47, 48, 48n25, 49, 50, 51, 52,
    53, 54, 55, 56, 57, 58, 59, 59n44, 63, 65,
    70, 78, 84, 93, 94, 95, 97, 100, 131, 140,
    142, 142n6, 143, 144, 144n9, 147, 149,
    152n32, 154, 154n36, 155, 156, 160, 162,
    164n63
Hesychius, 30
Heyne, Christian G., 8
Hieron of Syracuse, 93
Hipparchus of Athens, 79
Hippasus of Metapontum, xx, 72
Hippias of Elis, xx, 25, 113
Hippocrates of Kos, xx, 150n26
Hippocrates of Chios, xx
Hippodamus of Miletus, xx, 30, 30n69
Hippolytus of Rome, 38n39
Hippon of Metapontum, 72
Hölkeskamp, Karl-Joachim, 89n52
Hölscher, Uvo, 16n37, 41n16, 104n86
Homer, xix, 6, 7n10, 19, 25, 31, 32, 33, 41,
    42, 44, 45, 49, 54, 63, 87, 93, 94, 94n62,
    95, 96, 97, 98, 100, 105, 112, 113, 114,
    115, 116, 119, 121, 127, 134n60, 139, 140,
    142, 142n6, 143, 144, 150n26, 152,
    152n32, 154, 154n36, 156, 160, 161,
    169n81
Hornung, Erik, 17, 17n42
Horton, Robin, 65n3
Huffman, Carl A., 30n68, 128n44
Humphreys, Sally C., 42n17, 65n2,
    82n36
Hussey, Edward, 25n58, 63n53, 103n80,
    115n14

Iamblichus, 72
Ibycus, 96
Iccus of Tarentum, 72
Iles Johnston, Sarah, 124n33, 126
Inwood, Brad, 129n48
Ioli, Roberta, 147n16
Ion of Chios, xx, 121, 121n25, 122, 173

Irwin, William A., 7n11, 75n21
Isocrates, 175

Jacob, Christian, 90, 90n56
Jacobsen, Thorkild, 7n11, 75n22
Jacoby, Felix, 59
Jaeger, Werner, 4n6, 40n14, 43, 43n20, 86,
    86n47, 129, 129n46
Jaspers, Karl, xv
Jennings, Victoria, 173n94
Johansen, Thomas K., 22n51
Jouanna, Jacques, 174n47

Kahn, Charles H., 84, 84n40, 85n44,
    100n72, 101n74, 102n76, 107, 129n45,
    129n47, 134, 134n59, 162n60, 164,
    164n64
Katsaros, Andrea, 173n94
Kingsley, Peter, xiii, 130n50, 133n57,
    150n26, 152n28, 156, 157, 157n40,
    157n44, 158n45, 162n60, 163n60
Kirk, Geoffrey S., 54, 61, 62, 62n51, 116n17
Knox, Bernard M. W., 80n32
Körner, Reinhard, 108n95
Kouloumentas, Stavros, 109n97
Kouremenos, Theokritos, 123n32
Krämer, Samuel Noah, 7n11, 58n41
Kranz, Walther, 3n3, 5, 6, 23, 43
Krischer, Tilman, 66n4
Kurke, Leslie V., 71n13

Laks, André, xi, xii, 1n1, 16n38, 23n52,
    25n58, 50n31, 82, 82n36, 85, 85n45,
    123n32, 137n6, 157n42, 176n103
Lambert, Wilfred G., 14n30
Laotse, xv
Lasus of Hermione, 30n67
Ledbetter, Grace M., 144n12
Leon (Pythagorean philosopher), 72, 146
Lesher, James H., 145n14, 147n16, 159n46
Leszl, Walter, 2n2, 18n45, 45n21, 174n98,
    177n106
Leucippus, xx, 171
Lévi-Strauss, Claude, 69
Lewis, John D., 29n65, 42n18
Lightfoot, Jane L., 105n88
Lincoln, Bruce, 19n46
Lloyd, Geoffrey E. R., xiii, xiv, xvi, 19n46,
    29n64, 39n11, 46, 46n22, 46n23,
    46n24, 58n42, 60n47, 62n51, 64, 64n1,

65, 70n12, 72, 81n33, 161n53, 171,
174n97
Long, Anthony A., 31, 31n70, 137n64
Lorenz, Konrad, 16
Louguet, Claire, xi,
Lucretius, 161, 161n52, 173n95
Luraghi, Nino, 173n9, 175n101
Luzzatto, Maria Jagoda, 79n29

Machinist, Peter, 70n11
Maltomini, Francesca, 79n30
Manetti, Giovanni, 105n88
Mansfeld, Jaap, xiii, 18, 18n45,
25n57, 25n58, 101n73, 118n21,
172n90
Marincola, John, 171n88, 175n101
Martin, Alain, 165n67
Martin, Jochen, 89n53
Martin, Richard P., 29n63
Matson, Wallace I., 63n53
Maul, Stefan, 75n22
Mauss, Marcel, 10
Meier, Christian, 66n4
Mele, Alfonso, 50n30
Melissus of Samos, xx, 171
Metagenes, 84
Meuli, Karl, 121n26
Miller, Mitchell H., 35n5, 37n8
Miralles, Carles, 31n71
Mnesarchus, 101
Mogyoródi, Emese, 4n6
Momigliano, Arnaldo, 5n8
Morgan, Catherine, 88n51, 157n43
Morgan, Kathryn A., 20n47
Morrison, John S., 156n39
Most, Glenn W., xi, xii, 8n13, 9n14,
23n52, 36n7, 43n20, 53n33, 54, 55,
55n35, 56, 56n38, 59n44, 67n6,
78n26, 99n71, 123n32, 142n6, 153n35,
164n63
Murray, Gilbert, 9
Murray, Penelope, 20n47, 142n6

Naddaf, Gerard, 85n44
Nestle, Wilhelm, 3n3, 9, 9n14
Nieddu, Gian Franco, 78n27
Nietzsche, Friedrich, 6, 8, 9
Nightingale, Andrea Wilson, xiv, 175n100,
176n103
Nussbaum, Martha C., 115n13, 118n21

O'Brien, Denis, 131n52
O'Grady, Patricia F., 4n4
Obbink, Dirk, 125n37, 162n55, 164n64
Oenopides of Chios, xx, 173
Ong, Walter J., 78n27
Orpheus, xii, 33, 123, 123n30, 124n33,
157, 170n85
Osborne, Catherine, xiii, 129, 129n48,
130n50, 135n63, 152n33
Owen, Gwil E. L., 158n45

Padel, Ruth, 166n17
Palmer, John A., 22n51
Palumbo, Lidia, 161n54
Parmenides, xii, xvi, xx, 11, 18, 19, 22,
22n50, 29, 36, 40n14, 43, 59, 59n44,
73, 78, 80, 83, 93, 97, 107, 120, 130,
130n51, 136, 141, 151, 151n27, 152,
152n28, 152n29, 152n32, 152n33,
153, 153n34, 153, 155, 155n37, 156,
156n39, 157, 157n42, 157n43, 158,
159, 159n47, 160, 160n49, 160n50,
161, 162, 163n61, 161n62, 168, 169,
169n80, 170, 171
Patzer, Andreas, 25n57
Pausanias (pupil of Empedocles), 131n52,
136, 150n26, 161–62
Pausanias of Magnesia, 54
Pébarthe, Christophe, 74n20, 75n23,
76n24, 76n25
Peirithous, 72, 146
Peisistratus, xix
Pellegrin, Pierre, 177n104
Pellizer, Ezio, 91n58
Periander, 27
Pericles, xx, 67
Perilli, Lorenzo, 78n27, 108, 108n84,
174n97
Perses, 162
Petit, Annie, 72n17
Pherecydes of Athens, 60
Pherecydes of Syros, xii, xvi, xix, 6, 20, 51,
51n32, 52, 53, 54, 56, 57, 59, 60, 82,
82n36, 83, 84, 85, 122, 153n34, 168
Phidias, xx
Philippson, Paula, 36n8
Philistion of Lokris, xx, 176
Philolaus of Croton, xx, 72, 128n41,
128n44, 171
Philoponus, Johannes, 27, 28, 28n61

Pierris, Apostolos L., 49n28

Pittacus, 27

Plato, xii–xv, xx, 1–6, 11, 19–22, 25–26, 28, 33, 38n9, 44, 54, 56, 59, 67, 69n9, 72, 79, 80, 82n34, 90–91, 97, 116, 117n19, 118, 120, 123, 125, 127, 128n42, 137, 139–40, 150n26, 151–2, 160n50, 161n54, 168–71, 175, 176n103, 177

Pliny the Elder, 85

Plutarch, 40n13, 83, 165

Pollux, 29

Polycleitus, 30

Polycrates, xix

Popper, Karl Raimund, 61–3, 72, 110–12

Porphyry, 72

Prauscello, Lucia, 124n33

Primavesi, Oliver, 130n49, 131n52, 163n60, 165n67, 165n69

Protagoras, xx, 67, 172n90

Psammetichus I, 7

Pugliese Carratelli, Giovanni, 124n33, 156n39

Pythagoras, xiii, xvi, xix, 11, 29, 68, 81, 100, 101, 101n73, 119, 120, 121, 122, 132, 149, 150, 151, 156, 157, 159n47, 165, 168, 170, 175, 175n100

Ragone, Giuseppe, 94n62

Rangos, Spyros, 109n97

Rappe, Guido, 135n63

Raven, John E., 54, 116n17,

Renan, Ernest, xv

Riedweg, Christoph, 101n73, 133, 133n58

Rivier, André, 147n16

Robb, Kevin, 78n28, 103n79,

Robbiano, Chiara, 157n43

Rochberg, Francesca, 7n11, 75n22

Rohde, Erwin, 8

Romeyer-Dherbey, Gilbert, 145n13

Roochnik, David, 142n6

Roselli, Amneris, 173n92

Rossetti, Livio, 104n85

Rossi, Luigi Enrico, 77, 78n27

Roussel, Denis, 104n84

Rowe, Christopher, 58, 58n43

Rudberg, Gunnar, 97n66

Salmoxis, 119–21

Santoni, Anna

Sappho, xix

Sassi, Michela Michela, 8n13, 25n57, 39n12, 55n36, 67n5, 68n7, 87n49, 95n63, 98n69, 137n64, 147n18, 148n20, 156n39, 157n40, 163n61, 168n76, 170n84, 175n100

Scarpi, Paolo, 122n28

Schefer, Barbara, 104n84

Schenkeveld, Dirk M., 80n32

Schibli, Hermann S., 51n32

Schick, Carla, 82n35, 87n49, 171n89

Schiefsky, Mark J., 177n104

Schlesier, Renate, 10n18, 16n38

Schmalzriedt, Egidius, 82n34

Schnapp-Gourbeillon, Annie, 74n19, 74n20

Schofield, Malcom, 54, 116n16, 116n17

Schwabl, Hans, 16n37, 60n47

Scodel, Ruth, 142n6, 144n10, 162, 162n56

Seaford, Richard, 68–69, 91n57, 131n53, 157n40

Sedley, David, 116n17, 131n52, 135, 135n62, 135n63, 161n52, 166n70

Seligman, Paul, 112n6, 130n50

Semonides of Samos, 57, 144

Settis, Salvatore, 30n68, 85n43

Sextus Empiricus, 151, 163, 173n95

Sharp, Kendall, 29n63

Sibyl, 105

Sider, David, 109n97

Simplicius, 85n46, 86, 151

Sivin, Nathan, 70n12, 81n33

Snell, Bruno, 25n57, 27, 41n16, 70, 103n80, 113, 115

Socrates, xi, xx, 1–4, 6, 8, 26, 28, 38, 67, 80–81, 177

Solmsen, Friedrich, 35n5, 42n18, 151n27

Solon, xix, 27, 28n62, 29, 42, 57, 76–77, 89, 115, 140, 145

Sophocles, xx

Speusippus, 49

Staden, Heinrich von, 66n4

Stannard, Jerry, 63n53

Stehle, Eva, 166, 167n72, 167n73

Stobaeus, 148

Strabo, 104n84

Strauss Clay, Jenny, 31n1, 37n8, 143, 144n9

Svenbro, Jesper, 80n32

Tannery, Paul, 60n47

Themistius, 81

Theodorus (Greek architect), 84
Theodorus of Cyrene, 72
Theognis, 96, 162
Theophrastus, 85n46, 86, 112
Theron of Akragas, 133
Thomas, Rosalind, 76n25, 78n27, 172n91, 173n92, 174n97
Thomson, George, 68, 69n8, 104n84
Thrasybulus, xix
Thucydides, xx, 10, 19, 58, 69, 80
Timaeus of Locris, 20
Tortorelli Ghidini, Marisa, 124n33, 125n35
Trépanier, Simon, 163n62, 164n64, 165n69, 166n71
Tsantsanoglou, Kyriakos, 123n32
Tulli, Mauro, 155n38
Turrini, Guido, 147n18

Usener, Hermann, 8, 18

Valeri, Valerio, 50n31, 65n3
Van der Eijk, Philip J., 173n92
Van Dongen, Erik, 7n12
Vegetti, Mario, 112n7, 113n9, 129n46, 174n97, 177n104
Velardi, Roberto, 162n57
Verbeke, Gérard, 22n51
Verdenius, Willem Jacob, 22n51, 116n16
Vernant, Jean-Pierre, xvi, 15n36, 16, 47–48, 50–54, 65, 68, 169n79, 170–71
Vetta, Massimo, 96n64

Vidal-Naquet, Pierre, 10n19
Vitruvius, 84
Vlastos, Gregory, 89n53, 149n24
Voelke, André-Jean, 6n9, 54n34

Warburg, Aby, 8
Warren, James, 105n87
Watt, Ian, 73–76
Wesenberg, Burkhardt, 85n43
West, Martin L., 16n37, 39n10, 51n32, 54, 57, 123n29
Wilamowitz-Moellendorff, Ulrich von, 129
Wildberg, Christian, 130n50, 165n65
Wilson, John A., 7n11, 75n22
Wöhrle, Georg, 82n36, 96n65, 152n32
Wright, Rosemary, 152n33, 161n53

Xella, Paolo, 142n7
Xenophanes, xii, xvi, xix, 29, 33, 43, 57, 61, 67, 73, 78, 81, 83, 93–94, 94n62, 95–97, 97n68, 97n69, 100, 103, 111, 121, 121n25, 141, 146–47, 147n16, 158–50, 159, 169, 171

Yunis, Harvey, 80n31

Zaicev, Alexander, 66n4
Zeller, Eduard, 2, 5
Zeno of Elea, xx, 29, 80, 151–52, 171
Zhmud, Leonid, 72n17, 103n82
Zoroaster, xv, 5

A NOTE ON THE TYPE

THIS BOOK has been composed in Miller, a Scotch Roman typeface designed by Matthew Carter and first released by Font Bureau in 1997. It resembles Monticello, the typeface developed for The Papers of Thomas Jefferson in the 1940s by C. H. Griffith and P. J. Conkwright and reinterpreted in digital form by Carter in 2003.

Pleasant Jefferson ("P. J.") Conkwright (1905–1986) was Typographer at Princeton University Press from 1939 to 1970. He was an acclaimed book designer and AIGA Medalist.

The ornament used throughout this book was designed by Pierre Simon Fournier (1712–1768) and was a favorite of Conkwright's, used in his design of the *Princeton University Library Chronicle.*

CPSIA information can be obtained
at www.ICGtesting.com
Printed in the USA
JSHW022132230721
17200JS00003B/154